The Life *and* Strange *and* Surprising
Adventures *of* Daniel De Foe

J Taverner. Pinx.   M Vᵈᵉ Gucht. sculp.

Daniel De Foe
Author of ye Trueborn Englishman

The Life *and* Strange *and* Surprising Adventures *of* DANIEL DE FOE

By PAUL DOTTIN

Translated from the French by
LOUISE RAGAN

1971
OCTAGON BOOKS
New York

Published in France under the title
"Daniel De Foe et ses Romans"

Copyright 1929, Copyright © 1956, Emerson Books, Inc.

Reprinted 1971
by special arrangement with Emerson Books, Inc.

OCTAGON BOOKS
A DIVISION OF FARRAR, STRAUS & GIROUX, INC.
19 Union Square West
New York, N. Y. 10003

LIBRARY OF CONGRESS CATALOG CARD NUMBER: 70-154663

ISBN-0-374-92257-8

Printed in U.S.A. by
NOBLE OFFSET PRINTERS, INC.
NEW YORK 3, N. Y.

PREFACE

Every one has read *Robinson Crusoe,* but few have read that even more amazing story of adventure that is the life of its author, Daniel De Foe.

Working with the same magic tools that this English realist employed, I, too, have endeavored to re-create life, conjuring up the whole pageantry of the late Seventeenth and the early Eighteenth centuries in order to make De Foe live again in the midst of his contemporaries and against his own background.

From the pages of journals and pamphlets that De Foe himself read, from such older and more intimate historians as Rapin-Thoyras, Oldmixon, and Boyer, I have been able to catch the very spirit of the times. On the one side were the Whigs, for the most part merchants and shipowners; on the other side were the Tories, the landowners. The Whigs were Non-Conformists, or, perhaps, members of the Anglican Low church; the greater proportion of the Tories upheld the principles of the Anglican High church and hated Dissenters . . . they were sometimes called *high-flyers*. A third group, working in secret, were the Jacobites, followers of the Pretender, James III. They had not accepted the Protestant succession laid down by William of Orange and were accredited with Catholic and French leanings . . . they formed the right wing of the Tory party.

By visiting the old sections of London, by making pilgrimages to the places familiar to De Foe, by following his path and those of his heroes through the counties of England I have steeped myself in the very atmosphere in which he lived.

True, I have not voyaged to the mouth of the Orinoco nor to the Virgin Islands in order to see with my own eyes what Robinson Crusoe, Moll Flanders and Colonel Jack saw, but, as far as that is concerned, neither did De Foe. However, in spite of the fact that he often resorted to the inaccurate geographical data of his day for his locations, he does succeed in impressing his own personality upon every page that he wrote.

Here are glimpses of his happy, carefree childhood, passed in the midst of the debauchery of the Restoration. Here are suggestions of that ambitious urge that drew him into political intrigue and into expressions of religious animosity. This detail points to his knowledge of the corrupt rule of Walpole. There are passages that reveal his abundant energy, his tenacity, his persistent desire for knowledge, and his ability to come up fighting from one defeat after another. Surveying the whole story, one sees a man, rising from the lowest ranks to positions of eminence in the world of affairs. By a cruel trick of Fate, he slips and falls into the mire. . . . Disgraced, crushed, broken by a series of disasters, matched only by the biblical Job, he manages, nevertheless, to pull himself back to the recognition of his fellow men. Finally, he sought escape in a world he created for himself out of the great storehouse of his own experience . . . in his old age he produced those works of literature that have won him the laurel wreath of immortality. But it came too late for him to enjoy it.

The life of De Foe falls into three distinct periods. Up to the accession of Queen Anne, it is the merchant who dominates, but he has already become actively engaged in politics . . . he is a merchant with political interests. The second period covers the reign of Queen Anne; the political interest is to the fore with De Foe, but he continues his commercial speculations . . . he is a politician with commercial interests.

I have endeavored to unravel the political plots in which he became involved at this time, gaining a good deal of light from some forgotten manuscripts which I found and from the use of the recently published *Reports* of the *Historical Manuscript Commission* which contain nearly all the correspondence that passed between De Foe and the ministers who were his patrons. The last period extends through the reign of George I and the first years of the reign of George II. Without ceasing to give himself to business and politics, De Foe, during this time, is concerned first with his position as a writer and occupies himself primarily with producing the stories that have made him immortal. I have devoted some special chapters to a discussion of *Robinson Crusoe* and his other novels because these books are important, not only in the life of De Foe, but also in the whole development of English literature.

I cannot bring this preface to a close without expressing my indebtedness to the scholars who have preceded me in the study of Daniel De Foe and his works. There are too many to name them all here, but I owe too much to the writings of Prof. W. P. Trent not to make especial recognition of his help.   P. D.

TRANSLATOR'S NOTE

Three nations have contributed to the making of this book: there is first the Englishman, Daniel De Foe, who, two hundred years ago, lived a strange and adventurous life and created the universal character, Robinson Crusoe; a few years ago, a Frenchman, as a result of his study to understand his neighbors across the Channel, presented his view of the life and times of the great Englishman; an American now interprets the French version for English readers. Encouragement for the task of translating has come from many sources . . . from the author, whose help has been invaluable; from members of the English department at the University of Chicago who first called to my attention the French text; from a journalist and lawyer in Lafayette, Indiana, whose love for the first great English journalist made him enthusiastic about this modern study; and from a secretary at the American Embassy at Constantinople, who was interested in the international aspect of the work. These . . . and many others . . . helped.

L. R.

CONTENTS

LIST OF ILLUSTRATIONS

I. THE YOUNG PURITAN

F AR from London and its dirty, noisy streets, half asleep upon a broad bed of green and fertile meadow land, lies the hamlet of Elton, near Peterborough, in the county of Northampton. A tiny village, it is ignored by geographers and would remain wholly forgotten were it not the cradle of a humble family of yeomen that counts among its members the author of *Robinson Crusoe*.

The Foes,[1] originally from Flanders, had, undoubtedly, come to England in the second half of the Sixteenth century when Queen Elizabeth invited the Flemish who were being persecuted by the Duke of Alba to take refuge in her dominion. Responding to the cordial welcome of the English, the newcomers gave their allegiance to the sovereign who had befriended them and severed all continental ties to become loyal and useful Englishmen; they introduced a new industry . . . weaving, which was to become a source of later wealth to their adopted country.

The surname of Daniel was given to the child, who was to become so famous, in memory of his grandfather, Daniel Foe, who died at Elton in 1631. His will showed that he had been in moderately comfortable circumstances. As a good Protestant, he left ten shillings to the parish church; as a good father, he bequeathed 230 pounds to be divided among his four children, Daniel, Mary, Henry, and James; as a good husband, he charged his "beloved wife, Rose Foe," to administer his property until their children were of age.

---

[1] In Chapter IV is the explanation of how the author of *Robinson Crusoe* came to change his name from Foe to De Foe.

The eldest, Daniel, inherited the paternal fortune, but he did not profit from it long, for he died at Elton in 1647. The youngest, James, the father of the famous Daniel, was not baptized until May 13, 1630, less than a year before the death of his father. He remained under his mother's care until the great storm of the Revolution scattered many families and destroyed their homes.

The Civil War did not spare the peaceful Northampton village. The château of Woodcroft, of which the parish was so proud, became the arena for bloody conflicts. With the spirit of crusaders the English middle class fought for the right to interpret the divine Word by inspiration direct from the Lord.

In the wake of the storm James Foe came to London where he began the period of his apprenticeship. He identified himself with the Puritan group, drawn by their religious fervor and by their absorption in prayer to appease the wrath of a God to be feared rather than loved. His religious ardor was tempered, however, by his political moderation; republican principles appalled him; the tyranny of Cromwell's armies was repulsive to him. As a staunch monarchist he undoubtedly pitied from his heart the "Royal Martyr," Charles I. In 1653 he attended the funeral of a Presbyterian minister, Christopher Love, who was beheaded for having had a hand in "that horrible and fanatical plot organized for the return of Charles Stuart and the re-establishment of the monarchy." Fifty years later Daniel notes among the family possessions a ring of his father's commemorating this event, and he offers this in proof of one well-known Non-Conformist's attachment to the monarchical cause.

When James Foe's apprenticeship was ended, he established himself as a tallow-chandler in the parish of St. Giles-in-Cripplegate just outside the walls of London. In 1656 he married Alice, the daughter of a country squire, who had, at one time, been in affluent circumstances, owning horses, carriages, and hunting dogs. But the same Revolution that had driven James Foe to London had wrested from his future father-in-law his patrimony.

Because of the death of Daniel Foe in 1631, previous to the raising of the parliamentarian and the royalist armies, the story that the author tells of his grandfather's fine pack of hounds named after the generals in these armies, is now to be accepted as Alice's account of her own father. Undoubtedly she took occasion to impress upon her son a sense of his good birth, but that the maternal name was a great one seems unlikely. De Foe would have been only too proud to claim it; indeed he does claim for himself direct descent from Sir Walter Raleigh, a claim that has never been substantiated. In his taste for fine carriages and thoroughbred horses he did perhaps follow the lead of his maternal grandfather whose daughter was to come into a greater heritage than the holdings of an obscure British landowner . . . she was to become known as the mother of Daniel De Foe,[2] the youngest of her three children.

James Foe, a member of the Baptist sect, did not believe in the christening of infants, but he did attend regularly the religious services conducted by the Reverend Annesley at St. Giles' church whose register has yielded to careful search the following entries:

> "Mary, daughter of James Foe, tallowchandler, and of Alice; not christened, but born November 13, 1657."

and

> "Elizabeth, daughter of James Foe, tallowchandler, and of Alice; not christened, but born June 19, 1659."

[2] From now on he will be spoken of as De Foe, the name by which he has become famous.

It would be interesting for us to know the exact date of the birth of the one who was to become known as Daniel De Foe, the author of *Robinson Crusoe;* but no one has been able to discover it; therefore we are reduced to conjectures. Most recent biographers have given late in 1659 or early in 1660 as the approximate time of the birth of De Foe; such theories are exploded by the evidence of the birth of Elizabeth Foe in June, 1659.

The marriage license of "Daniel Foe," dated December 28, 1683, shows that he indicated his age at that time to be "about 24." But accuracy is not one of the virtues of the Seventeenth century. Take Mary Foe: she modestly declares in 1679 that she is "around 20 years of age," when the records show she was really 22. If we take Daniel's statement on his marriage papers to mean that he was entering his twenty-fourth year, then we may draw the conclusion that he was born before the month of December in 1660, an assumption that is not out of harmony with his later statement in the preface to *The Protestant Monastery:*

"Alas! I have but small Health and little Leisure to turn Author, being now in my 67th year, almost worn out with Age and Sickness."

These words have caused considerable perplexity to De Foe scholars because *The Protestant Monastery* is dated 1727 but really appeared November 19, 1726. The preface was written after De Foe had failed to place the work in any of the current periodicals and had resolved to publish it himself . . . probably in October, 1726. Looking back at the birth of Elizabeth in June, 1659, we may safely conclude that Daniel must have been born between July and October, 1660. Why, then, is there no record of this birth on the St. Giles' register? Without doubt because its Presbyterian minister, preoccupied by the political and religious situation arising out of the return of Charles II on May 26, 1660, had but little concern for such a trivial matter as the birth of the son of a Baptist business man.

Lacking documents of proof it is impossible to be more specific, but, if there is any significance to be placed upon De Foe's insistence upon an allegorical interpretation of *Robinson Crusoe,* it might lie in his naming the day . . . September 30 . . . that Crusoe was cast from the waves upon that unknown "Island of Despair." Life appeared to De Foe in his late fifties in a sorry aspect. England had proved an island of despair to him, and his advent upon it may have been truly indicated by this month and day which occur over and over again in his fictions.[3]

Later in life when Daniel was to become interested in astrology, he must have regretted that no one had studied the heavens at the hour of his birth to reveal to his parents the secrets of his destiny. When despondent thoughts took possession of him, he would perhaps allow his superstitious fancies to build up an imaginary horoscope for himself, filled with dire portents; so he could comfort himself with the thought that nothing he could do would change the course that Fate had charted for him.

Yet he was born at a joyful period; the country was just emerging from a state of anarchy in which it had long writhed; the crimes that a drunken soldiery had committed to the accompaniment of psalm singing had become no more than a frightful memory. The nightmare of the past years had flown away with a great flapping of wings like an immense bird of ill omen whose shadow had, for a long time, hovered over the city.

The lifting of this shadow let the sun shine down on all. Charles Stuart, the Liberator, was restored to his throne while

[3] De Foe was given to attaching superstitious importance to dates.—P. D.

merry bells pealed forth a glad welcome. The promise of new life stirred up business activity and brought out smiles on faces that had long been settled in gloom. And, to the Foes was granted a particular mark of Divine favor . . . a son was born to them.

The "Merry Monarch" as he was called, was naturally inclined to religious tolerance, but his advisers still cherished old prejudices. They scarcely waited for the first burst of joy to subside before they began to attack the Dissenters, or Non-Conformists, whose pathway to heaven took a different route from theirs. In 1662 an Act for the Uniformity of Worship required that every minister should publicly declare his conformity with the Book of Common Prayer or lose his benefice. The feast of Saint Bartholomew, August the twenty-fourth, was significantly chosen as the last day for the Presbyterian clergy to retain their benefices; on that day all of them who remained loyal to the cause of the reformed religion gave up their places to Anglican ministers. The Reverend Annesley was thus expelled from his beloved church of St. Giles; but, without loss of time, he hastened to found the Non-Conformist chapel at Little-Saint-Helen's-in-Bishopsgate. Nearly all of his parishioners followed him to this new location, including James Foe, who remained faithful to his pastor through good and bad fortune. The merciless Conventicle Act was passed May 16, 1664, punishing with seven years' deportation whoever had been convicted three different times of having attended any religious service which was not held in strict accordance with the regulations of the Established church; this measure brought about the usual results that follow an act of tyranny. The Dissenters, strong in their faith, regarded the tyrants who influenced the royal edicts against them, as servants of Satan. They continued to attend the services of their ministers, but they went stealthily and at nightfall as though they were conspirators. There were so many of them that the police dared offer little interference; yet these Puritans, aware of their handicaps and harried by the oppression of the times, prayed God to avenge their wrongs.

The Lord heard their prayer. When the measure of iniquity was full, he sent a pestilence to ravage the New Babylon. In Daniel's home there could have been but one topic of conversation . . . the plague. The foreboding comet, which preceded the outbreak of the disease, struck terror into all London, including surely the five-year-old boy who was later to find realistic expression for those early fears which, so little understood at the time, must, nevertheless, have sunk deep into his subconscious mind. How he must have shuddered at the harrowing visions that fanatics conjured up, deluding the credulous into believing that they, too, saw the Destroying Angel aloft in the heavens ready to strike with his flaming sword the accursed city; or he may have fancied that he, too, saw the white ghosts that the imaginative declared were passing disconsolately over the tombstones in broad daylight.

One by one, the houses in the neighborhood were closed; the door of each was marked with a large red cross and the inscription, "Lord have mercy on us." Low voices repeated the names of friends and of neighbors whose corpses were already rotting in the great common pit that had been dug, in the first weeks of the heavy casualties, in the fields of Finbury.

Daniel must have heard the heartrending cries of the plague victims who were left alone. He could have seen the reflected blaze of the purifying fires that were lighted in the different sections of the city. In his father's shop he would note that the customers placed the exact change for their purchases in pots filled with vinegar. When his father received letters, he sprinkled them first with alcohol and then read them from a distance through magnifying glasses. But the measure that must have most vividly impressed the young boy was the killing of the dogs and cats, the delight of the home.

It is probable that, as the pestilence reached its peak . . . September-October, 1665 . . . James Foe sent his wife and children to the upper floor of the house, joining them, after he had closed his shop, with provisions enough to last for some time. From there he communicated with the outer world only through a messenger who stood beneath the window ready to run on any errand. The day passed slowly in prayer and pious meditation. In the dead of night came the dismal ringing of a bell . . . not that of the watchman, however. A voice, dull and lifeless, would repeat monotonously, "Bring down your dead . . . bring down your dead." The grinding axles of a heavily laden wagon accompanied this dreadful chant that Daniel might have heard as an indistinct murmur of his childish dreams, but that he could scarcely have interpreted as the plague-stricken city's substitute for tolling bell and funeral rites.

James Foe and his family came out unscathed from this great trial by pestilence; the Lord had distinguished His own. When all danger was over and Daniel was allowed to sit out on the doorstep, he might have wondered at the streets covered with grass. He may have missed the pleasant-faced folk who had used to call him a greeting in passing but who passed no more and were soon forgotten. When accident uncovered the half-buried bones of those who, crazed by the disease, had fled from their homes and fallen in back yards and alleys, the child, horror-stricken, would be reminded of that God of Wrath to whom he appealed every evening for mercy and justice. He would have taken some comfort from the divine promises that his father read from the great black book and

HUGE BURIAL PIT IN ALDGATE
where victims of the Great Plague were buried. De Foe, a child during
its occurrence, was so impressed that in maturity he was able to write
of it in close detail.

that he said were meant for those who followed the commands of the Lord.

But the anger of the Lord was not yet appeased. During the night of September 2, 1666, a fire broke out in a house in Pudding-lane in the very heart of the city. Fanned by a favorable breeze, the flames soon devoured whole streets. The churches where the faithful had prayed that Sunday morning of September the third were transformed by evening into fiery furnaces. God had descended to preach there, even as He had on Mount Sinai. Senseless rumors, spread among the crowd, aggravated the panic: one had seen a number of Papists furiously spreading the fire; others asserted that French troops were going to raid the city and slaughter them all. Daniel saw the stream of victims flowing ceaselessly past his Cripplegate doorway. Not far from his father's was Moorfields, now become a vast camp, the refuge of those who had no other place to go. James Foe and his neighbors viewed that startling conflagration that obscured the whole southern horizon on the night of September the third and trembled with fear for their property. But the fire fighters, organized under the direction of the King, finally brought the flames under control. By September the fifth, the last flicker had died out close to the walls of the city, just sparing the parish of St. Giles.

The fire lasted three long days and was responsible for some flashlight pictures which were printed indelibly upon the child mind of the youngest Foe: there was the group of weary victims, standing stupidly by while the tigerish flames leaped upon their birthplaces and devoured them; there were the frantic fighters, pouring buckets of water into the burning mass that had been their homes and that hissed back at them in mockery at the futility of their efforts, until, burned by the intense heat, they gave up and joined the ranks of the hopelessly despondent.

Stunned by the catastrophe that struck at them all, the people of London forgot for a few weeks their domestic quarrels. The Non-Conformist ministers were allowed to celebrate their religious services in the open air quite unmolested. The Reverend Annesley preached upon the smoking ruins of the city.[4]

London was in ashes, and made a ruinous heap: It was a by-word and a proverb, a gazing stock and an hissing and astonishment to all that passed by; it caused the ears of all to tingle that heard the rumour and report of what the righteous hand of God had brought upon her. A mighty city turned into ashes and rubbish, comparatively in a few hours; made a fit place for Zim and Okim to take up their abode in; the merciless element where it raged scarcely leaving a lintel for a cormorant or bittern to lodge in, or the remainder of a scorched window to sing in. A sad and terrible face was there in the ruinous parts of London: in the places where God had been served, nettles growing, owls screeching, thieves and cut-throats lurking. The voice of the Lord hath been crying, yea, roaring in the city, of the dreadful judgment of plague and fire.

But in the heart of James Foe and upon his lips arose a hymn of thanksgiving to the One who had, time and again, spared him and his family. These catastrophes which had wiped out his competitors had left him more prosperous. He had now sufficient funds to set up as a butcher, a much more profitable trade than that of a tallow-chandler. He took a shop in Fore street, a narrow, business thoroughfare that ran along the wall of the city. So established, he soon gained the esteem of his fellow tradesmen and of the Corporation of Butchers, made up of Non-Conformists like himself. Conscious of his

[4] Cf. *The City Remembrancer*, 1679. By such sermons as this the Dissenters aroused the ire of their enemies and brought upon themselves the later accusations that they had been responsible for the fire, especially since they had so much regard for the day, September 3rd, the anniversary of the republican victories of Dunbar and Worcester.

standing among his fellows and of his parental obligations, he began to give some thought to the education of the son who was to carry on his name.

The child grew; the bright flower of his mind unfolded in the sturdy vase of his body. As an only son and as the youngest child, it would have been quite natural for his parents to have yielded to his every whim; but Puritan parents were strict and severe, even in their expressions of affection. His mother refrained from moralizing but taught him from the very beginning to master his fits of anger.

"If you vex me, I'll eat no dinner," said the young Daniel, naïvely believing he had won his own way.

"But," he acknowledges, "my mother taught me to be wiser by letting me stay till I was hungry."

His father, as long as his business allowed him the time, patiently fulfilled the rôle of religious instructor, as Puritan fathers believed they should do.

Every Sabbath evening the entire Foe family, attracting as little attention as possible, went to hear the Reverend Annesley preach the divine Word; the mystery with which they surrounded these night trips added to their fascination.

Daniel was placed under the care of the Reverend Annesley, who acted for a time as both pastor and schoolmaster to him. The boy was an intelligent and docile pupil; he kept always fondest remembrance of his old teacher whose death in 1697 called forth his enthusiastic verse:

> "His native Candor, and familiar Stile,
> Which did so oft his Hearers Hours beguile,
> Charm'd us with godliness, and while he spake,
> We lov'd the Doctrine for the Teacher's sake. . . .
> Meekness of soul did in his Aspect shine,
> But in the Truth resolv'd and masculine;
> A pleasing smile sate ever on his Brow,
> A sign that chearful Peace was lodg'd below."

As soon as Daniel knew how to read and write, his mother set him to copying long passages from the Bible. Then followed a more pretentious task: a rumor persisted among the Dissenters that the wicked Papists were going to use their influence at Court to confiscate and interdict all printed bibles. Daniel took it upon himself to see to it that his family should not be deprived, in such an event, of the blessed Word; he would copy all of the "Holy Book." He applied himself zealously and worked, as he says, "like a horse" until the whole of Pentateuch was transcribed. In his subsequent state of exhaustion he, no doubt, convinced himself that the rumor was false because he did not return to the task. But who can gage the effect of that earnest undertaking of his childhood? The simple biblical style of *Robinson Crusoe* is one of its greatest charms.

The clarity of expression that made him a master political pamphleteer may also be credited to an exercise of his youth. The Reverend Annesley required Daniel to take notes of his weekly sermons and then reconstruct his whole argument, point by point from the notes. Hostile critics were later to accuse De Foe of forever preaching in his *Review;* the truth in the accusation lies in this writer's moral tone and sustained biblical style. Through the long years of continuous, hurried writing that came between these laborious childish exercises and the finished product of an accomplished artist, how frequently did the early impressions prevail to guide the gradually developing genius?

The Puritan God is a God that takes a firm hold on youthful minds. Daniel felt himself lifted at times by a mysterious and irresistible force which his parents called Providence. They told him that he was made to glorify the all-powerful Divinity and to submit humbly to His decrees. When they described the misguided savages who still worshiped strange shapes of stone or crude wooden figures, he saw himself in fancy over-throwing these heathen idols with great thrusts of his lance and then being acclaimed the champion of the true God. Nor was he ignorant of the forces of evil. He regarded Satan as his personal enemy. He had listened to the servants' accounts of the awful machination of demons and sorcerers. With childlike logic he would surely ask himself why God, the infinitely good and sovereign Lord, did not kill the devil, the essence of evil? His continuous meditations upon the invisible and mysterious could not fail to make him superstitious and fearful; indeed, he remained, all his life, susceptible to supernatural influences.

He has left us a record of his early night fears when in the moonlight "every bush looked like a man, and every tree like a man on horseback." As soon as it began to grow dark, he would keep close within the family circle which was lighted by the flames of the hearth. How he welcomed the long drawn out family prayers, led by his father in a sonorous and assured voice. And how, later, he froze with terror when he was alone in his little bedroom. Often nightmares interrupted his sleep. He relates how once he awoke with the feeling that something alive was planted with all its weight upon his chest. He reached out quickly and lighted a candle; there was nothing. But he was persuaded that the Spirit of Evil had attempted to choke him in his sleep. In his adolescent years, he would lie awake, listening to the mysterious noises of the night in the sleeping city. The two watchmen of the district would pass, rapping at the doors with their iron staffs, monotonously re-peating, "Past three o'clock, and a rainy, wet morning." Then he would picture to himself the dark and empty streets, peopled, no doubt, by wraiths of the damned and his young heart would palpitate and grow cold with fear.

There were other influences at work in the life of the young Puritan. While he was still a child, he showed an eager interest in music and learned to play the two instruments most in vogue at that time, the viol and the lute. Later in life he was to boast of his early accomplishments as a musician. His boyish curiosity in the great city and its abundant life was satisfied by the inquisitive prowlings about London that he, with most of his playfellows, enjoyed in the daytime. Near his home stretched Moorfields with its large trees, dear to the heart of boyhood. In Silver street were the basket-makers, squatted in the open, bandying merry quips. There was a fascination in watching the baskets . . . great hampers or tiny flower-holders, take shape and grow under the quick, skillful fingers of the workers. Even greater were the marvels performed by the men who were erecting the column in memory of the Great Fire. This scene became the mecca for many a day's adventure, offering the more promise because the way there might, by some ingenuity, be varied each time, opening up new corners in London in the intricate passages and dark court-yards that made up the confused jumble known as the Royal Exchange. But it was towards the East, the Aldgate side that the boys were drawn, for there all was animated activity. The Minories led straight towards the menacing bulk of the Tower. To the left extended Goodmans' Field where there were likely to be enough fellows on hand for a game, after which it was easy to work one's way through the noisy crowd at Rag Fair.

In good weather there was chance for further exploration. He would start to run the whole length of Rosemary Lane, pausing for breath before the great glass-houses where he would look curiously at the little piles of warm coal-ashes heaped in corners; there young vagabonds might crouch to sleep at nights with some degree of comfort Off again until the fields of Stepney are reached. The open country at last! A treat after the clamorous demands of the city streets. But he would not miss the spectacle that Whitechapel offered on

Saturday afternoons. To see the aristocracy of London taking its weekly exercise on horseback drew gaping youngsters from all parts of the city. See that thoroughbred being deftly turned about! See them bow as they pass each other! Tired of play and sight-seeing, what more gratifying delight than to squeeze into the circle of tense and eager youths gathered about some old soldier who held them spellbound with the story of his exploits. Nearer the harbor the narrator might be a seaman with his strange tales of faraway lands where gold is more common than lead.

Daniel evidently showed too much boldness in these voyages of discovery in and about London, for his parents, in order to restrain his curiosity, told him terrifying stories of children stolen by the gipsies and afterwards condemned to lives of misery and disgrace. He was now old enough to make himself useful in the butcher shop, and often he went with his father to the city markets. He was particularly impressed by the grandeur of Leadenhall; later he loved to recall the remark of the ambassador of Spain which filled the butchers of London with pardonable pride. This foreign representative was credited with saying, "There is sold as much meat in Leadenhall in one month, as would suffice all Spain for a year."

Among the members of the Corporation of Butchers were many strict Puritans who kept alive the old republican spirit. In 1668 the butcher apprentices protested against the immorality of the Court by moving to demolish the brothels of the city, and they did not fear to say openly that they only regretted they could not demolish the great one . . . Whitehall. When Daniel was with his father's associates, he must have heard many destructive measures supported; but he was indifferent to political questions at his age; he was possessed, instead, with a passion for the small gossip of the neighborhood, such as, for example, the reports of the quarrels in the Milton household.

How Daniel must have reveled in the Great Fair of Saint Bartholomew, held every year at Smithfield at the end of Fore street! The Lord Mayor solemnly opened it and then deigned to accept a glass of lemonade, while the crowd poured in to make the round of the booths which were filled with attractive displays. Puritan though he was, James Foe could not refuse to allow his young son the pleasures of the Fair, with but one prohibition: he must not stop to view the puppet-show; that was a profane amusement contemned by the true disciples of the Lord. Daniel would listen to the caution, squeezing tightly the copper coins his mother had slipped into his hand while his father's back was turned. His eyes would gleam with satisfaction at the thought of a small treasured hoard, his earnings for errands run at the request of neighbors. Now, off for the Fair with all his savings, able to purchase the thing upon which he had set his heart for so long.

Daniel's parents would, most likely, send him to Bridewell to see the young thieves whipped before a public of children. That painful scene Daniel never forgot. There was the judge severely lecturing the culprits in a lifeless voice:

"There is but one end for the boy who persists in crime . . . he is headed straight for the gallows. Sooner or later he will be hanged."

Then came the howls of agony and the whistling of the leather lash which the man wearing a blue badge laid upon the young prisoner's back until it was all wealed and even bloody in places; he let up only at the sharp rap of the judge's hammer on the table before him.

But the young Puritan's reaction could have been only one of scorn for these petty thieves. He, himself, was of scrupulous honesty, and he had an excellent reputation; he was the son of a rich butcher of Fore street; he had a relative who had gained fame in the continental wars. And above all . . . what constituted in his eyes proof of his definite superiority . . . he had traveled about England. In 1668 he had gone to Harwich; then by boat up the river Orwell as far as Ipswich. What had impressed him most was not the striking contrast of colors that the furze heather of the slopes offered against the intense blue of the sea . . . it was the ships at anchor in the river, tall as mountains and more numerous than the ants of an anthill. He had also been to Bath and had drunk of the waters that guaranteed against dysentery and scurvy. These were great trips for a child, and he took pride in recalling them. But, deep in his heart, he acknowledged that nothing equaled the City . . . the City with its narrow, winding streets and its busy population! The City, where all life and activity were being constantly renewed . . . where the human element palpitated and changed while Nature remained immobile and dull. Such a boy was young Daniel: a little emotional, a little impresionable, but quick to yield gratitude to those who offered him a service . . . a practical lad possessed of some foresight. As he wandered about the streets of London, he would stoop to pick up pins that had dropped into the dust, so that, he tells us, he might never return home empty-handed. He was vigorous and born to lead. As captain of most of the organized games in his neighborhood, he defended his right to direct them by use of his fists. He was a ready fighter, by his own account, but he never knocked down his adversary, for to do that would be "beneath the dignity of a gentleman."

Gentleman! What a satisfaction to be treated in the shops like a gentleman, even if the merchant made you pay amply for the distinction. Daniel hoped, by his noble and generous conduct, to win the highest praises of his fellows. He liked to sit on his father's doorstep and watch the carriages of the nobles pass, picturing to himself the day when he, too, would appear in silken array topped with a great powdered periwig. He felt an instinctive respect for the nobility. He dreamed of becoming a real gentleman, but superior to the gentlemen of the Court whose habit of swearing he would not imitate, for he had been brought up in horror of such a vice. Nothing in the world could tempt him to take the name of the Lord in vain. He was quite set in his opinions; his large, square jaw indicates a bulldog tenacity. And he was always ready to leap boldly into the struggle for life. In an undefined way he already felt proud of belonging to the great English nation where God was worshiped as He wished to be worshiped, proud of living in the great city of London from whose harbor ships departed to bring back from every port in the world its richest and rarest offerings.

It is this child, bubbling over with vital energy, already smothering in the repressed home atmosphere, that James Foe, urged on by the Reverend Annesley, decided to set apart for the quiet ministry of the gospel. Obedient to parental authority, convinced, perhaps, that the Lord needed him, Daniel entered, in 1672 or 1673, an Academy, that is to say a seminary for young Dissenters who were studying to become ministers. He put into his studies the zeal and energy that he brought to every enterprise, but, later, in *Robinson Crusoe,* he blamed those who had not taken the trouble to discover his true vocational aptitude.

The Academy at Newington Green, a little village to the north of London, was directed by Charles Morton, a man of broad intelligence, whom De Foe must have had in mind when he came to describe "the compleat English gentleman." He was one of the pioneers of what we call modern education, attempting, in a small way, to counteract the extremely classic influence of Oxford and Cambridge. All of his courses were in

English, and he attached a great deal of importance to the
mother tongue. Daniel kept all of his class notebooks and re-
read them with pleasure, especially his notes on Civil Law; he
was later to call the attention of those who, like Samuel
Wesley, accused the Dissenters of propagating revolutionary
doctrines in their schools, to Morton's political system, entitled
Eutaxia, which was a masterpiece of moderation. Of course
Latin was taught at Newington Green, but it was not the principal course of the curriculum. Daniel was never a good Latin
student. His enemies frequently called him "an illiterate person
without education," the only insult that ever made him lose
patience.

Morton's academy was distinguished from other similar institutions by its emphasis on the practical. The study of logic
and mathematics was made secondary to shorthand, to the
modern languages . . . French, Dutch, Spanish, and Italian
. . . . to history, to the organic and natural sciences, to geography, and to astronomy; the last two never lost their fascination
for De Foe, for they allowed him to give free reign to his way-
ward imagination and offered him an escape from reality to
unknown lands and even to other worlds. The practice of
shorthand, the experiments in physics and astronomy, and the
study of the geographical maps absorbed the greater part of
the time of the pupils. But Morton never forgot to emphasize
the moral point of view in all of his lectures. He kept constantly before these children committed to his care the high
calling for which they had been chosen and for which they
must be educated. He stirred up debates upon theological questions that frequently led to hot disputes, prolonged, at times,
to late hours of the night. Daniel learned to speak extempore,
to spend serious thought on the writing of his discourses, and
to improvise easily. He became a master of polemics, an artist
at decisive argument, and, add his adversaries, an adept at

tautology. These exercises contribute greatly to make his future writings, whether romances or pamphlets, edifying tracts or scientific compilations, read like a vibrant sermon delivered in the open air.

Why could not Daniel become the Reverend Daniel Foe? Because none of the conclusions adopted by the pupils of Morton really satisfied him. Some, like Samuel Wesley, the father of the celebrated founder of Methodism, returned to the bosom of the Established church. This way was repellent to the loyal spirit of young Daniel, who clung to his religious beliefs. Others, like his fellow-disciple, Timothy Cruso, whose name he was later to immortalize, became humble Dissenting ministers, choosing thereby lives of trial and privation. But Daniel had no taste for martyrdom; he dreamed of an active life, of eminent posts, of incalculable riches . . . not of a wretched situation as a Non-Conformist pastor, tracked by the police and insulted by the crowd. Finally, he was not content at the Academy. Doubtless, he enjoyed the large garden, the well-kept bowling alley, the plentifully stocked fish ponds, and especially the large physics laboratory where there were suction and force pumps, thermometers, and telescopes. He took into account, too, the excellence of his master for whom he cherished a deep veneration. But his comrades displeased him by their violence and by their narrowness of spirit. Morton allowed his pupils to govern themselves; they had established a kind of democracy by which everything, even the penalty for an offense, was decided by a majority vote. In practice, this discipline left much to be desired; the conduct of certain drunken and debauched pupils at Newington became the scandal of the community. Moreover, in spite of Morton's counsels of moderation, they openly proclaimed republican principles . . . Cromwell was their God; Milton, their messiah. Daniel had been brought up to respect the monarchical principle of government, and he instinctively placed the character of Charles II above all discussion.

He was equally incensed at the religious intolerance of his classmates, who did not hesitate to repeat inflaming tirades against the Established church which they called the "great prostitute." They turned to ridicule the prayers of the Anglican liturgy and took delight in making personal attacks against the ministers. One night they organized a group on a hill near the Academy. After wakening the sleeping village by shouting into a speaking trumpet, they cried out for all the echoes to repeat some scandalous charges against the parish priest.

Such methods of argument deeply distressed the young Daniel, who had been reared to respect other people and their opinions. But in 1704 when the Non-Conformists academies were attacked by Wesley, De Foe publicly undertook their defense. He alone could do it, for Morton, after violent persecution, had taken refuge in America in 1685, where he became the vice-president of Harvard college. De Foe appreciated the fact that his experience at the Academy had had a decisive influence on his life; it was there that he had acquired the foundation of knowledge that made it possible for him to become a great writer. It is to be noted, too, that his reactions against the bigotry of his fellow pupils stamped him for the broader and more tolerant views that he was to take upon political and religious questions.

One of the great events of his adolescent years occurred in October, 1676, after his departure from the academy. His vacation was spent at Mickleham, a small village to the south of Epsom, where his great delight was in tracing the course, partly subterranean, of the Mole river, and of imagining, as he did so, that he was a great explorer. One day a sudden inundation surprised the people thereabouts. The lords of Beechworth Castle saw their fish ponds invaded by the river. Distressed at the loss of their fish, they got all the young men of the village to work, building up the slope of one of the meadows to form a basin that they thus detached from the raging torrent of the swollen river. This work done, the young laborers built crude huts, lighted great bonfires, and sent off to the Castle for a great supply of food upon which to feast while they remained encamped for two days. At the end of that time, the water which had submerged the meadow, had seeped, little by little, into the calcareous earth, leaving quantities of fish of all kinds and sizes scattered over the damp ground. These were quickly caught up and thrown back into the neighboring fish ponds. This miraculous catch stuck in Daniel's memory, not so much for the ingeniousness of the method employed, as for the large sum of money the sale of the captured fish might have brought. From then on, he viewed all objects in the light of their commercial value and dreamed of directing vast operations that would bring him piles of pistoles and doubloons.

II. TRAINING AND TRAVEL

JAMES FOE was forced to give up his high ambition for his only son. He was never to have the pleasure of hearing the Reverend Daniel Foe praised for his wisdom and his piety; he was never to know the exaltation of saying to an admiring world, "That is my son!" With complete resignation to the will of the Lord, he exclaimed, "Not my will, but Thine be done." Providence then, as now, moved in its own immutable, mysterious way.

Yielding to a pronounced taste for commerce, Daniel became apprenticed to Charles Lodwick, a merchant of Cornhill, who imported liquors and exported hosiery and cloth. There was no time to be lost; at eighteen a young man was too old to begin training for a profession, and Daniel was already sixteen. At the Academy he had received a general culture that made him superior to the majority of apprentices. He was treated more like a companion to Thomas Lodwick, his employer's son, than as if he were an ordinary clerk. He was soon exempted from the small tedious jobs which are generally given to beginners, such as weighing or measuring merchandise or tying parcels. He was intrusted with more difficult work and learned how to keep books and to make a good bargain. Following all of the suggestions made to him, he progressed in the confidence of his master and was, at eighteen, already in a trustworthy position with the firm; he was frequently called upon to deal directly with the leading business men of London.

Lodwick was a Dissenter, but he had not the strict, Puritan

outlook on life that James Foe had. With him business came
first; religion, next. He allowed a great deal of liberty, however, to his employees, who profited by it to take an active
part in the political and religious conflicts that kept the City
in constant turmoil. British business interests were distinctly
opposed to Roman Catholicism and an Absolute Monarchy.
The apprentices, like their masters, were against the succession
of the Duke of York, who stood next in line to Charles II, and
acclaimed the Duke of Monmouth, the illegitimate son of the
King, their hero. Many believed that the legitimacy of the
latter's birth would be established and his succession to the
throne assured. In the meantime, the Duke of York was extending his influence more and more in the management of
government affairs. There were distressing rumors among the
ranks of the good Protestants that the Papists were being supplied with French gold to form a conspiracy for the introduction of the Inquisition into England . . . their partisans were
said to be numerous at Court . . . their emissaries were supposed to be spreading out in the towns, devoting themselves to
intensive propaganda against the reformed religion. But the
Lord would not abandon His people; he was already raising
up a savior who was to rend the veil of imposture and expose
these secret maneuvers.

On the night of September 28, 1678, the people of Cornhill
were awakened by disturbing noises on the streets. When they
looked out of their windows, they were able to make out, in
the light of flaming torches, the police, entering certain houses
and making arrests. Their leader seemed to be a stout individual of surprising ugliness, who was known as Titus Oates.
It was his denouncement to the privy council of those connected with what he declared was a vast conspiracy of Papists
against the safety of the state that led to these midnight raids.

A few days later the judge, before whom Oates had made his first deposition, was mysteriously assassinated.

The situation offered the young apprentices of the city many excuses for a proper outlet of their animal spirits. Organized in numerous bands, they would rouse themselves to a fury of virtuous indignation and descend upon the brothels in Moor-fields, utterly destroying them, as they had done once before in 1668. With their passionate thirst for expression still un-quenched, they would scatter to the taverns in search of some victim that could be pommeled with impunity . . . a stray Jesuit, perhaps. Failing to stir up any legitimate quarry, they might pounce upon any chance for diversion. Daniel tells of an unsophisticated gentleman, whom he and his companions overheard asking the landlord of the tavern where they were all gathered, for news of the conspiracy. His fearful manner, as he made his cautious inquiry, amused the bold company of young apprentices; one of them, urged on by his mates, stepped up to the timid gentleman and seriously volunteered the in-formation that six Frenchmen had attempted to carry off the Monument, but that the guard had arrested them at the last minute and had forced them to put it back. If he wanted proof, he could go and see the crowd watching the workmen busy refastening the stones. The too-credulous questioner shook his head, as he went his way, at this bit of news which he took in good faith, while his merciless hoaxers doubled up in ill-bred mirth at his expense.

There were frequently more serious matters for this volun-teer militia. Under cover of the general disturbance, profes-sional robbers grew bolder. Lurking in the dark alleys of the city, they rushed out to leap upon passers-by and to rifle them with little or no consideration. To the single-track minds of the apprentices, all such thieves could be no other than Papists in disguise; consequently, their duty was to police the streets of the city and protect the citizens from violation by pursuing everyone of a suspicious character. Their weapon was a simple one, consisting of two clubs joined together with a leather lash; they called it "the Protestant flail." Daniel never went out, even for a walk, without carrying his flail, which, he claimed, was more effective than any kind of a pistol. No doubt the disguised Papists were of the same opinion because, whenever they were about their night time mischief, they prudently managed to keep out of his way.

Religious fanaticism grew more violent during 1679. In every town of England there were arrests of all who were suspected of being Jesuits. Two professional informers, Bedloe and Dugdale, stimulated by the success of Titus Oates, declared that they had just uncovered some new proofs of the great conspiracy. They told of having been threatened with death by certain individuals against whom they were supposed to have information. Such methods of intimidation stirred the people of London to a fierce sympathy for the informers whose stories they swallowed whole. Great meetings of protestation against the enemies of the reformed religion kept the popular fury inflamed. Daniel was often in the front ranks, getting his first lesson in methods of reaching and holding public attention. All the strength of his young lungs went into this first burst of enthusiasm for the redressing of a wrong. But saner afterthought questioned the over-exaggerated and violent language of the orators. Just how sincere, for example, was this Oates, with his ugly face which fairly exuded hypocrisy, meanness, and debauchery; his vulgarity and his equivocal attitude soon became repulsive to all honest souls. Daniel, upon reflection, came to regard with a skeptical air this too-vehement reformer who was the first to use the term "tory," an Irish word for robber, with which to ban anyone less radical than he.

"How," he asked himself, "could these Catholics, who form

scarce a thousandth part of the population of London, attempt to massacre all the Protestants?" After having firmly believed for some months in the reality of the great conspiracy, his robust common sense convinced him of the inanity of the accusations brought by Oates and his followers. Still it was a splendid occasion for making a great stir! All this shouting in public gatherings, this intriguing with bewildered idlers, this evening pursuit of suspects, waving his Protestant flail, was too agreeable a diversion to the young apprentice to be foregone for the sake of a twinge of conscience as to the justice of it all.

He began now to feel the restless urge of young blood to be up and about, seeing the world. He burned with curiosity about the people, the places, and the things that were only names to him. The close of his period of apprenticeship offered him the opportunity to satisfy some of this urge; it left him free to visit the commercial ports of England and of the continent so that he could study first hand the agricultural and industrial resources of the principal countries of Europe. He probably first joined a company of traveling-merchants, who served as a kind of middle-man between the importer and the city shopkeeper. As Daniel was all his life a tireless horseman, he must have enjoyed this active life in the out-of-doors. Added to that was the thrill of unforeseen incidents and even dangers, since there was no security on the open road in those days. At almost any turn an impromptu gibbet might give evidence of vengeance taken against some unlucky highwayman. In 1680 he visited Liverpool and greatly admired its wide streets. When he returned there many years later, he was filled with wonder and surprise at its rapid development.

He spent the greater part of the next two years on the continent. The actual facts concerning his movements during this time can only be guessed at from the wealth of suggestive material that found its way into his writings. De Foe, particularly in his old age, loved to recall incidents and impressions from the travels of his youth. It is probable that he went to Portugal on a coaster which cleared the principal ports of the peninsula from Oporto, Portugal, to Cadiz, Spain. During his long stay in Spain he crossed the country, passing through Madrid and Pampeluna, in the company of a caravan of merchants. He appears to have spent the succeeding months in the south of France; from there he crossed the Alps to visit the large commercial cities of Italy. He returned to London by way of Paris and Calais.

He spent only enough time in his beloved London to arrange his business affairs before embarking on a vessel, chartered by some British merchants, bound for Normandy. Concealed by the fog, they passed unperceived, the custom officials who, from the forts of Tilbury, guarded the mouth of the Thames. Reaching Caen without any untoward happening, Daniel continued on his way to Paris; but he was taken ill and went to Aix-la-Chapelle for the water cure. He reports finding there "bathing-places perfectly installed." It seems likely that he went from there to Holland, where he made a long stay before embarking for Harwich, and thence, home. He returned, conscious of his new wealth of knowledge and eager to become his own master in the future. He was never again to leave the shores of his native land.

There is an old adage that says, "Travel forms the young." It is aptly illustrated in the youthful De Foe, who traveled to complete his business training rather than for any personal pleasure. When age forced him to seek an armchair satisfaction in his passion for strange lands and peoples, he revealed but little taste even then for long sea voyages. The heroes of his romances are all victims of severe sea sickness; he depicts their sufferings with such realistic detail that one must conclude he wrote from actual experience. Not until he was safe on dry land, was he able to regain his interest in business and in the life about him.

He was quite capable, however, of making up for lost time by turning a business deal which served several purposes. In successfully putting through a commission entrusted to him by some London merchants, he gained three objectives: The profitable disposal of England woolen stuff in a foreign market; the investigation of a new market for English products; and the introduction into England of some rareties, including musk, which he was later to import to his own advantage.

During his stay in Spain he was the hero of a petty transaction which he relates with much gusto in *The Compleat English Tradesman.* He had an important order from London for some good brandy and called upon a merchant whose address he had. Although the dealer was away, De Foe was asked to come in and taste from a number of casks, some of which appeared excellent to him and which he, consequently, had set aside. The next day the dealer, whose employees had told him of the matter, came to call upon Daniel. The two discussed the price of the amount ordered, and, reaching satisfactory terms, the merchant agreed to send off at once the casks that his customer had had set aside. But Daniel, never loath to make matters doubly sure, proposed to taste the liquor again before ordering its delivery. He did well to do so, for the second sampling was not to his liking. Little suspecting that he was being made the dupe of a dishonest deal, he simply stated that his taste must have deceived him, and he refused to take the brandy, in spite of the merchant's threats and entreaties. A few days later he found out that the liquor in the casks he had first selected had been diluted during the night because the Spaniard believed the Englishman would never find out about it.

The young traveler did not have any very kindly judgments

to pass upon England's continental neighbors. His British self-satisfaction made him biased and severe in his regard for other ways and customs than those of his own people. He had a very bad opinion of the Portuguese; he called them "A proud and effeminate nation whose commerce had declined." Among his fictitious characters are Portuguese robbers who are cruel and cowardly. He scorned them for being poor sailors and despised them because he found among them proof of the vilest submission to their masters and of utmost tyranny to their inferiors . . . they are "worse than the Turks," he declared. He goes so far as to say that he found in their features the characteristic traits of the black race, and he concludes, rather hastily, that this nation is a mongrel race, exhibiting all the vices of the whites as well as those of the negro.

The Spanish pleased him much more. He recognized the nobility of sentiment and the somewhat haughty politeness which they had inherited from their ancestors, the Moors. He looked with suspicion, however, upon their boastful pride and noted that they were vindictive and ferociously jealous of their women . . . not without some cause, he conceded, for he severely questioned the virtue of the señoras. The indolence of these people seemed to him their chief fault; they lacked persistency in their efforts. Yet the most nonchalant of Spaniards became a very demon incarnate when his religious passion was unchained; and along with this passion of attachment to his faith was a deep fear of the Inquisition which made him crafty and cruel. Spanish fanaticism filled Daniel with disgust and horror; the macerations, fasts, and vigils of Holy Week seemed to him outrageous customs. The cessation of all work at the ringing of the Angelus bell filled him with an indignation he had difficulty in restraining.

De Foe, man of the North, granted to the people of the South only one great quality . . . their sobriety. For this he particularly admired the Spaniards and the Southern French. Of them he said, "Wine mingled with water is the ordinary Beverage or Drink for mere necessity or food; but if they take anything to exhilarate or raise the Spirits, it is brandy; which yet they very rarely drank to excess."

He was also pleased with the politeness and the courtesy of the French. Their constant gaiety, even in the midst of misery and misfortune, seemed to him remarkable. He was envious of their wide knowledge and their fine taste. But he contemned the common people for their economy, which seemed to him sordid; he says, "'Tis a very unusual thing to have them part with their money." In general he considered the French volatile and sprightly, impulsive and unstable, lacking in calmness and poise; at times he would gently mock their outbursts of temperament.

The Italians scandalized him by their lax morals; their licentiousness, which he believed was caused by their misuse of spices, offended his rigorous Puritanism. Their hypocrisy aroused his extreme wrath. The intolerable pride of the Venetians was to him the last straw; it confirmed him in his dislike of the Italians. Indeed, the very mention of the name of Italy was ever after to bring forth a reaction of disgust on his part.

Rarely in his works does he mention the Germans or the Dutch. He had but little contact with the former . . . only enough to label them drunkards. As for the Dutch, he held for them, not only the highest esteem, but also the greatest affection. Here were thrifty minds and loyal hearts with which he felt akin.

In after years in spite of the distractions of intense political interests, Daniel was still able to recall those matters that had struck him most forcibly upon his early voyages on the continent. He had gone out of his way to find out the various methods of capital punishment used by the ecclesiastical and civic authorities in the countries he visited. In Portugal he had actually witnessed the torture by fire of the Inquisition, but he had contented himself by looking on from afar, for he had no desire to take any chances among the Papists when their passion for cruelty was unloosed. He describes in detail a hanging in Spain; the long procession of monks, the dismal wail of the fiddles, and the beautiful badge of the hangman, all impressed him. He admired the skill of the hangman who threw himself down the scaffold to hang on to the condemned man and break the vertebrae of his neck with one jerk. He did not neglect to visit the Place de Grève at Paris where he saw an execution; nor did he overlook the Châtelet upon which he gazed with mingled fear and respect. The German executioner won his admiration for his efficiency . . . he boasted of never taking more than two strokes to cut off a head. Then there was the house of correction at Amsterdam which appeared to him a marvel of ingenuity. The prisoners were kept locked up under such conditions that they had to pump with all their might to prevent being drowned; in such manner did the authorities make certain of having an important public service performed.

Trifling details of his voyages did stay with him . . . the passage of a great number of eagles, the fall of a cloud of locusts, his examination of an ingenious machine for irrigating gardens, his study of different types of cisterns. He speaks, too, of the beauty of the Castilian women, and of the distress he experienced in hearing the nasal twang of a guitar. He admired Paris for its relative cleanliness . . . an agreeable change from the Spanish streets, covered with filth. He never forgot the magnificent uniforms of the Swiss guards who drilled in front of the gate of the Louvre. The palace of Louis XIV and the superb residences of the French nobles were flies in the ointment of his national pride. He admitted Versailles was magnificent, but he would not concede that it was more so than Hampton Court; the castles of the nobility were vast and sumptuous, he agreed, but not more so than Rangers Lodge at Ham Park. The smiling and varied country which extended around Paris, sprinkled with its well-kept gardens and beautiful buildings was certainly worth a visit; but he preferred the uniquely picturesque environs of Richmond. There was only one thing he saw in France with which nothing in England could compare . . . not even the women promenading in Nottingham could hold a candle to the exquisite ladies taking their airings in open carriages in the garden of the Tuileries.

Daniel was generally too much absorbed in his practical interests to have the leisure to act as sightseer in the countries he visited. He found the time, however, to witness a bullfight, which he found somewhat diverting. His sympathies were with the bull, who appeared to him to be unfairly matched against numerous and aggressive adversaries. He did appreciate the Spanish wines . . . for two reasons, their excellence and their cheapness; he found them equalled only by the light wines of Troyes, France. He viewed everything in the light of its commercial value; he judged every town from the amount of business that it transacted, subordinating every other quality to the one that dominated his own angle of vision. Consequently, Rome fell far down in the scale of his values; the ruins appeared to him to take up valuable space that might be used to much better advantage for shops. Furthermore, he was ill at ease in the city of the popes; he passed so many priests that he began to think he was in Pandemonium, the capital of hell. Madrid, with its ramparts of dirt . . . Valladolid, where business had to be conducted in the early hours of the evening, since its citizens had to seek shelter from the hot sun during the day . . . the Hague, surrounded by deep motes . . . all impressed him as being dead towns without interest to an enterprising British merchant.

He was really happy in the seaports: Lisbon, Cadiz, Bordeaux, and Marseilles with their large wharves; Leghorn, Genoa, Naples, Venice, Amsterdam, and Rotterdam. He ignored the towns of the interior unless their position was made favorable for business by their being located on a crossing of routes, close to a mountain pass, or on a large canal.

He tolerated the presence of rivers on the earth's surface, but upon the condition that they were navigable and not, like the Guadiana of Spain, in part subterranean. Rivers did not interfere with traffic; they made, indeed, an ideal passage for ships. They did not offer any real obstacle to the pedestrian, who could cross them by fords or bridges. Daniel could name and locate the principal bridges that he saw upon the continent . . . there was the bridge over the Manzanar, near Madrid, its immense skeleton rising over a dry river bed; and there was especially the Rialto at Venice. He had to admit that the latter was more imposing than the bridge at York, and his patriotism suffered a slight setback until he discovered that the central arch of the bridge between Glasgow and Stirling had a diameter thirteen feet greater than that of the great arch of the Rialto.

But by what singular mental aberration or what forgetfulness of His most sacred duty to mankind, had the Creator placed upon the land such high mountains, which inconvenienced merchants and interfered with the progress of travelers? The Alps particularly excited the disapprobation of the youthful Daniel. Eager to show that his own country could outdo all others, even in matters of inconvenience, he did not rest until he could show that the Britons, too, suffered from the eruption of these monstrous blotches on the face of Mother Earth; to him the Welsh mountains, while not as high as the Alps, were fully as terrible. In such manner did he regain his sense of superiority, which was subject to deflation in the most surprising way.

The hand of Providence was discernible even here, however, for these impenetrable masses of mountain, Daniel was to see, were cleft here and there in such fashion that shortcuts were made available; this seemed of real value to a commercially-minded individual. But he paused, alarmed, before such a wild defile as the Pertuis Rostan, near Briançon, which appeared to him to be more the work of the devil, who might have hacked it through in satanic rage at this impassable rock. Such furious rage Daniel could understand; he felt it, too, in the presence of the mountains of Savoy or Dauphiné, or even the hills of Wales and Scotland.

"Frightful, horrible, appalling," were some of the epithets that he hurled at these giant obstructions that loomed before him. Traveling through a hilly country was, to Daniel, even worse than crossing the seas. He was not happy until he reached the plains.

What transports cause his heart to palpitate . . . what hymns of joy rose to his lips when he saw the shores of his native land rise again before him! The dishonest merchants of Harwich who had exploited the travelers coming from Holland put a bitter taste into his homecoming; because he was always chagrined when someone else got a good bargain at his expense. But even this disagreeable memory disappeared when he saw once more the familiar streets of his own city. He was just twenty-three, and he had already met life squarely in a practical struggle for existence. He was vigorously determined to follow his own ambitious urge and become his own master. The world was his. He had returned to his native town . . . the only place where he felt at home, possessed with the idea of becoming a real factor in the commercial life of his country.

His prosaic soul grew lyrical at the very name of London. The pure sky of Italy, the play of color in Spain, the exquisite courtesy of the French, the enchanting beauty of the women of Versailles . . . had no place in a heart that beat with emotion only at the sight of the dilapidated steps that led down to the Thames; at the mysterious, dark mazes of the Bank section of the city; and at the smoky taverns where, in the half-light, seated at crippled tables before jugs of beer, the English business man made his important transactions.

III. THE HOSIER OF CORNHILL

IN Cornhill, in the parish of St. Michael's, there opened up one day, in the year 1683, the twenty-third of the reign of King Charles II, a new place of business conducted by one "Daniel Foe, merchant." His establishment occupied a place in Freeman's court in front of the entrance to Change-alley. He, doubtless, had the backing of his former master, Charles Lodwick, and it was, perhaps, upon the latter's advice that this location in the busiest section of the city at that time was selected. The fire of November 10, 1759, which swept over all of Cornhill, destroyed the building in which the author of *Robinson Crusoe* hopefully believed he was achieving the high destiny of his life.

The shops of the period were far from having an æsthetic appeal; there were no show windows, nor was there an attempt at any kind of display. In them could be bought a little of everything. The tradesman stood upon his doorstep, calling out his wares, proclaiming their excellence, and inviting passers-by to enter. But Daniel was not one of these small retailers who, with the painstaking labor of an ant, succeed in accumulating enough for comfortable old age; he belonged to the aristocracy of business men, acting more as an agent, or middle man, between the English manufacturer and the foreign merchant. He traded principally in hosiery and, for that reason, was later accused of being a "seller of stockings," an insult which cut him to the quick. He was really a hose factor, but he also followed Lodwick's example . . . exporting materials and importing wines; and he was ever on the look-

out for a chance to turn a good business deal, not neglecting
to take advantage of any bargain of importance. Some years
later he began trading with the Dutch. It was from Holland
that he bought drugs or perfume, particularly civet, for which
reason his enemies enjoyed calling him a "Civet-cat merchant,"
implying that he traded in the pelt of the animals.

Daniel did not turn out to be a perfect business man; he did
not spend enough time behind his counter, bending over his
account books. He had an eye for the big things, but he dis-
dained the petty details that seemed to him beneath his notice.
The Jewish merchant, who never neglected a profit, no
matter how small, struck him as ridiculous. Besides, Daniel
was ambitious in matters that were outside his professed voca-
tion . . . he was credited with a reputation as a wit, a keen
connoisseur, and a man of letters. Time which should have
been devoted to the demands of his business, he gave to reading or to discussing the politics of the moment with a circle
of admiring friends. If there was some connection between his
interest in the guns on the "Royal Charles" and a navy sufficient for the protection of the merchant vessels, there would
seem to be but little excuse for his delight in quoting long passages from the licentious poems of Rochester, who was his
favorite author at that time. He came to prefer Milton, but
the light verse of Rochester, that so aptly hit off the levity and
the skepticism of the period, stuck in his memory for many
years. Cut loose from the family apron strings, he could indulge himself in reading *Hudibras,* the burlesque poem by
Butler, which would have been anathema to the home circle
for its crass blasphemy against the old Puritan leaders. The
classicism of Roscommon appealed to De Foe . . . indeed, it
served as a model to him, for it is probable he was even then
writing bits of verse which he would read to his most intimate
friends. It was the golden age for visionary projects, for fanci-

ful utopias; to De Foe, as to others, came the urge to present his ideal state, to formulate a scheme for the administrative and social reorganization of his country in order to wipe out all of its evils.

It was not long until he began to feel the need for some gentle and helpful companion . . . a sympathetic and obedient helpmate . . . a wife. His two sisters were already married: Mary, the older, on May 20, 1679, to Francis Bartham, a shipbuilder; Elizabeth, the younger, to Robert Davis, an engineer. The fifty-year-old James Foe had been longing for some time now to hear that Daniel had chosen a wife; he had to look to this only son to carry on the family name. His prayer was to be quickly answered . . . too quickly, perhaps, for Daniel appears to regret his early marriage. On the register of St. Botolph's-in-Aldgate there was entered on January 1, 1683, the names of Daniel Foe and Mary Tuffley, with the information that they were married by the Reverend Hollingworth. The record for the application of the license on December the twenty-eighth gives these interesting details:

> Charles Lodwick, of St. Michael, Cornhill, applies for Daniel Foe of the same parish, 24 and a batchelor, marchant, and Mary Tuffley, of St. Botolph Aldgate, 20, spinster, with consent of her father.

The winter was an exceptionally cold one . . . there had been skating on the ponds and rivers; the Thames had been so thoroughly frozen that a fair had been held on its glassy surface. But when the bells of St. Botolph's rang forth their signal that the marriage ceremony had ended, a crowd gathered as near the church door as possible in order to greet the new bride and groom in the customary fashion; the funmaking was all the more vigorous because of the extreme cold.

Daniel did not marry for love; he disregarded so dangerous and impractical a passion, to be ruled instead by the dictates of cool reason, mature reflection, and sound judgment. Mr. Tuffley was a pious Non-Conformist, who settled later in Newington, where he conducted a conventicle. He gave his daughter a dower of 3,700 pounds, a goodly "dot" for those days. Unfortunately, it was all too quickly absorbed by Daniel's ill-advised speculations.

Mr. Tuffley had two sons: Charles, who had become a sailor; and Samuel, who was in business at Hackney. The latter prospered and aided his sister in her all too frequent needs for both material and spiritual help. As a consequence, Samuel Tuffley came to regard his brother-in-law with a not wholly unjustified lack of confidence.

Mary, herself, was a perfect wife for a city business man; deeply religious, she was, at the same time, endowed with adaptable energy. She aided her husband as far as she was able in all of his enterprises and managed his household with enthusiasm and good taste. Daniel sincerely liked his young wife; but he believed too much in the superiority of his own sex to accept from her any more than the most casual of suggestions. Who knows? Perhaps it would have been better for him had he referred more often to the good common sense of his wife; she would have known how to take care of the family fortune.

The marriage of "Daniel Foe and Mary Tuffley" was generously blessed by the Lord. They had eight children: two sons, Daniel and Benjamin; and six daughters, Mary, Hannah, Henrietta, Maria, Martha, and Sophia. Two of them died quite young: Mary, in 1688; and Martha, in 1707. The others grew rapidly in strength and beauty. The paternal instinct was never developed to any great extent in Daniel; he left the care of the children to his wife. His restlessness, which was almost a disease, led him far from home. It drove him in every direction, either in pursuit of financial gain, for pleasure, or for mere distraction. Near the close of his long life, he had this to say to young fellows just starting out:

"If he (the tradesman) has a family, he will make his excursions upstairs, and no further." The suggestion seems to come with all the more force and sincerity because he must have deeply regretted that he had not followed it himself.

But he appears to have had no scruples about taking every opportunity to get away from home. All the great fairs lured him, even those that were farthest from London; the one held at Leeds particularly interested him. Here all transactions were carried on in a low voice and as quickly as possible to prevent the dealers from entering into competition by underbidding each other. Between 1684 and 1688 De Foe traveled over most of the highways of England; he came to know them so well that he could discuss them in detail, noting all of their defects, in his *Tour of Great Britain* and in the articles that he later wrote for his own magazine, the *Review*. In the course of his business trips he made many other profitable observations and gathered much valuable material for his writings. He looked upon his country with the curious eyes of a stranger, eager for knowledge. The lower classes interested him more than did the nobility; the factories, more than the castles. His usual companion was an old woollen-traveler; the two enjoyed getting into long-drawn-out arguments, especially during the periods when they paused to rest their horses.

One day his old traveling companion started a defense of the Anglican clergy, declaring they were right to require that Dissenters should receive the sacrament *kneeling;* De Foe, of course, supported the contrary view. As their way led past Windsor, he suggested stopping to see the Royal chapel there. The first thing to catch their eye as they entered was a large painting of the Last Supper which showed the disciples *seated* around Christ. De Foe exultantly pointed out this feature and took the occasion to make the matter indicative of the tyrannical methods employed by the Established Church in forwarding its doctrines, many of which, he claimed, could not be substantiated.

De Foe's frequent journeys necessitated his having a well-filled stable. Since his circumstances now made it possible for him to possess horses and carriages, he never failed to look over the different animals at the fairs he visited. It was not difficult for him so to arrange his business trips that he might take in all the more important races, particularly the ones at Newmarket which the King honored with his presence. De Foe saw the Duke of Monmouth carry off many first prizes, mounted, in spite of his weight, on the swiftest of horses. This same Protestant Duke was to be seen at the Aylesbury races where he mixed familiarly with the crowd, displaying such charming interest in all about him that his popularity was increased twofold. De Foe, too, came under the influence of this royal personality and, from then on, he was an enthusiastic admirer of Monmouth, untiring in his devotion to his hero's cause. Although he believed that horse-racing was the only sport really worth the notice of a leading young business man like himself, he did condescend, out of mere curiosity, to go to the cock fights. They seemed to him cruel . . . just the sort of thing to appeal to the crowd. But his innate regard for energy, under whatever form it presented itself, called forth his appreciation for the tenacious courage of these game little fowl.

"I was at several of these combats," says De Foe, speaking of the cock fights he attended, "and I never saw a cock run away."

Nevertheless, he felt uncomfortable in the Cockpit at Whitehall for a number of reasons: the people who hemmed him in were repugnant to him; his deeply engrained Puritanism revolted at the sport. . . . He knew that his forebearers held all animal combats to be criminal; moreover, his thrifty conscience reproached him for spending so much time in idleness, throwing away his shillings for unprofitable pleasure and giving in to unproductive emotions. When he became bankrupt a few years later, he attempted to account for the disaster by running over the various ways in which he had lost money; it was then he came bitterly to repent the hours he had wasted at the races and the money he had spent on useless pleasure.

But in his heyday, when Daniel had a well-filled purse, he was eager to be off to one of the fashionable watering places. . . . Tunbridge Wells or Epsom, where his purse was emptied all too quickly. It is quite likely that he brought his family to Epsom several times at the height of the season. He himself would go up to London on horseback early in the morning, take care of his business affairs in the city, and return in the evening at the very hour when the smart little village was reviving from its stupor of the hot afternoon. There was just the right kind of conviviality for De Foe at Epsom; groups of talkers, drawn by their common interests, would gather upon the rustic benches, half hidden by the arbors; there they would drink of the refreshing beverages and enjoy their conversation until sunset. Those who had horses and carriages would drive out in the cool of the evening to the hills near by; others would seek diversion at the bowling-alleys or would listen to a musical concert. Later in the evening all would assemble in the town hall where there would be dancing for the young folk until sometimes as late as eleven o'clock.

All this was intoxicating to De Foe . . . this British Capua where one might rub elbows with any number of the highest nobility of the land. He never counted the cost of that which added to his sense of his own importance. When he was at Epsom, he was not the tradesman of 'Change-alley. Any one passing this neatly and correctly dressed gentleman, carrying himself with a haughty and superior air, would have been impressed with his appearance and would have imagined him to be attached to the retinue of the King.

Indeed, De Foe had some reason for considering himself a person of consequence now; his reputation as a wit and a brilliant orator was well established by this time among his friends, the business men of the city. He had become the oracle of many of the Whig clubs, which were made up of merchants ready to rebel at the very idea of one of the hated 'Papists' falling heir to the throne of England. The object of their particular resentment was the Duke of York. In the coffee-houses where the news of the day was eagerly seized upon and discussed, De Foe pretended to take an independent stand. But his air of nice aloofness was not always pleasing to his more serious friends . . . those who were uncompromising in their non-conformity, in politics as well as in religion. When the Turks in 1683 sided with the Protestant Hungarians and marched upon Vienna, the Whigs were in high glee at the situation . . . a Catholic emperor thrown upon the mercy of the Turks right in his own capital. De Foe declared that they were wrong to exult at this, that the Papists were, after all, Christians and, as such, deserved the consideration of all followers of Christ against the Turks who "had rooted out the name of the Christian religion in above three-score and ten kingdoms." He wrote a short treatise on the subject which he no doubt read in the coffee-houses and had circulated among his acquaintances. His point of view was defendable, but it was too full of Tory sentiments to please his political friends.

It was no doubt dictated by his desire to be original and by his love of paradoxes. He came bitterly to repent having allowed himself to develop such dangerous inclinations.

Charles II died February 6, 1685, much lamented by the Whigs because his successor, James II, was the King of the Tories and the Catholics. The Protestants of London showed their opposition by stirring up frequent rebellions which were mercilessly put down. While this trouble was brewing, De Foe continued his trips about England. Early in June he was in the Western counties, probably at Wimborne or at Martook, where he had some relatives, when he heard a rumor which filled his heart with elation. . . . Monmouth, his hero, had landed at Lyme and was proclaiming himself the champion of British freedom and of the reformed religion, preaching a holy war against his uncle, the King. A proclamation was issued by the leaders of the army of rebellion in which they denounced the "Duke of York," now the reigning king, James II, as the one responsible for the great fire of London and the murder of Godfrey, the upright judge who had received the first deposition of Titus Oates. Like a train of powder, the news of the revolt spread through the region where the Dissenters were in the majority; they flocked by the thousands to join the ranks of the rebels. But Monmouth made a mistake in proclaiming himself King upon his own authority; he should have waited for Parliament to confer upon him the crown. It was his own hasty act that lost him the sympathies of the great Whig lords. Alarmed at his show of independence, they began to reflect a little; their reasoning took some such form as this:

James is already an old man; his oldest daughter, Mary, next in line as the legitimate successor to the throne, is the wife of William of Orange, the pillar of Protestantism in Europe; better remain patient than rush into an unsatisfactory and, perhaps, dangerous alliance with this pretentious adventurer. But the West county people were not capable of such complex reasoning; they enlisted without hesitation in the army of "King Monmouth." To them it was sufficient that Monmouth was a good Protestant . . . James, a hated Papist. De Foe, too, was carried away by the general enthusiasm. He followed the impulse of the moment; deaf to the voice of cool reason, he leaped upon his horse and enrolled under the banner of insurrection.

What was the part he played in this brief campaign? No one knows; but it could not have been very important nor very glorious. De Foe was never burdened with modesty; had he taken an active part in this rebellion, he would certainly have boasted of it as an heroic and impetuous episode of his young manhood. Instead he makes but a brief justification of his conduct in *The Appeal to Honour and Justice,* written some thirty years later. It seems apparent that he did follow the maneuvers of Monmouth's army at close range, possibly as a prudent spectator. It was an unequally matched combat with disorganized and undisciplined bands of volunteers pitted against the well-trained soldiers of the King. De Foe describes with his usual minutia of realistic detail the various skirmishes undertaken to capture the vanguard of the enemy. He must have been present at the battle of Sedgemoor, probably in the cavalry of the insurgent army . . . one of those who scattered at the first charge of royal musketry. The work horses that most of the rebels rode were startled by the shot and fled wildly across the fields. De Foe could not have regretted that his own horse bore him in safety far from the scene of butchery that followed.

A few days later he trembled with fear when he heard of the capture and arrest of Monmouth and of the frightful means that "bloody Jeffrey" was using to quell the rebellion and prevent any further support for the unlucky Monmouth. One discomfited tradesman must have been enveloped in terror when he was told that three of his former classmates at the Academy had followed their unfortunate leader to execution. What sudden panic must have seized him at the disgraceful punishment meted out to one of his acquaintances, John Tutchin, a young Whig politician, who was condemned to be whipped in public through all the towns of Dorset every year for seven years. All these were unnecessary and unfounded fears on Daniel's part because these victims had been much more involved in the revolt than a certain cautious "Daniel Foe," who had not drawn attention to himself by any brilliant and heroic deeds and who was almost wholly unknown in and about Bridgewater. He was known only to a schoolmaster in Martook, a relative, who had offered to give him a refuge. De Foe escaped the claws of Jeffrey and returned to London after successfully covering up all traces of his own share in this inglorious undertaking. He continued prudently to follow his business leads which took him away from London quite frequently so that he was able to avoid much of the hateful persecution inflicted upon the Dissenters of the city. It was at about this time De Foe rented a country house at Tooting, a small village to the south of London. Here his family lived for several successive summers, while De Foe continued to keep up his business establishment in 'Change-alley.

Meanwhile, James II proceeded to carry out his double design of restoring absolute monarchism and Catholicism to England. Since he kept the latter of the two motives in the background, he had at first the support of the High church clergy in all of the London churches; they always upheld the divine right of kings and preserved an attitude of "non-resistence" and "passive obedience" towards the legitimate sovereign. De Foe vouches for the fanatic preaching of clergymen who called upon their parishioners to bow down like slaves to the sovereign's will. He says in an issue of his *Review:*

"I have heard it publicly preached that if the King commanded my head and sent his messengers to fetch it, I was bound to submit and stand still while it was cut off."

The Whigs began a secret agitation against the despotism of the King. In March, 1686, a subscription was started in the country for the benefit of the Huguenot refugees; this gave the English Protestants a chance to show their dislike for the Catholicism of Louis XIV. James II was at first astonished at the success of the collectors, at.the large sums subscribed; he took his revenge by frustrating the distribution of the money as far as he was able to do so. The Dissenters' clubs in the city plucked up courage and held some secret meetings in the coffee-houses. Daniel was to be seen at these gathering places and it was at one of them he ran into an old companion of Academy days . . . John Dunton, who had married a daughter of the Reverend Annesley. Dunton had just returned from a hurried trip to America where he had had an opportunity to visit their old teacher, Charles Morton. With their common background of early associations De Foe and Dunton became fast friends and united in leading the forces that stood for civic and religious freedom.

In April, 1687, James II was brought face to face with the fact that he could never reconcile anglicanism and popery. His second Declaration of Indulgence met with the united opposition of the clergy.

He turned about and, with a front that was ostensibly for toleration first, urged a coalition of the Catholics and the Non-Conformists. He encouraged the latter to go back to their conventicles and promised them his protection. But Daniel put his fellow Dissenters on guard against premature rejoicing. With a perspicacity that did honor to his youth and his training, he pierced the crafty cunning of the King. He cautioned them that, once the penal laws and the Bill of Test were abolished, the Catholics would be free to hold the highest places in the government. That accomplished, the Established church could count its days numbered, and the Dissenters would stand no chance at all beside the triumphant Papists . . . the country would pass again under Roman control.

While De Foe was leading the opposition of the country against the Declaration of Indulgence, he did not hesitate to profit by it. The Non-Conformists of Tooting where his new summer residence was located, had no well-organized congregation. Like a good pastor, De Foe brought together the scattered flock of sheep, bought a small house for them to use as a meeting place, and, recalling his early training, presided himself over their first services. In 1688 when it became necessary for him to give up his Tooting place and return to London, he left his faithful followers in the hands of an excellent minister, the Reverend Joshua Oldfield. The thought of his work among these people was always a source of satisfaction to him; it may have been he felt that this temporary post as a minister was a fine preparation for the more active pursuits to which he was ever turning. To play an important rôle in politics seemed to him now the very peak of attainment; the growing demands of this ambition began to supplant his earlier dreams of acquiring a vast personal fortune. Instead of adding to his personal wealth, he strove to increase his historical knowledge so that he might become a great Whig pamphleteer. He frequented the booksellers of Paternoster Row and never forgot, unfortunately, a sentiment that he picked up from one of them to this effect, that if he would have a book sell well, he must have it contain something scandalous or seditious so that it would be condemned and burnt by the common hangman.

Encouraged by his success as an organizer at Tooting, Daniel began to see himself as a great tribune of the people, a prophet listened to by his own countrymen. King James's tyranny, his bigotry, and his inquisitorial measures seemed to him the very prods that were needed to awaken the spirit of independence and the love of liberty that had slumbered for the last three years in English hearts. There were times when he lamented the cruel fate of Monmouth; but he awaited with confidence the liberator to be sent by the All-Highest. In such an exalted mood he would see pass before him the shadowy faces of the great Puritan regicides.

He could distinguish upon the horizon the approaching storm that could not but sweep the kingdom. This seemed to him the proper time for him to become a "free citizen" of London, the better to realize his political aspirations. His father's connection made it easy for him to be registered as a member of the Corporation of Butchers. Upon the books of the association, under the date of January 26, 1688, is the following entry:

At a court held in Pudding-lane, Daniel Foe, son of James Foe, citizen and butcher, of Fore-Street, Cripplegate, attended to apply for his admission by patrimony, and was admitted accordingly, and paid in discharge of serving all offices, £ 10 15 s.

To-day the memory of Daniel De Foe is commemorated in the Hall of the Butchers by a large stained glass window, representing the distinguished author in a majestic and dignified posture, arrayed in court attire of an elegance that he would surely have approved. Under his arm is a three-cornered velvet hat worthy to be worn upon the head of a king.

In the meantime events moved rapidly. Seven Anglican bishops who had petitioned against the acceptance of James's second Declaration of Indulgence were imprisoned. The King,

**STAINED GLASS WINDOW IN
HONOR OF DE FOE**
in Butcher's Hall. De Foe was chartered a master
butcher, in his day one of the most respected trades.

infuriated, ordered their trial for seditious libel. Their acquittal
was a grea triumph. For the first time in years the effigy of the
Pope was burned in public. All factions were united against
the King. There was feverish activity among the Whigs . . .
messengers departed for the towns of the provinces; couriers
arrived with unexplained peed from Holland. In the midst
of all this agitation, a part of it, was one man, a prey to alter-
nating depression and exaltation . . . intriguing, haranging,
preaching, running with news, spreading his hatred of the
tyrant, and announcing that the Messiah was near at hand;
this man was a certain hosier of Cornhill, well known among
Dissenters by the name of "Daniel Foe."

Meanwhile, the unfortunate Puritans of the West kept looking anxiously out to sea, hoping, like the Celts who had
strained their eyes for the return of Arthur, to see the ships
of Monmouth rise upon the waves. On November 4, 1688,
their patience and faith were rewarded, for on that date one
even greater than Monmouth, sailed into Torbay, come to save
British liberty. William of Orange landed upon English soil
on the anniversary of the day of his birth and of his marriage
. . . to the Seventeenth century mind, particularly to the mind
of De Foe, this was of vast significance. It seemed to insure the
ultimate success of the Protestant cause. Indeed, such an assumption seemed justified. Even in the army of James II, concentrated at Salisbury, there were soldiers who drank openly
to the success of the liberator, as he was called by the English
who welcomed his coming. A great crop of orange ribbons
which betokened each wearer's allegiance to William sprang
up in no time on the streets of London. The disappearance,
on November twenty-sixth, of the Princess Anne, the youngest
daughter of the King, was first explained by the rumor that
she had been assassinated. Armed soldiers mingled with the
crowd, muttering of a bloody vengeance to be taken upon all

the Papists of the Court, who were, of course, blamed for the alleged crime. To quiet the people there was read to them Anne's letter, saying that she had left the palace and joined her brother-in-law, William, of her own accord, because she wished to identify herself with the reformed religion.

De Foe made himself conspicuous at the head of the rejoicing populace by loud cries and gesticulations of welcome to the new order. Indeed, he did not stop at that; leaping again upon his horse, as a rebel to the reigning King, he rode towards the army of the liberator in order to witness the historic occurrences that were under way. He had already reached Windsor when he heard news that caused him to pause for reflection: the Irish dragoons of Lord Faversham, beaten by William's forces in a skirmish near Reading, had scattered about the country, swearing that they were going to spread fire and bloodshed in their way. They did, in fact, march upon Maidenhead, Uxbridge, and Colebrook, but when they found the citizens armed to the teeth and ready to receive them, their resolution melted; scattering in all directions, they threatened dire vengeance. The people of Colebroke warned the country side of the bloodthirsty pack; the neighboring villagers, panic stricken, abandoned their cottages in the middle of the night and, in the pelting rain, sought refuge in the nearby cities of Kingston, Hounslow, Bratford, Egham, and even Windsor. The terror spread, De Foe reported, "like the undulations of the waters in a pond, when a flat stone is cast upon the surface." That December twelfth offered, perhaps, one of the most extreme examples of panic known to history.

Meanwhile De Foe remained prudently at Windsor. When he had picked up enough courage, he decided to make his own investigation as to the extent of damage done by Lord Haversham's dragoons. By doing this he thought he would be able to bring the latest news to the army of the liberator and, perhaps, draw the attention of William of Orange to himself. Early in the morning he started for Maidenhead, which, he was told at Slough, was in ashes, as were also Uxbridge, Reading, and many other cities. But he found that Maidenhead, though in pretty much of a hubbub, was still standing; consequently, he began to question all reports as exaggerated and indeed wholly unfounded. He pushed on to Reading where he was told again that Maidenhead was on fire, Oakingham destroyed, and more matter of the same sort. He had gone as far as was necessary to convince himself from now on that there was but little faith to be put in rumors. Without pushing his investigation any further, he returned to Henley in time to see the second detachment of the Dutch army enter the town that afternoon. Those to whom he reported were already informed of all the facts he had witnessed; he, on the contrary, was astonished to learn that James II had fled from London and had been arrested at the port of Sheerness. Recognized by the crowd at Faversham where he had been taken, the King was suffered to endure insult and mistreatment without any interference on the part of the priests and the gentlemen of his retinue who accompanied him. At last he was brought back to London.

Eager not to lose touch with the least among these momentous happenings, De Foe galloped into Faversham, which was still in a state of agitation. From the excited crowds on the streets he was able to pick up most of the details concerning the capture and return of James II. His account of this historical event, which he uses a number of times in his writings, he says comes from eye witnesses.

De Foe returned to London just in time to take part in the triumphal entrance of William and Mary on December the eighteenth; he mixed with the retinue of the King, his horse adorned with the significant orange ribbons. The Protestant bells rang out at full swing, Protestant throats sent forth hoarse cheers, and, in the evening, millions of Protestant candles died bravely at their posts so that the good folk might prolong their rejoicing long into the night. Daniel joined in the singing at the top of his voice of the revengeful verses of the popular anti-Jacobite song called *Lillibulero,* pausing only to drink, kneeling, to the new "Saint William."

While gaiety and merry-making prevailed in celebration of the coming of William, the royal James, turned out by his country, waited at Rochester until the twenty-third of the month, when he embarked for France. He was never again to see the country where he had dreamed of becoming a second Louis XIV.

Parliament assembled to consider the national crisis. De Foe listened in feverish excitement to all the discussions; he says that he was present at nearly all of the debates in both houses. Upon the twenty-second of January, he heard the House of Lords adopt a resolution that the Commons had sent to them. He was almost beside himself with joy at the words of the resolution that "it is inconsistent with the constitution of this Protestant nation to be governed by a Popish prince." By February the sixth the last vote had been cast, making William and Mary, king and queen of England. This is another date that strikes De Foe as fatalistic; he calls attention to the fact that it was on a February sixth that Charles II died, that Queen Anne was born, and that James II lost his throne.

The political revolution of 1688 was accomplished quite peacefully and rapidly. It proved to Europe that the English people, through their Parliament, were sovereign. In less than fifty years, they had killed one of their kings and exiled another.

The coronation took place on February the thirteenth. It was the signal for demonstrations of the wildest Joy. Shouts of loyalty burst from the people with torrents of noisy acclaim. Beer flowed freely as the nation toasted the new sovereigns. The great overflow of the national drink filled the gutters of the streets and collected between the paving stones. One great laugh shook the Puritan city. The feasting continued into the autumn; on October the twenty-ninth the King and Queen were invited by the Lord Mayor and the Corporation of the city to a great banquet at Guildhall. A corp of volunteer cavalry, many of them the richest merchants of the city, rode in pomp to Whitehall to invite the royal couple. In the cortege an envious pamphleteer notes a young man splendidly garbed in whom he recognized, "Daniel Foe, the hosier in Freeman's Yard, Cornhill."

IV. THE PHŒNIX

"THE English tradesman, though unfortunate, is a kind of phœnix," says De Foe in the *Compleat English Tradesman*, "a phœnix, who rises out of his own ashes." And he adds the advice that "if he is prudent, he makes the ruin of his fortunes a firm foundation to build his recovery upon." It is advice that he himself has been wise enough to follow at times in the course of his long and varied career.

It was success and overwhelming joy that should have made him wary. Instead, confident that all good luck must attend the national era of good feeling, he plunged into the wildest speculations. Fortune yielded to his bold and persistent onslaughts, and he began to multiply his gains. In 1690, he made a fruitful voyage to Liverpool and then sat back to count up the safe reserve of capital that he felt he had amassed. But the moment of self-satisfaction is the moment for caution. Who so fickle and variable as Fortune? She is ready to give place to an ugly Nemesis upon the least or upon no provocation. Within a few months a series of reverses had eaten up the careful accumulations of ten years. At first De Foe could find ready enough excuses for his small losses.

Having imported a large quantity of Spanish wines, he was obliged, in order to pay the duty upon it, to borrow a goodly sum from a Lombard street goldsmith; the latter demanded that the wine be kept in his cellar as security for the loan. Difficulties arose at once and grew more complicated. De Foe was actually forbidden to retail his merchandise. Vainly he sought for some wealthy business man to put up enough

money to save his wine; but weeks passed without the needed
help turning up. The interest on the loan accumulated; the
wine began to spoil. The goldsmith finally sold the whole lot
at auction for a ridiculously small sum and De Foe lost more
than £600 on the whole transaction.

It was at about the same time that De Foe became the victim
of some bold swindlers who, furnished with false letters of
recommendation, bought from him on credit some valuable
material and ordered it delivered into the section of London
known as The Mint. This quarter was the refuge of criminals
of all sorts who were so strongly entrenched that the police
even were powerless to bring them to justice. They were so
bold . . . these robbers of De Foe . . . as to come the very
next day to his shop to defy him openly and to mock at his cre-
dulity. It was too much. . . . De Foe was in a fury of righteous
anger at such rascality. He was next the dupe of men who
pretended to be inventors; playing upon De Foe's well known
taste for novelty, they wheedled him out of some money and
then disappeared, leaving no trace behind them.

But it was the war with France that made commerce and
business more and more uncertain. So many ships were captured by the enemy that it became necessary to place an "assurance," as it was called, upon all cargoes. And the cost of this
insurance made trading almost prohibitive. Daniel tells, for
example, of paying 100 pounds for protection on merchandise
which he sold for a net profit of fifty pounds. These troubles
began to prey upon his mind; he faced the reality that all of
his fame as a poet and an orator was not enough to assure him
of credit as a business man among his associates. He went every
day in great distress to the postoffice in Lombard street. Fever-
ishly, no doubt, he walked up and down the yard and waited
for his mail. The men who sorted it always seemed so slow
to him. But the bad news came inexorably . . . the ships

which Daniel had helped to fill had never arrived at their destination: one of them had been cast by a tempest on the coast of Galicia where it had been plundered by the Spaniards; the other had been captured by a French frigate. Crushed by the disaster De Foe, for the moment, lost courage. In a short time his creditors began to demand what he owed them; but he was unable to pay. By the close of 1692, he was driven to bankruptcy for the considerable sum of 17,000 pounds.

At this time bankruptcy was punished with implacable severity. A business man who was so unfortunate as to fail must stand by and see his family turned out of home and all his property seized. If he did not wish to spend all the rest of his own life rotting in some dungeon, he could choose one of two alternatives . . . flight or suicide. De Foe felt that most of his creditors had confidence in him, and he justified such confidence by putting all of his assets into their hands without any reserve. But even so there were those who might pursue him for personal reasons . . . those who had come to hate him for his superior accomplishments and his cutting sarcasm. He believed it would be prudent for him to disappear at the first threat of arrest and wait until the matter had blown over. He took refuge, as did many other insolvent tradesmen in The Mint, where he found himself plunged into the midst of a heterogeneous mass of swindlers, thieves . . . petty and great ones . . . highwaymen, and widows trying to capture a new husband. The bankrupts who had the means would bribe the guards to permit them to bring carts of merchandise into their asylum during the night; they would squander money that should have been turned over to help pay their debts upon the lowest type of prostitutes. The debauchery of this resort disgusted De Foe so much that he did not neglect, when he had the opportunity later, to expose the intolerable abuses that

were permitted here right in the heart of London . . . even
though the place had offered him a sanctuary when he needed
it most. The privileges it afforded the insolvent tradesman
were granted him. That there was need for just such a place
was recognized by the founding of such an asylum on the
other side of the Thames when The Mint was closed to such
unfortunates a short time later.

According to the rules of The Mint, De Foe was secure for
one month; at the end of that time, the police had the right
to arrest him even though he took refuge in a church. Consequently, when his month was up, De Foe made a cautious
departure for Bristol, where he kept himself out of the way
for many long months; the only break in the monotony of his
voluntary exile from London consisted in the welcome visits
from faithful friends. He went out only in the evening; and
then, only after assuring himself that no officer of the law
was lurking in a nearby doorway to grab him by the collar
and march him off to imprisonment. Only on Sunday could
he walk about freely, for no policeman could make an arrest
on the Lord's Day. So it was he became known to his landlord and close associates in Bristol as the "Sunday Gentleman."

His wife and some influential friends united to procure an
amicable settlement that would clear his name with all of his
creditors. The latter were brought to see that they could gain
nothing by insisting upon imprisonment. How much better for
them to let him go free so that he might recover his business
connections and endeavor to repay them for the losses they
had suffered at his expense. De Foe resolved to merit this confidence placed in him and to reimburse his creditors, at least
in part. Returning to London, he threw himself energetically
into repairing his fortunes; only so could he make up for the
sense of failure that haunted him. Evidently his friends noted
his spirit with satisfaction, for, in just a short time, he was

given proof of their reliance on his business ability and good judgment; he was asked to take a remunerative post as representative to Cadiz. It was a tempting offer, particularly because of the mark of confidence it showed in him. De Foe explains his refusal of the offer in the *Appeal to Honour and Justice,* which was written many years later. He says,

"But Providence, which had other work for me to do, placed a secret aversion in my mind, to leaving England."

De Foe made it always a point of honor to follow the dictates of those quick and often irrational impulses that swayed his will; he believed, with Socrates, in an invisible spirit, a sort of mysterious emanation of Providence, a guardian angel sent by the Lord to serve him in particular. He speaks of a supernatural being that stood at his side and breathed into his ear the counsel that he should follow for his own best interests. There was another and more evident motive that kept De Foe from going abroad . . . he was beginning to gather the fruits of his devotion to the Whig and the Orange cause. Many of his old friends had now come into power, and they did not forget him. They remembered how clever he was; they sought him out now for original ideas. When he saw how well received his suggestions were, he began again to dream great dreams . . . he visioned himself rising once more to position and influence.

But the brilliant future that he had once conceived for his own destiny was now forever clouded by his lamentable bankruptcy in 1692. He would always carry the blot of failure; he could not overcome the fear that stalked with him . . . at any moment one of his old creditors might rise up before him with an order for his arrest. It was the nightmare of his maturity, no less disturbing to him than the fearful visions conjured up by his youthful imagination. It put the taste of bitterness into every good fortune that came his way. It made him a recluse, caused him to practice deception, threw out of line his whole system of morality so that he now looked on life as one steeped in a sense of his own inferiority and was ready to take every advantage that came his way. Such necessity as he had been in seemed to him sufficient justification for any action that would save him from a repetition. His efforts at sublimation led him to draw comparisons between the "poetic license" of the poet and the "white lies" of the unscrupulous merchant. Such is the only possible explanation of the inconsistencies in De Foe's later conduct.

Perhaps the most serious consequences of De Foe's bankruptcy lay in its furnishing his enemies with a formidable weapon against him. Here was the chance for retaliation where old sores still hurt and unpaid debts of another order still rankled. There were many to take the word. He was subjected to all sorts of accusations . . . dishonesty, suspicious dealings, duplicity. Among all these early attacks only one was well-founded:

The author of the pamplet, *Observations on the Bankrupts' Bill,* regretted that the measure gave such advantages to the insolvent class, among whom he names "Mr. Daniel De Foe." "If they could have set bounds to their desires and not been too projecting, in all probability [they] might not have had occasion to crave the benefit of such a law."

De Foe hastened to excuse himself by saying that the principal cause of his ruin was the state of war that interfered so disastrously with maritime commerce. Indeed, De Foe's name is to be found on the list of merchants which the Commons had proposed to indemnify for the losses which they had sustained during the hostilities. But this measure of February, 1694, was, unfortunately, not adopted by the House of Lords, and Daniel continued his struggle unaided by his government. It required the greatest effort on his part to free himself of all his obligations, especially since he set out to pay his creditors in full, although the law held him only to pay a certain percentage of his indebtedness.

He took immense satisfaction in relating the following incident which occurred in a coffee-house where the mention of his name had brought down a storm of execration. One man arose to make this declaration:

"Gentlemen, I know this De Foe as well as any of you, for I was one of his creditors, compounded with him, and discharged him fully. Several years afterwards he sent for me, and though he was clearly discharged, he paid me all the remainder of his debt voluntarily and of his own accord; and he told me, that as far as God should enable him, he intended to do so with everybody. When he had done, he desired me to set my hand to a paper to acknowledge it, which I readily did, and found a great many names to the paper before me; and I think myself bound to own it, though I am no friend to the book [1] he wrote, no more than you."

In between times he published his first pretentious work, *An Essay upon Projects*. During his exile at Bristol he had given much thought to the political and social problems that he felt were interfering with the prosperity and the greatness of England. His own painful position as a fugitive bankrupt caused him to give first consideration to measures that would relieve the embarrassed or unfortunate business man. He was further concerned with the development of instruction in England; he urged, for example, the creation of a body of men, selected for their wisdom, similar to the French Academy. He struck a modern note in advocating the higher education of women; his plan was to give them a general and yet complete course of instruction in some kind of a Protestant nunnery. When he took into account the great number of books appearing

---

[1] *The Shortest Way with Dissenters.*

each year and considered that the government finances did not permit the subsidizing of these works for purposes of aiding the authors or giving them charity, he offered the suggestion, unconscious of the humor in it, that authors be required to pay a special tax which would go towards maintaining a lunatics asylum. In the last part of the *Essay* he advanced many practical methods of conducting the war for the greater glory of British arms.

Since all of the improvements and reforms pointed to the increase of power to William and his ministers, reward was not slow in coming to the author of them. Daniel was presented to the Queen and was one of the company that went with her when she gave orders for landscaping the new gardens at Kensington. He became a frequent visitor at Hampton Court which had been restored by the new rulers.

Following these marks of honor and distinction came more remunerative posts. On May 1, 1695, parliament voted a tax on glass. Thomas Dalby, who was entrusted by the King with selecting a commissioner to collect the new impost, at once made up his mind to enlist the aid of Daniel. The latter, quite unaware of the good fortune in store for him, was away on a business trip. Imagine his great surprise when he received word that he was named for the official position of commissioner on the glass duty. He held the place until April 25, 1699, when the tax was removed upon the protest of the English glassmakers.

In every difficulty, it seemed, the government was to turn to him for help. When the royal coffers began to look alarmingly empty, the public lotteries were established. The English were gamblers by instinct; when a drawing of the lotteries was scheduled, there would be such a tumult on the streets of London that one would think a fire was destroying at least a section of the city. *The London Spy,* a satirical journal of the period, thus reports the excitement that accompanies a drawing:

The Gazette and Post-papers lay by neglected . . . and nothing was purr'd over in the coffee-houses but the Ticket-Catalogues. . . . People running up and down the streets in crowds and numbers, as if one end of the town was on fire, and the other were running to help 'em off with their goods. One stream of Coachmen, Footmen, Prentice-boys, and Servant-wenches, flowing one way with wonderful hopes of getting an Estate for 3 pence. Knights, Esquires, Gentlemen, and Traders, Marry'd ladies, Virgin-maidens, Jilts, Concubines, and Strumpets, moving on foot, in Sedans, Chariots, and Coaches another way; with a pleasing expectancy of getting six hundred a year for a crown. . . . The Unfortunate crying out as they went along, A Cheat, A Cheat, a confounded Cheat! Nothing of fairness in it! The Fortunate in opposition to the other crying 'Tis fair, all fair, the fairest Adventure that ever was drawn!

One can judge from such a description of the importance of the lotteries in the life of a Londoner of the day. Imagine, then, the respect that was accorded the organizers by the buyers of the tickets, or the "adventurers," as they were called. Daniel had the honor of being twice chosen as manager trustee of the royal lotteries; the first time was in October, 1695; he was one of the men selected for the trustworthy position of overseeing the drawing of an "adventure" that offered great profit to the lucky ticket holder who would win 50,000 pounds upon the wager of twenty shillings. In March, 1696, he filled the same office for a more popular lottery for which the tickets sold at a half-guinea.

It was in connection with the announcement of a lottery in an October, 1695, issue of *The Post-Boy* that Daniel's last name occurs for the first time with the aristocratic preposition prefixed to it. The tradesmen whom the Commons in October, 1694, had named for indemnification for his losses sustained in business during the war was called, "Daniel Foe;" but the important individual whose presence was requested in order to assure the success of the operation of the royal lotteries was designated as "Mr. Daniel De Foo." For some years he continued to use both names . . . the tradesman, appearing under the title, "Foe" . . . the literary man and the courtier, responding to the more dignified cognomen, "De Foe," written by him originally as two words. The second form began rapidly to be the dominant one, though his enemies would often maliciously use the original form in order to send a barbed shaft into Daniel's proud heart. Contemporaries were inclined to put the worst interpretation upon his affected change in his last name; they forgot the time when the change occurred and imagined the most extravagant reasons for it.

There is not much doubt that Daniel was actuated by personal vanity and the somewhat adolescent desire to show off. Also he was sensitive about the disagreeable puns to which his paternal name made him the frequent butt. Now that he was becoming intimate with royalty, he felt that he had the right to a name that would command the recognition and the respect of the gentlemen of the Court. "De Foe" seems to be of Norman origin, and it is possible that Daniel was descended from an old family in that country. He had apparently studied the matter for some time, as he was quite sound in prefixing the preposition "de" to the "Foe" in a real effort to restore an ancient family name. His ancestors in Flanders might have been called Defau or Defawe, a normal derivation from the Latin, *fagus,* meaning beech-tree. There is a natural tendency to shorten names of people, so that the descendants of the family Defau or Defawe, might have used simply Fau or Fawe. Such onomastic developments of proper names is well exemplified in analogous pairs of names . . . Delaunay and Launay; Dechesne and Chesne; and Delaune and Laune. As for the vowel formation, the "oe" might easily have been influenced by the common noun meaning enemy. In the *Tour thru' Great Britain,* De Foe tells of a Warwichshire family, "De Beau Foe," a name whose etymology is quite obvious. And De Foe himself indicates his awareness of the possible origin of his own name by the frequency with which he returns again and again to this very Warwichshire family. The fact that there were Huguenot refugees in London by the name of Deffoe or Defo may have helped to point the way to him. Nevertheless, there is no denying the share his own vanity played in his adoption of two words for his last name. Were other proof wanted, there is the care he expended in planning a coat of arms for himself, who had no real right to one. When it was finally made legally his in 1706, it consisted in an elaborate device: *Per chevron engrailed gules and or, three griffins passant counterchanged.* To which he added the Latin inscription from Juvenal of which he was quite proud: *Laudatur et alget.*

Slowly but surely De Foe mounted one by one the steps of that long ladder which leads to the highest honors; at about the same time that he was making his climb, he was also taking steps to open a new business enterprise which succeeded so well that he became more prosperous than he had ever been before. He got hold of enough capital to build at Tilbury a factory for making bricks and pantiles. He called himself the "secretary" of the establishment; that meant that he was the manager, as well as the owner of it. The exact location of this most profitable of all De Foe's ventures may now be seen on the north bank of the Thames in front of the fort which guards the entrance to the mouth of the river. In 1860 at the time of some excavations for the purpose of enlargin; the depot at Tilbury, there were unearthed some bricks and broken tiles which were shown to be the remains of the old factory operated by De Foe; they serve as proof of the durability of the product for which he was responsible.

It was a courageous undertaking, for the English were accustomed to buying their bricks and tiles in Holland. The new industry had to meet foreign competition right on the home market. Furthermore, it was necessary to educate the public who, invariably, preferred the half-burnt bricks of a red color, called sammel, to the hard, grey and white bricks that were well burnt; having chosen against expert advice, they were, nevertheless, ready to complain at the inferior quality of their choice. Daniel, fortunately, had connections with the right kind of people who were able to get him several important orders; for example, in 1697, he was appointed by the government to furnish bricks for the Greenwich hospital. De Foe believed in his business; he put into it every bit of his salary as commissioner of the glass duty, and later added the gifts he received from the King. The success of the undertaking must have been the one salve that would heal the old sore of his bankruptcy. How he must have thrilled as he tended his infant industry and watched it expand so that it became necessary to make extensive additions to it. He was soon giving employment to a hundred families and making an annual benefice of 600 pounds which made it possible for him to begin paying off his old debts. When circumstances made it imperative for him to close his factory in 1703, he records that it meant the loss at one stroke of more than 2,500 pounds.

The management of such an industry was no easy thing. Daniel had trouble in finding workmen; he even made an attempt to hire the beggars who knocked at his door, but they impudently retorted that begging was more profitable and less fatiguing. When he did succeed in getting workmen, he complained about them, lamenting their half-hearted and sluggish way of going about their tasks. Their drunkenness disgusted him; every Saturday evening they took their pay . . . from sixteen to twenty shillings . . . and made straight for a wine shop where they drank until they were intoxicated, in which state they remained until Monday morning, spending their last penny and even going into debt to satisfy their craving for liquor. Their state was appalling . . . they had no shoes to walk in and but a few ragged clothes to wear. Their wives and children lived at the expense of the parish. De Foe considered it a matter of the gravest concern that the English workman was poor and miserable on a wage of nine shillings a week, while a Dutchman could become prosperous on the same earnings.

The hard school of experience had taught Daniel how to watch closely the transactions of his new enterprise; he did not intend to go into bankruptcy a second time. Therefore, although he had an energetic overseer, he did not fail to inspect the brick-yards himself. He tells of a violent quarrel he overheard one day between two of his workmen. In one of the issues of his *Review,* he describes in detail the entire conflict, which seemed to him to offer a fruitful lesson:

"One of the two brick-makers whose name was Peter, had the other down and beat him unmercifully. The fellow that lay under him cried out, and as I was at some distance, I ran with some servants to part them, thinking he had cried murder; but coming nearer I understood him better, and found he cried out, Pay me Peter, pay me Peter! 'Twill be my turn bye and bye! Peter did his best and being a very strong fellow, mauled him sufficiently. But at last when Peter had beaten until he were out of breath, the fellow's turn came; he got up, and Peter was undermost, and the other used him accordingly." De Foe maliciously dedicated this anecdote to the Anglican high church when it turned again to persecuting the Dissenters.

Daniel was a master who was certainly demanding and hard to please, but he was just and reasonable. Without doubt, he wanted to get the greatest amount of work for the lowest cost. This appeared to him only a proper measure in the light of his practical common sense. But his enemies were not slow in making use of any matter that might reflect to his discredit. They accused him of employing what came later to be called the sweating system; that is, of gaining great wealth through the sweat and toil of his employees, of being, in other words, an exploiter of the working class. Seeking for a catch phrase that would hit off this attempt to vilify his character, they managed to give wide circulation to the quip that he "did not, like the Egyptian, require bricks without straw; but, like the Jews, required bricks without paying his labourers." A choir of envious fellow-tradesmen took up this exaggerated refrain and spread its evil suggestion so broadly that De Foe was never able to rid himself of the opprobrium it attached to his name.

Yet what importance can be granted to criticism that is dictated by envy; Daniel, exulting in the success that crowned his efforts, was oblivious of the evil reports spread about him. Trade, "that everlasting spring," had enabled him to recover his fortune. Scarcely four years had passed since his bankruptcy, and he was already able to buy back his horses and carriages. He was once more leading the life of a gentleman, but this time he was managing his affairs more prudently. As an official, he was now in a position to receive many flattering invitations; a part of the summer of 1697 he spent in Sussex at Steyning, the sumptuous estate of Sir John Fagg. A zealous courtier, he felt that he must be present at all the great demonstrations organized in honor of the King; he did not hesitate to break off a business deal at Yarmouth in order to join the triumphant procession that on November 16, 1697, escorted William, just returned from Holland, through the streets of the city. Of course, Daniel would not, for anything in the world, miss the races at Newmarket, particularly not the brilliant ones that followed the peace at Ryswick; he always recalled them with enthusiasm.

He lived in London only a part of the time, and his family saw very little of him these days, for he took his meals, as did all the prominent men, at Pontack's, the renowned tavern where a delicious dinner was served for four or five shillings with old wine at seven shillings a bottle. He had just bought another house in Westminster which he had to look after quite frequently as the tenants were very poor pay. He had a good deal of contention with one of them, a butcher, one of his own connection, who kept putting off the settling of his rent upon the pretext that he was waiting for money from Lord X . . . or Lord Y . . . until finally he ended in bankruptcy without having paid his irate landlord a penny. A good share of the year Daniel must spend at Tilbury. He had built near his tile factory an up-to-date country-house, and, whenever he was there, he spent his leisure hours boating . . . he had purchased a pretty little sailing vessel of which he was quite proud.

Success turned his head; forgetting the lessons of misfortune and the strict principles of his youth, he, who had been once on the point of becoming the Reverend Foe, now gave himself up entirely to the pursuit of fleeting pleasures and distractions. In his effort to imitate the licentious Rochester, he took to composing light and amorous verse after the style of his model. The manuscript of one, entitled *Good Advice to the Ladies,* he had circulated among his friends and admirers, although he endeavored to suppress it after it was published in 1702. In it he counseled beautiful women not to hide their charms and give them only to "that thing called a husband." De Foe takes his place among the poets of his day as master of the lampoon, leaving tragedy to Dryden, comedy to Congreve, lyrical verse to Wycherley, the ballad to D'Urfey, the panegyric to Prior, and religious poetry to Tate. If he had stopped with this light pastime, he could have been accused only of frivolity, but he, who had once aimed at the ministry, must now let practices of a most compromising nature enter into his life. To escape the reproaches of his wife, the censure of his serious-minded, Non-Conformist friends, and the pursuit of old creditors, he took a number of different apartments in the city, and changed his residence so frequently that even his coachman was not always able to say where his master has spent the night. To add to his list of questionable actions, he set up at Tilbury an acknowledged mistress, in imitation of the custom of the nobility. But, if we are to believe Pope and Savage, the lady was one who followed the honorable calling of "oyster woman." The son, born to this illegitimate union, as a living reminder of the sin, came later to add to his mother's name (Norton), the name of his father, when the latter became famous.

This period of irregular living did not last long. Daniel's Puritan conscience was not really dead, and it began to make itself heard in protest to a manner of living that he had been taught to abhor. Daniel bemoaned the fact that the flesh is weak, and temptations are strong; he deplored his past errors and proved his repentance by his earnest recommendation to others, in *The Serious Reflections of Robinson Crusoe*, that they should not follow his wickedness; he drew the nice analogy that "the man who has been sick is half a physician." His humility quieted his conscience so that he was able to answer the Presbyterian minister, Mr. Howe's reproaches concerning his misconduct by the pious assumption that, since God had repaired his material fortune, He must certainly have forgiven his follies and indiscretions. Nevertheless, he quite prudently drew the curtain over his life of sin so that

no one would have been aware of these regrettable episodes
had his political enemies been as discreet as he was.

He did, however, give a great deal of space in his writings
to curious anecdotes connected with his life as a rich manufacturer of Tilbury. One of the most amazing was the descent,
one day, of a great cloud of winged insects from the marshes
of Essex upon the streets of the town; they covered the surface
of the Thames, filled his boat, moored on the river bank, and
fell in such quantities down the two chimneys of his house.
that he scooped up from his two fireplaces enough of the
insects to fill his hat. To him it was the most extraordinary
thing he had ever seen, and he delighted in dwelling upon
the details of the phenomenon. With similar extravagance of
detail does he relate his experiences on the river. It became
necessary for him to make a series of business trips, which
he called "dangerous adventures," although they appear to
have been merely taking the ferry which passed Tilbury on
its way from Gravesend to London. It was only when the
matter was most urgent and the tide was most favorable that
he undertook this trip, as he was far from being comfortable
on the water where the slightest wave appeared to him "enormous" and "monstrous;" the temerity of the boatmen, too,
seemed to him the height of foolhardiness. The ferrymen
through laziness and indifference were accustomed to guiding
the boat towards the middle of the stream where the strong
current that pulled towards the sea carried them along. There
was always the prospect of danger from the backwater; whenever there were any other passengers, De Foe would protest against the maneuver and, finding himself supported,
would threaten to cut the boatman's throat if he did not seek
the shore and employ either his sail or his oar in making their
way down-stream. But one evening as he was returning from
London, he discovered that he was the only passenger on

board. The wind rose and the water became quite choppy; De Foe was concerned about the safety of the boat; he realized, however, that the least display of alarm on his part would only arouse the spirit of bravado in the boatman with, perhaps, fatal consequences. Distressed beyond measure, he, nevertheless, managed to control himself and appear indifferent. He even stretched out in the bottom of the boat and pretended to be asleep. His tactics were successful; the boatman proposed, of his own accord, to stop at Blackwall until the weather cleared. De Foe agreed with apparent regret, while, in reality, he could scarcely repress a sigh of relief; as soon as his feet touched land, he offered thanks to Providence for his safe delivery.

V. THE CONFIDANT OF THE KING

IN business and in politics De Foe had now found himself.
Straddling the topmost rungs of these two ladders, he
smiled as he saw the star of an even greater ambition just
within his grasp, or so it seemed to him. The linking of his
name with the names of other great writers of the period
brought the warmest glow of satisfaction to his heart. It was
the unbroken friendship with his old classmate, John Dunton,
nicknamed the preaching Weathercock, that led to this distinction so early in his career. Dunton, who had just set up as
a bookseller, was somewhat eccentric, quite vainglorious, and
always busy about something; one of his hobbies was search-
ing for odd bits of fact that would contribute to the sum total
of human knowledge. He and his friends established, in 1690,
a literary club to which they gave the pretentious name, *Athenian Society*. Daniel was one of the most interested and most
active members of the group; he was always glad to mingle
with educated men who might add to his own meager knowledge of Greek and Latin. The Society published, over a period
of seven years (1691-1697), a journal, first called the *Athenian
Gazette* and then the *Athenian Mercury;* it pretended to be a
kind of literary clearing-house, a forerunner of such modern
publications as *Notes and Queries*. There had never been anything like it in England, but it had probably been suggested to
Dunton by the *Journal des Sçavants* and the *Acta Eruditorum,*
continental journals in circulation at the time. The editorial
staff of the *Mercury,* made up primarily of Dunton, Samuel
Wesley, and Richard Sault, announced that they would have

the aid of the "great writers of the times, Tate, Mottreux, Swift, and De Foe." The latter speaks proudly in his *Essay upon Projects* of being an "Athenian." Posterity cannot speak so proudly of his attempt to celebrate the glory of the Society in an execrable ode after the manner of Pindar. De Foe generously proffered his aid to the editors in answering the numerous queries addressed to the Society . . . not hesitating to propound his theories upon almost any subject, theological, literary, scientific, and gastronomic. Here is a sample of the kind of questions addressed to the Athenian Society which De Foe attempted to answer:

"Is there such an animal as a Unicorn?

"Shall negroes rise at the last day?

"Which is the greatest sin, Fornication or eating Black Pudding [1] on Good Friday?"

De Foe was soon accepted by the crowd as an infallible oracle. Every new problem that caught the public interest was passed on to him; his answer was awaited breathlessly . . . nor did he fail to have his say, usually in the form of a trenchant satire that took hold of the fancy of the public. The "Reformation of Manners" and "Occasional Conformity of Dissenters" were two topics of concern at the moment. The reign of the two strict Protestants, William and Mary, had brought to a close the unhampered excesses of the Restoration; the King made clear his attitude towards vice and immorality in his very first public address. And, indeed, there was cause for national alarm over the liquor question; the break in business relations with France in 1689 had given impetus to British manufacturers, including the distillers who made a bid for popular favor with a new drink, called gin, which they were able to place on the market at a price that put it within the reach of the poorest laborer. Daniel liked good wine and good

---

[1] The answer to the last was: "The first excludes from heaven, the second does not."

beer, but he protested without ceasing against the introduction of this vile mixture which was, he said, poisoning the nation . . . he called gin one of the great banes of life, along with the devil, the Pope and the Pretender. He threw the whole force of his personality, whether writing for publication or volubly declaiming before a more intimate audience, into the Puritan warfare against the unrestrained license of the last two reigns. He contributed to the "Societies for the Reformation of Manners," founded by the Queen. These organizations soon became influential enough to demand the closing of the brothels, to establish institutions for the care of abandoned children, and to insist upon keeping holy the Lord's Day by forbidding all games, celebrations, and noises of any kind on the Sabbath. In 1698 De Foe published a resounding pamphlet, *The Poor Man's Plea,* from which the ministers freely drew long extracts for their sermons. The author, hiding behind the disguise of a pauper, presented his ideas clearly and dogmatically.

"With regard to the reformation of manners," he said in substance, "why not begin with the wealthy, who should set an example? It is always the poor who are censored for vices that are excused in the upper classes. Or why not reform the magistrate first? Is a man to be blamed for protesting against a sentence at the pillory for drinking, when the judge who pronounces the sentence is tipsy? Who will graciously pay a fee for letting slip an oath or two when the magistrate who demands the penalty does so with a vehement,

" 'God damn him, the dog must pay!' ?"

The lower classes have become better mannered, De Foe says, because they have had to accept the dictum imposed by those of wealth and position.

This tirade was far from pleasing to the ones affected by it, and De Foe was made to feel their displeasure. He was before the public eye now, and must suffer the consequences of his public utterances. It was, perhaps, suggested that he could give more valuable aid to the Society by leaving his neighbors alone and reserving his reform measures for himself; he remained silent for a few years but returned to the charge with a savage satire in verse, called the *Reformation of Manners,* in which, despite the hypocritical assurances in the preface, he indulged in personal attacks on certain judges and Anglican ministers whose names he suggested by initials. He did not hesitate to load these victims of his pen with such epithets as: libertine, rake, seducer, Sodomite, blackguard, and so forth. Less than a year after the publication of this poem, when his boldness had put him in a difficult position, Daniel was the first to be amazed at the blind fury of the magistrates and the clergy against him. He posed as a martyr, but humbly admitted that he had been in the wrong in yielding to the impulse to attack debauched judges, drunken clergymen, and blaspheming atheists. It was outraged virtue, not prudence that had governed him, he said. But never . . . no never . . . would he have thought of criticizing any one in particular. It was not his fault if certain magistrates and clergymen had recognized themselves under such initials as S . . . . n, or B . . . . s, letters he had chosen at random to indicate types of the ridiculous and the wicked.

The uncompromising quality of De Foe's Puritanism is well-illustrated by the stand that he took at this particular time upon the question of occasional conformity. It might have been that he wished to show those who knew of his misdeeds how he had changed, to cover the scandalous acts of his private life by assuming a sternly moral attitude in public. Whatever the motivating force, he chose for attack the custom of certain Dissenters who held official positions in following the letter of the law by "occasional conformity to the rites of the Church of

England;" they would attend every Sunday the services of the Established church, as they were supposed to do if they held public office; then, having fulfilled that requirement, they would go, as unobtrusively as possible, to one of their conventicles. But in October, 1697, the Lord Mayor of London made the mistake of attending a Presbyterian service wearing all the insignia of his office. The "outrage," as it was called, aroused a storm of protest and vituperation; the Tories took this as an opportunity to light upon the Whigs, who were, in the main, Dissenters, and to demand that the odious practice of "occasional conformity" be abolished. They declared that, if a Dissenter wished to serve the government, he must drop his observance of a religious form that was out of harmony with the principles of the State church. With his usual delight in paradoxes, De Foe joined the chorus of Tories against his own party, but he stamped his remarks with his own point of view.

"An upright man," he said, "has only one religion, and he cannot prostitute his conscience for worldly advantages; he dare not play hide and seek with the Almighty."

He insisted that one must either sincerely accept the dogmas of the Anglican church or else regard its teachings as detestable heresies; he urged the abolishment, in the name of loyalty and for the honor of religion, of these "amphibious creatures" who try to be at the same time conformist and nonconformist.

As De Foe went his way, wrapped in his fine uncompromising cloak, his conscience clear, he was serenely indifferent to the approaching storm, nor could he have anticipated what a tempest of personal insult he would stir up for himself. Outstanding among his assailants was the famous Presbyterian minister, John Howe, whose attack upon Daniel had most serious consequences; it led the Dissenters to a conclusive break with the presumptuous pamphleteer who had made common cause with their persecutors. A few years later when the question of occasional conformity again came up, De Foe took a different stand in order to atone for his earlier lapse and to work himself into the good graces of his Dissenting friends; it was too late. His first offense was never either forgiven or forgotten. When a Non-Conformist minister saw fit to quote from De Foe's works, he always studiously avoided mentioning the name of the author.

If De Foe had given a little more thought to the matter, he would have realized that his fondness for paradox could not but bring him into trouble; but he lived too much in the present to bother his head about the distant and problematical consequences of the play of his wit. At the moment he sought fame above everything . . . why not accept the recognition that his dangerous and brilliant talent brought him . . . who could be expected to forego expressing so pronounced a gift for satire! The most paradoxical of all his works, the one that established his reputation as a great writer of the times was his long poem, published in January, 1701, *The True-Born Englishman*. From the moment of its appearance it caught and held public fancy; Daniel was always proud of being spoken of as the author of *The True-Born Englishman*.

De Foe's verse was never melodious; it was generally labored and often inaccurate; yet he boasted of his poetic talent and was regarded by his fellow citizens as "one of the great poets of the period." That is not so surprising in view of the fact that the reign of William was, perhaps, the most prosaic in English history . . . all the creative activity of the nation was being absorbed in war and business . . . and that the poet laureate of the reign was one Nahum Tate, whose verse is certainly equalled by De Foe. There are, in fact, surpassing passages in the *True-born Englishman* that save the poem from oblivion . . . that show a verve almost epic and that contain striking lines, turned with the neatest rhythm. The piece was written, however, to fill a passing need. John Tutchin had published a satirical poem, *The Foreigners,* in which he had scornfully stigmatized William by declaring:

"It is intolerable for a true-born Englishman to be governed by a Dutch king."

The statement was a red flag to De Foe's bull-like temper. He could not stand having his idol so mishandled; in addition, he might have sensed in the attack a thrust at his own Flemish origin.

"A true born Englishman, indeed! Who is a true-born Englishman?" he demanded, and proceeded to pour out a scathing reply: Whoever knows history well, knows that there is no such person in existence. From whom would he have descended? The first inhabitants of Great Britain were barbarians whose vices indicate that they were direct descendants of Satan. Then came tribes of invaders, the scum of the European nations, Romans, Saxons, Danes; all of whom left behind offspring whose race would be hard to define. The Normans came next, easily conquering the country. Our "old nobility" forget too readily that they are descended

"From the most scoundrel race that ever lived;
A horrid crowd of rambling thieves and drones."

Who knows but that his great ancestor was a French cook or an Italian whore! Let us examine this "heterogeneous thing," called an Englishman . . . first the product of the eager rapes committed by Roman brutes upon the native Britons; upon the female offspring of this mixture, the Danish pirates engendered a "mongrel half-bred race" whose "rank daughters" submitted to the will of the conquering Norman soldiery. This is the foundation of the "well-extracted brood of Englishmen," says De Foe. A Turkish horse better understands his family history than does a great English Lord. And it is this amphibious nation that shows its disgust because its ruler is a "new-come foreigner." De Foe could only shrug his shoulders at such inconsistency.

His shrug found the Britons in sufficient good humor to enjoy a joke at their own expense. The word, *jingoism,* had not been invented at the beginning of the Eighteenth century. De Foe's satire was all-inclusive . . . it mocked at the vanity of the aristocracy, but stepped on the toes of no one in particular. Well-filled bellies could shake with laughter; The *True-Born Englishman* was the best-seller of the times. In 1701 alone nine editions, selling at one shilling a copy, were disposed of; between 1701 and 1704 there were twelve pirated editions put out by unscrupulous book-sellers. De Foe estimated that more than 80,000 copies of these unauthorized editions, badly printed on shoddy paper, were sold throughout the kingdom at one or two pennies apiece by peddlers; he declared that he would be worth many thousands of pounds if his property had not been so unceremoniously stolen from him. But he did not grieve over his financial loss to any great extent, since it was the wide circulation of his poem that won him his last great ambition . . . a secure place among the great writers of his age. Every one from the struggling young apprentice to the wealthy and established merchant could quote long passages from his poem . . . his phrases were in every one's mouth. The pack of enemies to the crown frothed at the mouth in rage and barked with all their might in protest. Pamphleteers of the opposition rained a perfect torrent of invectives upon De Foe's head. It was insinuated that a "Billingsgate Amazon" had supplied the choice words in the author's vocabulary in order that the poem might have the proper flavor of filth to catch the fancy of the crowd. They called De Foe "an ill bird that defil'd his own nest." They declared that he had been "got by a Dutch Pot-hero upon an English fishwife," that he was "the spawn of both nations, a loathsome thing, shap'd like a toad with spots and scabs," and more of the same sort. More moderate and better-mannered journalists accused De Foe of having dragged the nation in the dirt in the eyes of the world, of having destroyed the regard of the lower classes for the nobility, in a word, of having done an unpatriotic thing. They were not far mistaken, either, for, two hundred years later, the Hindus used *The True-born Englishman* as a means of propaganda against their oppressors. But nothing at this time could disturb De Foe's self-satisfaction. . . . Was he not the great poet sacrificed on the Cross of Fame? He had made forever ridiculous the expression "the true-born Englishman;" his verses had been read aloud in the streets; from all directions expressions of envy and of admiration were showered upon him; finally came the highest honor . . . the King sent for him in order to tell him personally how much the poem pleased His Majesty.

No two men of this period could have been found who, by the similarity of their mentality and their taste were in more perfect harmony than were William of Orange and Daniel De Foe. Both of them were practical and realistic; both were strict, but unbigoted, Protestants; both of them liked business and gardening; both hated the Devil, the Pope, and Louis XIV. William was instinctively drawn to De Foe at this first meeting; he recognized the bond of deepest sympathy between them. As for Daniel, from that moment, he worshiped the King as a demigod; he could no more see defects in the King than he could distinguish spots on the sun; he was faithful to his hero-worship of William to the end of his life. Every year on November the fourth, "the initial day of Europe's liberty, the great dawning of the Age's glory," according to De Foe,

KING WILLIAM AND QUEEN MARY

De Foe was one of King William's secret counsellors and had an almost
fanatical devotion to that monarch, writing: "Can an Englishman go to
bed or rise without blessing the name of King William?"

there appeared an edition of his *Review* dedicated to the memory of William of Orange, the mention of whose name was alone sufficient to call forth from Daniel a lyrical eulogy rare from his pen. One such expression of enthusiasm that appeared in an issue of his magazine follows:

Can an Englishman go to bed or rise up without blessing the very name of King William? . . . When you sit down to eat, why have you not soldiers quartered in your house, to command your servants and insult your table? 'Tis because King William subjected the military to the civil authority, and made the sword of justice triumph over the sword of war. When you lie down at night, why do you not bolt and bar your chamber to defend the chastity of your wives and daughters from the ungoverned lust of raging mercenaries? 'Tis because King William restored the sovereignty and dominion of the laws, and made the redcoat world servants to those that paid them. When you receive your rents, why are not arbitrary defalcations made upon your tenants, arbitrary imposts laid upon your commerce, and oppressive taxes levied upon your estates? . . . 'Tis because King William re-established the essential security of your properties, and put you into that happy condition, which few nations enjoy, of calling your souls your own.

This was only one step short of numbering this benefactor of England among the saints; De Foe took that one step in his long philosophic poem, *Jure Divino,* when he says of William:

"A guard of glorious lights form'd his ascent,
  And wond'ring stars adored him as he went."

It was Daniel who usually rose in the gatherings of Dissenters and in the Whig clubs to propose in a voice, trembling with emotion, the time-honored toast:

"To the Glorious, Pious, and Immortal Memory of the Great Deliverer . . . who rescued us from Popery, Prelacy, Brass Money, and Wooden Shoes."

To this the Puritans would add in an undertone their peculiar litany, "From Plague, Pestilence, and Famine; from
Bishops, Priests, and Deacons; Good Lord, deliver us!"

William's effort at fixing the order of succession to the
crown of England in such a fashion that the Catholic Stuarts
could never get hold of it was blessed by the Whigs long
after his death.

Mutual sentiments of sympathy and admiration put the relationship of William and De Foe on the most cordial basis from
the very start. At the end of a few months they had become
quite intimate. William was keenly aware of the importance
of the economic angle of affairs in Europe; moreover, he could
gain nothing but profit from conversing with an intelligent
and well-informed business man who had already given many
proofs of his devotion to the Protestant cause. Henceforth, it
was not necessary for De Foe to seek aid from influential
friends for advancing his ideas; he could take his ingenuous
projects straight to the attentive ear of the King. His first important suggestion was to shift the scene of the war with Spain
from the continent to the enemy's possession in South America.
By the beginning of the year (1702), he was ready to lay before
William an exact plan for an attack upon the Spanish colonies; he proposed first the conquest of Chili where he would
establish a strong basis of operations upon which the English
army might depend in its invasion of the American continent
to the north and the east. At the same time he would have a
large fleet seize Havana and make this port a source of supplies for troops that would go from there to the Mexican shore
where the Spaniards would be unable to resist a well-planned
invasion. In this fashion the famous old route of the Spanish
galleons would be cut in two, and the source of inexhaustible
riches to the successors of Philip II would be dried up forever.
De Foe had in mind, also, an accompanying project that would

yield, he believed, important subsidies for the continuation of the war; he urged on the conquest of Guiana, a country with the richest of resources; he describes their rivers, veritable Pactoluses, rolling with nuggets of gold. De Foe had charts that showed conclusively how this country might be taken almost at once without striking a blow. William was dazzled by the prospects that his humble adviser opened up to him; he was accustomed to directing his foreign affairs himself, consulting only the two Hollanders among his counselors, Portland and Albermarle.

These two men were also captivated by the originality in Daniel's views, William took the first step in following De Foe's suggestions by insisting, in his treaty of alliance with the Emperor, Leopold I, that all the land taken in the West Indies should remain English possessions. After more careful study and examination of De Foe's projects, he was preparing to carry them out to the letter when his premature death put an end to the whole matter. One can only imagine the high position the originator of these plans might have attained had they proved successful.

Important as these services were they were not enough to make Daniel the real "confidant of the King." There was a secret undertaking, at times quite dangerous, that bound him yet more closely to his sovereign. In the latter's service he consented to act as informer, or, as his enemies put it, as a spy upon his fellow citizens . . . a service for which he was well repaid. It was his duty to catch the spirit of public opinion, to report upon the proceedings at the gatherings of those who were antagonistic to the court in order to point out who were the most stubborn and the most dangerous to the peace of the administration. The Whig party was, at this time, divided into two factions, of which one, known as the "old Whigs," was hostile to the royal policy; it was this group that was subject to the most careful watching on Daniel's part.

From old letters that have been recently published by the Historical Manuscript Commission of England, there has come to light De Foe's part in this espionage. Several times his intimacy with the King is revealed by the frank advice that he offered him in critical moments, as in the following extract of a message to William when the latter, overwhelmed by the violence of parliament, had grown despondent:

"Your Majesty must face about, oblige your friends to be content to be laid by and put in your enemies, put them into those posts in which they may seem to be employed, and thereby take off the edge and divide the party."

De Foe knew by experience the value of such advice, division for the sake of governing . . . and he knew, too, that almost everybody has his price if one is willing to pay it. It is not likely that De Foe was in possession of any great state secrets, but he was made familiar, through the King, with the worst side of the political situation as it stood at the end of William's reign. He jealously guarded his intimacy with his sovereign, but could not refrain from boasting at times of his knowledge of political secrets, carrying such a knowing air that he aroused the suspicions of certain of the nobility who were made uneasy by his manner. De Foe did not hesitate to avouch having the confidence of the King; he would proclaim to whoever would listen to him that,

"I had the honour to be trusted, esteemed, and, much more than I deserved, valued, by the best King England ever saw. . . . I am not at all vain in saying, I had the honour to know more of his Majesty than some of those that have thus insulted him knew of his horse. . . ."

His repetitions became boresome, and his modesty subject to question in such statement as this, "It has been my honour to be heard and valued by the best King that ever reigned over you, and I can, with a boasting not contrary to modesty, write it on my grave, as the true character of my life:

"By wise men courted, and by fools despised."

Feeling certain of the King's backing, De Foe cast aside all prudence; he openly took part in the movement instigated by the Whig faction that supported William. Revolutionary measures were undertaken to bend the Tory parliament of 1701 to the monarch's will. The people of Kent were preparing to protest formally against the Common's delay in giving William the vote of credit he had asked for in order to prepare for a new war with France. The Kentish petition was brought to London by five men, led by one Colepeper. The Commons was greatly disturbed by the implications in this independent act; every possible means was used to scare the men out of presenting the petition, but Colepeper persisted and, with his companions, made his entrance during the session of May 8, 1701. Wild with rage and fear, the enemies of the King sought to arrest these five men of Kent upon the pretext that their petition was unlawful.

But the Whigs were prepared for just such an emergency; they made the best possible use of the incident to turn the crowd against the Commons for trampling under foot the most sacred rights of every British citizen. The whole town was excited in the interest of the five martyrs; they sold thousands of copies of their pictures and composed songs in their honor. De Foe took advantage of the moment when the passions of the people were most stirred up to write a violent lampoon which he called: *A Memorial from the Gentlemen, Freeholders, and Inhabitants of the Counties of ———, in behalf of themselves and many thousands of the good people of England;* he signed this satire with the threatening words, "Our Name is Legion, and We are Many More."

The text of this strange pamphlet consisted of an enumeration of the fifteen grievances of "Loyal Englishmen;" that is, of those who were followers of William, against a parliament that was tyrannical, corrupt, insolent, traitorous, negligent, unlawful, scandalous, debauched, and so forth. Before giving general circulation to this statement, De Foe copied it, disguising his handwriting; he then drew up a letter to the Speaker of the Commons, Robert Harley, challenging him, in the name of 200,000 citizens, to distribute the *Memorial* among the members of his assembly. At the head of sixteen armed men who were ready to draw their swords in his defense, if need be, he went boldly to the House of Commons. In the midst of the disturbance caused by their entrance, he handed over to Harley the pamphlet and the letter of admonition. Could it have been possible that, at this critical moment, Harley was subconsciously impressed by the character of this man who was later to become his most trusted assistant? It might have been that he made up his mind right then to engage the aid of one who was capable of such courage.

The members who were hostile to the royal policy were afraid. The most violent of them, one Jack Howe, declared dolorously that he feared for his life. The greater part of the Tories who had been but a short time before ready to fight, were now of a mind to try the country air for the sake of their health. The Commons, after a timid and formal protest, found it wiser to concern themselves with other business. The five men from Kent were freed and a great banquet was prepared for them. A disgruntled Tory journalist, describing the acclamation with which the appearance of these men was greeted, wrote:

Jove, when he appears in an Assembly of the Gods, cannot have more homage paid him. . . . Next the Worthies was placed their Secretary of State, the author of the *Legion Letter;* and one might

have read the downfall of parliaments in his very countenance. . . .
The journey-men and apprentices ran for one whole day from their
masters. This was even as bad as a Lord-Mayor's show. Hither came
the good man and good woman who brought her child along with
her, and went home very well satisfied, and thanked God that her
child had seen a Kentish Worthy.

This was the way William gained his end; feeling himself
sure now of public opinion, he did not hesitate to dissolve his
intractable parliament. He was generous in his expressions of
gratitude towards those who had aided him at the risk of
their liberty and even of their lives.

Daniel De Foe, the favored of a great monarch, the prince
of satirists, the master of the lampoon, what is to become
of you? What high place can you not obtain with your talent
for vigorous expression and your clarity of intelligent thought?

Alas! An implacable Nemesis ruins all his hopes by bringing about one of those casual accidents which so frequently
change the destiny of individuals and of nations. On February
21, 1702, while William of Orange was taking part in his
favorite sport, hunting, his horse stumbled at a molehill and
threw the King so violently to the ground that he broke his
collar bone. The fracture was such a shock to his body, already
undermined by overwork and worry, that he never recovered
from it; after several weeks of severe torture, he succumbed to
Death which he had so often faced defiantly upon the battle
field.

As soon as the news of his decease was noised about in
London, the Tories indulged in expressions of the most inde-
cent rejoicing. Toasts were given in public to the King's horse,
"worthy of having a star named after him" for having had
the fine idea of throwing its rider. Many cups were emptied
also in honor of the "little gentleman in velvet," that is to say
the mole, who had been lucky enough to be the cause of the

fall. De Foe grew white with wrath at these slanderous words. He set to work at once composing a long memorial poem to avenge the wrong done his idol; his sincere sorrow and unlimited veneration for his hero shine through every verse of this work of love. But he was soon convinced that no detraction could dim the glory of William's achievements, and he satisfied himself with laughing at the futile efforts of the Tories, "dogs who bay the moon." He said of them, "They make a noise and look up; but the beauteous planet shines on and suffers no eclipse from their rage. The glorious and immortal memory of the King will shine to the end of time."

VI. DE FOE FANS A BREEZE—ENCOUNTERS A TEMPEST

D E FOE looked with suspicion upon the accession of Queen Anne, the second daughter of James II. His fears were justified, for it was not long until a change became apparent in England . . . a subtle change that permeated the atmosphere with a sense of unrest and insecurity. Anne was inclined to be weak- willed and artful, but she was strongly biased in her religious outlook and wholly devoted to the cause of the Established church. Certain of royal favor again, the High church leaders celebrated their triumph by urging a drunken crowd to destroy some of the Dissenters' meeting-houses and molest their ministers, if any were bold enough to venture out into the streets.

Anne followed the foreign policy of her predecessor in declaring war upon France, but her domestic policy showed signs of being retroactive. She soon found excuse to remove the Whig ministers and lent her royal support to the agitations against the Dissenters that were led by a certain fanatic clergyman, named Doctor Sacheverell. Under the pretext that "the Church was in danger," the Commons attempted to revive the old problem of occasional conformity. But the Lords who had been named by William successfully blocked the whole vexatious measure. De Foe lined up this time with his fellow religionists, but he did not succeed in winning his way wholly into their good graces.

In that great powder magazine that was the London of the moment, the least spark was sufficient to cause a tremendous

91

explosion. De Foe cast into it a flaming torch. Hiding behind the mask of a *high-flyer,* by which was meant an extreme partisan of the High church group, he presented his discussion; it carried to the point of absurdity the very ideas that Doctor Sacheverell was propounding each Sunday in his sermons; the latter had been imploring the nation to raise the "bloody flag and banner of defiance" against the Dissenters. De Foe, in the twenty-nine-page pamphlet which appeared on December 1, 1702, entitled *The Shortest Way with Dissenters,* proposed a religious unity in Great Britain to be achieved by a violent suppression of all Non-Conformist sects. He wrote:

"This is the time to pull up this heretical weed of sedition, that has so long disturbed the peace of our church and poisoned the good corn. . . . "

But, he continued, objectors say, that would be simply a throw-back to the days and the methods of the Inquisition.

"I answer," says De Foe, "it is cruelty to kill a snake or a toad in cold blood, but the poison of their nature makes it a charity to our neighbors to destroy those creatures, not for any personal injury received, but for prevention; not for the evil they have done, but the evil they may do."

As he goes on, this supposed high-flyer, carried away by a sacred enthusiasm, plunges into this vehement peroration:

Alas! The Church of England! What with Popery on one hand and schismatics on the other, how has she been crucified between two thieves! Now let us crucify the thieves; let her foundations be established upon the destruction of her enemies: the doors of mercy being always open to the returning part of the deluded people, let the obstinate be ruled with a rod of iron! . . . And may God Almighty put into the hearts of all the friends of truth to lift up a standard against pride and Antichrist, that the posterity of the sons of error may be rooted out from the face of this land forever!

QUEEN ANNE
in whose reign De Foe passed through his most difficult period, being
at one time pilloried and spending several terms in prison.

In putting on paper these resounding phrases, De Foe was really giving himself much amusement. He regarded his work as a timely bit of foolery that would hold the high-flyers up to ridicule in the eyes of all sensible folk and so create some public sentiment in favor of the Dissenters. But he had forgotten that irony is rarely appreciated by the general run of people. The furor of discussion that followed this publication really frightened the author of it at first.

As a matter of fact, religious feeling had become so hysterical that no one was able to say just what the much-talked-of article really aimed at . . . whether it was parody or satire. Some took the blood-thirsty tirades just quoted seriously; the high-flyers lauded its merits and lamented that such a remarkable writer should choose to be anonymous. A young Tory clergyman to whom a friend had sent a copy of *The Shortest Way,* acknowledged the receipt of the book in a letter filled with the most extravagant praise. He wrote:

"I join the author in all he says, and have such a value for the book, that, next to the Holy Bible and the sacred Comments, I take it for the most valuable piece I have. I pray God put it into Her Majesty's heart to put what is there proposed into execution."

As for the Dissenters, they were at once convinced that the pamphlet was the work of one of their worst enemies. They, De Foe says afterwards, "never saw the irony of the style but began to look about them to see which way they should fly to save themselves." One of them attempted to match *The Shortest Way* with *The Surest Way,* in which he pleaded for mercy for the Dissenters. The president of one of the Non-Conformist clubs of London made a public declaration that if he knew the author of the inflammatory pamphlet, he would denounce him, not for the sake of the reward he might obtain, but just for the satisfaction it would give him to perform a duty against one who was guilty of advocating such measures. An "honest colonel" presented himself as a hangman ready to dispose of the fanatic high-flyer who clamored for innocent blood.

Aroused by one such explosion of fury, De Foe decided that his little joke had gone far enough; he published *A Brief Explanation of a late Pamphlet entitled the Shortest Way with Dissenters;* and so all of England learned that the famous pamphlet had not been written by a high-flyer at all, but by some prominent Non-Conformist who was really mocking at Sacheverell and his followers in order to show that fanatics of that type would stop short of nothing to gain their ends.

The Whigs held their sides with laughter. The high-flyers frothed with rage. The Dissenters remained suspicious and uneasy; they could not forget the attitude that one of their number had taken earlier upon a question that affected them so nearly . . . that of occasional conformity; and they were not at all convinced of the irony and the satire in *The Shortest Way.* One of them questioned in this wise:

"He must have a very transforming maw or a very good slight of hand, that will spew us up claret or blood, Knives or Daggers, and at the same time to make us believe 'tis all the same wine and sugar-plums that he swallow'd before."

The enmity against De Foe, who was easily guessed to be the author, did not let up; far from it . . . and, to put him on trial, an anonymous young blood addressed him in a pleasantly written piece entitled, *The Shortest Way with Whores and Rogues,* in which he offered to meet De Foe in a private field "with an arm brighter than the pen." But by the time this challenge appeared, De Foe was being tracked by the police, so that the challenger cannot be said to have run any great risk of being taken up.

The Count of Nottingham, secretary of state, understood

from the first that *The Shortest Way* had but one objective, the ridiculing of the leading clergy of the Anglican church, and that it could have but one result, the throwing of the Dissenters into a panic so that they would attack the high-flyers before they themselves were attacked. Already some of their ministers had been molested . . . prompt and energetic action must be taken against a public agitator. As soon as the name of the author of the disturbing pamphlet was being mentioned with some assurance, there was no question but that he had acted for the Whig politicians who were opposed to the ministers. Nottingham was responsible, then, for the order, issued January 3, 1703, for the arrest of Daniel De Foe, declared guilty of "high crimes and misdemeanours."

Fortunately, Daniel was kept well enough informed with regard to the activity of the ministers that he was able to elude this order and to burrow into one of the many haunts that the city held for criminals who were sought for by the police. His wife alone knew of his hiding place; she visited him often to bring him the latest news of the world of affairs and to try to help him keep up his courage. De Foe was really wild with terror; accustomed as he was to take long walks or ride horseback in the open, he could not bear the idea of being couped up in a prison cell. He who feared no one when he was out-of-doors, trembled with fright at the thought of the brutality of jailers. He was afraid of dying, especially of dying in prison of the mysterious malady known as jail fever which carried off regularly its quota of the inhabitants of Newgate. This famous old prison was badly aired and but poorly supplied with water; it was, moreover, too small to accommodate all the prisoners who had been sent to rot there. De Foe, too, was well aware of the ruin that his imprisonment would cause to his business; his tile factory, in which he had invested all the money that William had given him, would have to be closed. He was ready for anything that would save him from this disaster.

On January the ninth, in the hope of calling off his pursuers, he wrote Nottingham an abject letter, couched in platitudinous terms of submission:

"I had long since surrendered to Her Majesty's Clemency," he wrote, "had not the Menaces of your Lordship's Officers possessed me with such ideas of Her Majesty's and your Lordship's resentments, as were too terrible. . . . My Lord, a body unfit to bear the hardships of a prison, and a mind impatient of confinement have been the only reasons of withdrawing myself; and, my Lord, the cries of a numerous ruin'd family, the prospect of a long Banishment from my native country, and the hopes of Her Majesty's mercy move me to throw myself at Her Majesty's feet, and to intreat your Lordship's intercession. I beseech your Lordship to assure Her Majesty that I am perfectly free from any seditious Design. . . . With the lowest submission I intreat Her Majesty's pardon for this mistake, from which I am ready to make any publick acknowledgment, and further humbly beseech your Lordship in making a proposal on my own Behalf."

The poor petitioner promised to answer in writing any questions as to his past political rôle that were put to him. He brought up once more the prison and the pillory that he feared "worse than death," and recalled that criminals had been spared to accept service in Her Majesty's armies; he offered to serve at his own expense as a volunteer in the royal cavalry in the Low Countries for one year or longer. He intimated that he would be more liable to die there in Her Majesty's service than he would be to die in prison. He closed with the suggestion that, if Her Majesty was generous enough to pardon him in full, he would raise, with his own resources, a cavalry troop, and, heading it himself, he would give the rest of his life to Her Majesty's service.

Mrs. De Foe took this humble missive straight to Nottingham and added her supplications to Daniel's. But the minister of state turned a deaf ear to it; he even went so far as to insult the bearer and offered her money to reveal her husband's secrets and his hiding place. She turned from him in disgust, resisted all of his overtures, and was, from then on, bitter in her denunciation of this tyrannical minister. The latter's conduct can be explained on the ground that he felt vaguely there was a vast conspiracy on foot against him and his party. He was aware of the fact that the friends of the deceased king were engaged in suspicious dealings with Robert Harley, Speaker of the Commons, a rising figure in politics, one who was unusually clever and who did not scruple to plot in secret. Moreover, Nottingham knew that De Foe was surely informed of all the Whig secrets; and he might have known or at least suspected that Harley had already sounded out De Foe through a mutual friend, William Paterson, and had attempted to draw him into a closer party affiliation. By catching De Foe, Nottingham believed that he would be catching the chief instrument of the intrigue. Consequently, he ordered the pursuit of the fugitive to be continued with redoubled vigor.

The very next day the *London Gazette* published a proclamation offering fifty pounds reward to any one who would furnish information leading to the arrest of one Daniel De Foe. The description that accompanied the notice was:

"He is a middle-sized man, about forty years old, of a brown complexion, and dark brown coloured hair, but wears a wig; a hooked nose, a sharp chin, grey eyes, and a large mole near his mouth."

On January the fourteenth, Nottingham gave an officer the order to go to Croome, the printer of *The Shortest Way,* and to seize the manuscript and all the copies of the offending pamphlet and to put them into the hands of Her Majesty's Advocate-General. At the following session of the assizes (February the twenty-fourth), *The Shortest Way* was declared a "seditious pamphlet;" the Commons ordered it burned in the public square of New-Palace by the common hangman. The printer and the publisher of it were arrested, but the author was still in hiding.

It was soon apparent to De Foe, however, that he could not remain forever concealed in London. Nor could he go safely to any other city where his presence would be immediately noticed. He endeavored through his friends to make a number of approaches to the ministers, but none of them were successful. In April he played his last card . . . he wrote his friend Paterson a long letter, begging him to induce Harley to intercede for him with the Queen. This letter from beginning to end is a touching appeal in his own defense . . . it is one long cry of desperate anguish. De Foe laid before his friend all the circumstances of his terrible situation, showed the whole anguish of his heart, and complained of the ingratitude of his Non-Conformist friends for whom he had fought and who "like Casha (*sic*) to Caesar lifted up the first dagger at him." He protested that he had not had the least idea of opposing the government when he had written his pamphlet which was aimed at such fanatic high-flyers as Sacheverell and Stubbs. He repeated the offers of service he had made to Nottingham, stating specifically that he would undertake any work, no matter how menial it might be, provided only that it be honest. He even let himself go to the lengths of a confession that must have been painful to his pride. He wrote:

"Gaols, pillories, and such like, with which I have been so much threatened, have convinced me I want passive courage, and I shall never for the future think myself injured if I am called a coward."

He made many protestations of his respect and his devotion for Harley; he lamented that he had at one time offended him with his Legion pamphlet and assured his future benefactor of his eternal gratitude and of his good conduct for the rest of his life.

Paterson, whether he could not meet Harley, or whether he did not find circumstances favorable to do so, did not intercede for De Foe at once. It was not until he heard of the unfortunate fugitive's arrest that he made up his mind to put the humble letter of supplication before Harley. It is more than likely that the latter, at the very moment that he received the appeal, resolved to bind De Foe to his own interests by coming to the aid of the harassed man. The surprising relationship between the crafty minister of state and the talented pamphleteer dates from the last of May in the year 1703.

After having remained hidden for nearly five months, De Foe was finally denounced to the police who made the arrest on Thursday, May the twentieth, at the home of a French weaver of Spitalfields in the East End. The informer, who took care that his own name should not be known, sent to the minister for the fifty pounds reward. The sum was granted him on the twenty-fifth of May; but he did not call for it in person, fearing, no doubt, the vengeance of De Foe's friends. All of the writings that De Foe had with him in his retreat were seized; among them was a pamphlet entitled, *Advice to All Parties*. This was published by the author, when, after a long and careful examination, all of his manuscripts were returned to him. On the twenty-second of May, after a brief questioning to establish his identity, De Foe was imprisoned at Newgate upon the demand of the Count of Nottingham.

De Foe was, at the beginning of his imprisonment, quite

philosophical about the matter, being certain that his political friends would look after his release. Here at Newgate was a new bent for his insatiable curiosity; this strange and sordid company of highwaymen, pick-pockets, and prostitutes was both attractive and repellent to him. The cynicism of those who were condemned to death staggered him; mixed with his horror at their indifference was a little bit of wondering admiration at it. He who had been so in fear of death could not but be astonished when during the night he heard the husky vioces of those who were to be led to the gallows the next morning at dawn; he would listen to their obscene songs and their drinking songs, but soon all the various voices would unite in a formidable chorus bellowing forth the famous Newgate hymn:

> If I swing by the string,
> I shall hear the bell ring.

Ineffaceable pictures were stamped upon De Foe's mind to be used twenty years later in *Moll Flanders*.

What was most satisfying to De Foe was the fact that, while he had the leisure and the opportunity to observe at first hand this swarming mob of prisoners, he did not have to suffer any actual contact with them; furthermore, as a political prisoner, suspected of being the holder of important secrets, he was treated with the greatest respect, and stood high in favor with the jailers who were always susceptible to bribery. Like Bunyan, he employed much of his time in prison in self-communion, but there was a difference in the conclusions that the two men drew from their meditations in captivity; where Bunyan came forth resolved to devote himself to the service of the Lord, De Foe made up his mind that the object of his life should be material gain and that, in order to obtain it, it would be necessary for him to ally himself with the men

NEWGATE PRISON

as it was in the 18th Century when De Foe was one of its chief political prisoners.

in power; from then on, opportunism became his political creed.

He passed his day in prison reading and writing, stopping only to receive relatives and friends to whom he intrusted his manuscripts for the printers. He had made a selection of his best pamphlets and was beginning a long political poem in twelve cantos which he called *Jure Divino;* it was directed against the doctrine of the divine right of kings. His ability to keep busy and the sympathetic atmosphere he felt about him enabled him to hold up valiantly under the monotony of those long summer days spent in a torrid cell.

Nevertheless, there were dark clouds that troubled the serenity of his spirits. He was, in the first place, disturbed by the ingratitude of his fellow religionists, who were unable to cast aside the fear that his *The Shortest Way* had evoked. He attempted to dispel this by writing to three Dissenting ministers, among them the Reverend Howe, inviting them to come and pray with him, begging them humbly to forgive all his past offenses. They replied that God would pardon him if He pleased to do so . . . they never could. They declared that his request was an example of rare impudence, scarce meriting the formality of a refusal. Passing by his cell, they went to pray with a horse thief named Witney who had just been condemned to death. De Foe cried out against such persecution, but he cherished the memory of the affront as a precious token of the wrong he had suffered and sought his vengeance later by letting fly some poisoned arrows against the Dissenters and then denying that he was responsible for them.

What gave him the most concern was the precarious financial condition of his family, that could look to him alone for support. He had never known how to economize so that there was no reserve fund upon which his wife might draw, and, now his business at Tilbury was ruined, practically every source of income was cut off. He was even caught up in a lawsuit concerning the payment for some casks of beer that had been distributed in the brickyard to his factory workers. He disposed of this new complication as quickly as possible by a private arrangement because the July assizes were about to open, and he awaited with impatience the decision to be made here, as he believed it would free him.

But he was to be undeceived at once. Sir Simon Harcourt, the advocate general, showed an extreme prejudice against him; he accused him of "paving his way with the skulls of churchmen," and attempted to frighten him into openly confessing that he was indeed the author of *The Shortest Way;* but that De Foe obstinately refused to do. De Foe's defense, William Colepeper, the instigator of the Kentish petition, was disturbed by the prosecution's unjust attitude, but Colepeper let himself be convinced that the best tactics for his client to follow were to acknowledge his authorship and throw himself upon the mercy of the Queen. It was a tragic mistake; De Foe lamented it bitterly, and Colepeper did his utmost to make amends for it by insistently pleading with the Council for mercy for his client. But the judges were just waiting for this confession on De Foe's part before passing the sentence that had been decided upon much earlier. De Foe, as if in a dream, heard himself condemned to pay a fine of 200 marks, to stand three times in the pillory in a public place, to stay at Newgate as long as the Queen deemed it proper, and finally, upon his release from prison to offer guarantees of his good conduct for the succeeding seven years. It was an extremely severe judgement, dictated probably by Nottingham, who had political reasons for his implacable enmity against the unfortunate pamphleteer; but there was also among the ministers who pronounced the sentence, Rochester, against whom De

Foe had levelled the most serious accusations of immorality in his satire, *The Reformation of Manners.*

The condemned man, a prey to the most profound despair, was led back to his Newgate cell. As long as he had been assured and reassured that he had only a month to spend in prison, he had kept up a good face, but now, when the future looked so dark and the blessed hour of his deliverance so uncertain, he gave in to an overwhelming depression. Like his own Robinson Crusoe on his deserted island, he peopled his cell during the night with funereal apparitions and horrible visions. He pictured in his imagination the coming scene at the pillory, that "nut-cracker" as the London thieves ironically called it. The prospect made him shudder. He knew the custom of the brutal street crowds who delighted in pelting the helpless victim caught in such a ridiculous position. Their missiles were whatever came to hand, often the most disgusting of objects . . . rotten eggs, spoilt meat, horse dung; he had even known facetious housewives to catch up their pots of urine and fling their contents into the face of the pilloried wretch.

De Foe did everything he could think of to escape this shameful part of his punishment. Two Quakers who had come to Newgate in order to convert the prisoners had called upon Daniel in his cell. One of them, William Penn, just then in good standing at Court, had promised to aid him. There was not a minute to be lost, as the carrying out of the sentence against him had been set for July the nineteenth. De Foe had loaded Penn with a long list of measures that might be effective for his relief. On the sixteenth, Penn went to the Marquis of Normandy, the Lord of the Privy Seal and laid the matter before him, saying,

"De Foe is ready to make oath to your Lordship of all that he knows, and to give an account of all his accomplices in whatever he has been concerned, provided by so doing he may be screened from the punishment of the pillory and not produced as an evidence against any person whatsoever."

Penn went the same day to Lord Treasurer Godolphin who conferred the very next day with the Count of Nottingham. The Queen, in turn, was also told of the matter; she deemed it of enough importance to call a special session of her ministers for the following day. The Council decided that De Foe's declarations were of sufficient concern to bear examination by the Count of Nottingham and by Lord Godolphin and that, as a consequence, it would be necessary to delay the execution of the sentence against him. As soon as William Penn heard this good news, he wrote to the Lord-governor of Newgate for fear the latter would not be informed in time to prevent the execution of the punishment; but it was an unnecessary precaution, for, at the same time that Penn's letter arrived, there came the command from Nottingham specifying that it was the Queen's pleasure the prison authorities should postpone the punishment of Daniel De Foe until July the twenty-third.

The Court was, at this time, at Windsor. Nottingham sent, on the nineteenth, commanding the prisoner to be brought to him for examination. Now, if De Foe had once got outside the city limits of London, he would have had the right to refuse to return to Newgate; his condemnation could not then have been made subject to the law. De Foe may even have counted upon escaping in this fashion through the thoughtlessness of Nottingham, but, if so, he was doomed to disappointment. His jailers were on their guard and let Nottingham know that, if he wished to examine their prisoner, he must come to Newgate or else make out a writ of *Habeas-Corpus* against him. Nottingham chose to take the latter method and asked, on July the twentieth, for such a writ from the Lord-governor.

The Whigs had grown uneasy about what revelations their

champion might be able to make, and they made up their minds to act energetically in his behalf. They sent him an assurance that they would protect him in the pillory against the crowd and that they were organizing a demonstration in his honor, as well as working actively for his release. As a result, when De Foe was taken, on July the twenty-first, to Windsor, he revealed no secrets that were not already common knowledge through-out England; and he maintained his own point of view with asperity when the ministers asked for an explanation of one of the manuscripts seized in his hiding place that contained questions capable of a seditious interpretation; such was this one:

"Whether Her Majesty was not as much an usurper as King William?"

Later De Foe even boasted of having triumphed over Nottingham in their discussions.

De Foe's so-called confession was brought before the Queen, who judged it of no consequence; but, because she was a weak, irresolute individual and because she did not wish to displease Penn, she said that his case should be referred to the Lords of the Committee, who would decide whether he should suffer his penalty on July the twenty-third or whether it should be put off until later. Since nothing had been decided by the twenty-third, Nottingham wrote, on the morning of that day, to the officials of Newgate, advising them that it would be best to wait until "the final decision of Her Majesty" was known. It was not until the twenty-seventh that he wrote them again, announcing that the Queen had declared their famous prisoner must suffer the full penalty of the sentence against him. In conformance with that, it was decreed that De Foe should be exposed in the pillory on July the twenty-ninth in Cornhill in front of the Royal-Exchange; on the thirtieth, in Cheapside near Conduit; and on the thirty-first, at Temple-Bar.

VII. THE HERO IS WORSHIPED AND THEN FREED

A MONG the Whigs Daniel had come to be looked upon, to a certain extent, as a hero; they praised his loyalty to the memory of William of Orange, whose secrets he had refused to betray, even at the cost of his own freedom. De Foe himself was not blind to the fact that it was this stand that he had taken which had set him up at once as the idol of the common people. Knowing the value of winning as many laughs as possible for his own side, he wrote, within a few days, some ironical verses which he called *The Hymn to the Pillory*. He planned to have this sold on the streets the first day of his public chastisement.

Everything took place exactly as De Foe had foreseen it would. On each of the three days, a guard of honor escorted him from Newgate to the place where he was pilloried and back again. It was not a condemned wretch who was being dragged to ignominious punishment, but a conqueror who was being led to his triumphal arch. The London crowd was slow to grasp the idea, but when it did come to understand that De Foe, in writing *The Shortest Way,* had played a good joke on the "powers-that-be," the high-flyers, it displayed the most riotous good humor with this victim of governmental chagrin. And, while De Foe accepted the demonstration thankfully, he was not misled as to the depths of its sincerity; he knew that only a few weeks before, this same jovial crowd had carried Sacheverell through the streets in triumph and had gleefully set fire to the Dissenters' meeting houses. To-day they were as boisterous in their acclaim of a champion of the Whigs and of the Non-Conformists. There was no guessing who would ride the crest of popular esteem on the morrow. In the meantime De Foe's friends were keeping well stirred up this widespread enthusiasm for him . . . a martyr of official intolerance.

From his elevated position on his disgraceful platform, De Foe tasted the joys of a triumph that made him forget his physical discomforts. . . . Although his head was held in a strained position by the heavy instrument of torture, he smiled around at all this crowd that tossed flowers at him instead of throwing mud in his face. Upon the third day, when he was to stand near Temple-Bar, the crowd reached the point of hysteria before the arrival of the hero of the day; his pillory was covered with garlands; shouts of "Long Live Daniel!" kept up throughout the hours that he stood before them; the women wept while the men declaimed the injustice of the ministers. Jugs of beer were passed around among the good citizens who drank, with one knee on the ground, to the health of Daniel and the confusion of his enemies. The prisoner's bright eyes surveyed the whole crowd, taking in each individual; then, lighting on the heads, rotting on top of the gate of Temple-Bar,[1] they closed in horror at the thought of what his own fate might be. When his guards released him for the last time, the acclamations of the people were redoubled; all of them saluted him with their pewter cans filled with wine or beer; those who were near, threw wreaths of flowers over his head. He returned to his prison dead tired, but with a heart triumphant . . . he had shown the Queen's government that the "pen was mightier than the sword." Within three days he had become the most idolized man in London. His riotous satirical *Hymn* had caused the ministers more trouble than a cabal in the Commons would have

[1] The heads of great criminals and regicides were fastened up on this gate.

caused; everyone had a copy of it, for the crowd swarmed about the pillory where the street vendors were continually crying it for sale . . . this clever bit of journalistic strategy so enraged the Tory pamphleteers, who had counted upon the degrading punishment of the pillory to discredit forever their dangerous rival, that they had to pour out their bile in a torrent of pamphlets against him.

"Thou great destroyer of men's fame!" exclaimed one of them.

" . . . to raise contentious heats and feuds I know
No instrument more useful than D— F—"

"The next time thou makest thy tower in the Pillory, mayst thou be plentifully endued with a double portion that Figure (a scribbler) exposes thee to, may rotten eggs like March hail shower on thy head!" was the kindly wish of another of the tribe of rival journalists.

A third indignantly averred: "The Whigs have of late made use of the scurrilous prostitute Pen of an infamous stigmatiz'd Incendiary, one who lives by Defamation, and by writing to the level and capacity of the Mob is become a bold impetuous popular demagogue, and the admired oracle of the deluded people."

The whole Tory clan pretended, as time went on, to forget the triumphant scene that had changed De Foe's punishment into a glorification; they allowed themselves to remember but the one fact, that De Foe had suffered the same disgraceful penalty that was visited upon those condemned for dishonorable offenses. Swift negligently and disdainfully referred to him as "that fellow who was pilloried." That the Tories held a lasting grudge against De Foe is proved by the fact that twenty-five years later Alexander Pope, the greatest of their literary supporters, wrote Daniel De Foe, the great Whig champion, down for posterity with a rancor that reveals its

DE FOE IN THE PILLORY

Instead of a humiliation as his enemies expected, it was a great triumph
for De Foe, the populace serenading him and offering him flowers.

origin. He names De Foe in his *Dunciad,* but to meet the exigencies of his politics and his poetry, he does not hesitate to twist the truth:

"Earless on high stood unabash'd De Foe"
wrote the "wasp of Twickenham," who well knew that De Foe had never suffered any such mutilation. Nor could it have been poetic jealousy that caused Pope to let fly these poisoned arrows. De Foe could not pretend to any great heights of poetic inspiration. He must be content with a place beside Prynne and Withers, mediocre versifiers, who served as his models, according to Pope. But the latter returns, in his essay on "The Art of Sinking in Poetry," to his petty haggling. He compares De Foe to one of the *genus,* ostrich, "whose heaviness rarely permits them to raise themselves from the ground; their wings are of no use to lift them up, and their motion is between flying and walking; but they run very fast."

In all of Pope's attacks there was no question of actual political rivalry; it was simply that no Tory could forget the party's disappointment in the old matter of De Foe's triumphing over a disgraceful situation. When he should have been loaded with ridicule, he had turned the weapon back against them, his enemies. More unpardonable yet, from the political angle, he had used his personal popularity to unite all the factions of the Whig party. Even Tutchin, the editor of the *Observator,* who had always looked upon Daniel as a dangerous rival, had backed him whole-heartedly. As one disgruntled high-flyer wrote: "thanks to him [Tutchin] for summoning the Mob to keep off Rotten Eggs and Chanell Salutes from De Foe's pretty face."

Meanwhile, Robert Harley, Speaker of the Commons, had reached the conclusion that such a talented journalist as Daniel De Foe was could be of real service to him. Harley's deep-seated ambitions were of the calculating type; he would first

strive to discredit Nottingham, whose place he then planned
to slip in to. All the time that he was keeping himself prudently behind the scenes, he was egging on the Whigs and the
Dissenters to open rebellion against the leaders of the High
church party. By August, 1703, the stage was set for the appearance of a moderate Tory, like Harley. Lord Treasurer Godolphin had got into some difficulties with Nottingham and
wished to clear his ministry of all high-flyers.

De Foe's vibrant mood, feeding upon every detail of his
public triumph, held over for a few days, and then left him
in the throes of a depression in which he viewed with despair
the uncertainty of his release from prison; his confinement had
become more oppressive to him than ever before. Nothing, not
even his pretentious poem, *Jure Divino,* could rouse him to
activity. Imagine then how his heart leaped with joy and renewed hope when, about the middle of August, James Stancliffe, a messenger from Harley, came into his prison cell to
put this question from his patron:

"Ask that gentleman what I can do for him."

De Foe was in sufficient control of himself to make no immediate reply. He asked for some time to consider, and he did
weigh carefully the reasons for and against an alliance with
Harley. But he cut short his musings; after all, Harley was a
moderate who had friends in both parties; he was a rising politician, who was sure to climb to the highest positions in the
control of the State; he was, moreover, known as one of the
most generous patrons of learning . . . there could be nothing
but advantage in serving such a man. De Foe made up his
mind quickly to accept the straw offered him; but he acted
cautiously, always suspicious of his jailers, and resolved not to
make a misstep. The message that he sent to Harley could
have no meaning to one who was unaware of the approach

that had already been made to an understanding between them. It read:

"Lord, that I may receive my sight."

With this in hand, Harley set to work to get De Foe's discharge from prison, and he worked the more persistently to this end when he sensed that Nottingham would regard its accomplishment, a veritable slap in the face. Harley first wrote Godolphin a preparatory letter, couched in suggestive phrases:

"It would be of great service to have some discreet writer on the Government side, if it were only to state facts right; for the generality err for want of knowledge and being imposed upon by the stories raised by ill-designing men."

Next he had some small sums of money sent to De Foe to relieve the needs of his large family.

These initial measures did not fail to excite the suspicions of certain ever-watchful high-flyers. Two of their lords, one of whom was Harcourt, the Attorney-General, the other, probably Nottingham himself, made a secret visit to Newgate one day about the middle of September. They asked to be taken to De Foe's cell where, for several hours, they put its occupant through a severe cross examination, using the most frightful threats to try to drag from him all his secrets. But De Foe refused to divulge anything; as soon as they were gone, however, he sent word to Harley that he had about reached the end of his physical and moral endurance. Harley wrote at once, September twentieth, to Godolphin, stating that it was high time to act if the Government was to gain the services of such a valuable writer as De Foe, whose friends were already talking of getting up a subscription to pay his fine and a petition to the Queen for his release. Harley proposed that De Foe be given his freedom and his fine be cancelled; but that it be impressed upon him that he owed his release to the infinite kindness of the Queen.

"This may perhaps engage him better than any *after* rewards, and keep him more in the power of an obligation," ended Harley, showing that he had estimated the character of his protégé at its true worth.

It was now necessary to enlist the interest of the Queen in De Foe's fate. It was not an easy task, but Godolphin used all of his influence and his tact to gain it. Anne had but one passion . . . her religion. She had been told that De Foe had attempted to excite the people against the leaders of the Anglican church, and so she had given Nottingham a free hand in putting down the bold pamphleteer. The Court was at Bath when Godolphin approached Her Majesty with Harley's letter. At first the Queen would not even listen to anything he had to say in the matter, but gradually, her timidity getting the upper hand, she evaded the issue by putting all the responsibility for action upon Nottingham. Godolphin persisted in his appeal; he called forth the sympathy of the Queen for the unfortunate prisoner and his innocent family, painting in pathetic terms their abject misery; he touched lightly upon Nottingham's unnecessary cruelty, and praised Her Majesty's spirit of forgiveness for which she was blessed by all her subjects. He ended by an appeal to her self-interest, showing how Harley had guaranteed that this unparalleled pamphleteer should devote himself to Her Majesty's service from now on. Anne yielded without a great deal of compunction because she had but recently suffered in silence some instances of Nottingham's petty tyranny. From her own purse she took a large sum to be sent to Mrs. De Foe, and she ordered Godolphin to pay De Foe's fine as well as the costs of his release. Upon the twenty-sixth Godolphin wrote Harley that he had but to say the word and De Foe would be out of Newgate.

Harley, however, moved with extreme caution in order not to alarm the high-flyers. He felt that De Foe should remain in prison one more month so that the agitation aroused by *The Shortest Way* would have been completely forgotten. He did, however, let De Foe know that his deliverance was near at hand, and he even gave the restless prisoner the impression that he could look forward to a confidential post in the Government.

Harley set to work then among De Foe's friends, looking for some one who would be willing to be surety for the latter's good behavior during the next seven years. He managed so discreetly that no one in the political world had any inkling of Harley, as the power behind these amicable maneuvers. By the fourth of November, Harley let Godolphin know that all was ready; the latter replied briefly:

"I have taken care in the matter of De Foe."

With the gaining of his freedom, Daniel blotted out of his memory the five long months he had passed in captivity at Newgate. It was like having a nightmare dispelled by a ray of light. He was again eager for the struggle of living, aglow with the joy of being alive. His spirits rose in a great hymn of happy thanksgiving to those who had been instrumental in opening his prison gate. He wrote to Harley on November the ninth, offering him his thanks in the most ardent of terms and begging him for the names of all of his benefactors in order that he might thank each of them individually. He wrote also to Stancliffe, asking him for advice with regard to the publication of the pamphlets he had written at Newgate. He said that he did not wish to circulate one word that would displease his benefactors, not even to justify himself and his own acts.

His overflowing activity had soon a chance for exercise. The shift of scenery from the monotonous four walls of a prison cell to a London disaster equal to the plague and the great fire was alone sufficient to stir the emotional depth of this singularly responsive man. During the last week in November, 1703, an unusually violent storm created a great deal of havoc in the South of England. On the twenty-fourth, which was a Wednesday, the people of London grew anxious about the heavy wind that rose about four o'clock in the afternoon. As evening came on, it became strong enough to dislocate loose pieces of wood and stone. De Foe tells how he just missed being killed by a falling piece of wall while he was on his way home. During that night and the following day the wind increased in violence; the streets were heaped with debris, but there still appeared to be no danger for those who remained quietly at home. Friday conditions became much worse. De Foe, kept, perforce, to his small brick house near the walls of the City, began to be alarmed. About ten o'clock in the evening, he noticed that the mercury of his barometer was abnormally low. He could not believe his eyes and concluded that one of his children must have been tampering with the instrument; but about an hour later the whole town was in an uproar; no one could sleep in the midst of the savage howling of the wind. As its strength increased, it capsized a number of buildings whose crashing added to the frightfulness of the terrible night. All at once, De Foe felt his own house shaken upon its foundation. Terrified, he drew his family around him and considered what was to be done. To stay on in the building might mean that they would all be buried under its ruins; on the other hand, where could they fly? He opened the door to the garden; outside all was blackest night, no moon, no stars, only the fearful swirls of wind that carried everything before it . . . stones, tiles, pieces of timber, iron and sheets of lead. To venture out meant more certain death than to hold to the shelter of their tottering house. Fortunately, about eight o'clock in the morning, the hurricane let up; the Londoners stuck their noses out of their half-open doors to look at the sky; the bravest of them plucked up enough courage to call to their neighbors that the storm was over. But towards evening, the wind began whistling again, and the night was filled with fitful windstorms accompanied by thunder and rain; the unsettled weather continued up to the following Tuesday, during which time the wind rose again and again, tearing off the roofs of the houses that the people had just repaired. They were not entirely free from danger until Wednesday afternoon, when the unleashed elements showed signs of being under normal restraint. De Foe started out as soon as possible in order to estimate the amount of damage that had been done throughout the City. His first visit was to the London harbor, which had been wrecked by a prodigious tide; all was a jumble of masts and timber; many ships had broken their cables and had been washed out to sea by the current; others, filled with water, had sunk. All business was suspended for the time being. De Foe's description of the wreckage caused by the storm runs as follows:

"The ouses look like skeletons, and an universal air of horror seemed to sit on the countenances of the people; all business seemed to be laid aside for the time, and people were generally intent upon getting help to repair their habitations."

The price of tiles rose from twenty-one shillings a thousand to more than six pounds. De Foe bemoaned the fact that he no longer owned his tile factory at Tilbury. . . . It would have been a splendid chance to amass a large fortune. He made up his mind to get some profit from the storm, however. . . . If he could not sell tiles, he would sell ideas. Some Dissenting ministers had already had printed their sermons on this great catastrophe in which they called it, after their peculiar fashion, a "Warning." The Lord, they said, had spoken through the wind to the English people. De Foe took the word, and set to work with his usual rapidity on a didactic poem in which he personified the wind. "Reform," was the cry he had it shout to the whole world, and he proceeded to make lengthy comments; not forge ting the main issue, he passed from reflections upon the hurricane, to laudation of Harley's pacifist policies. Then he launched a yet more pretentious scheme. . . he would preserve London's disastrous experience with the devastating element, by writing a detailed history of the November storm. Early in December, John Nutt, who had agreed to act as De Foe's publisher, had a small notice inserted in all of the leading journals of London, in which he asked those who had witnessed any unusual happenings during the storm please to send him an accurate account of the event. De Foe himself undertook to survey Kent in order to judge the amount of damage that had been done outside London. He was first struck by the great number of trees lying on the ground; the destruction of the fruit trees appeared, to his business instincts, a severe blow, but he was even more distressed at the sight of the wreckage among the great shade trees in the parks. He had never lost his enthusiasm for landscape-gardening; the sight of a neat lawn bordered with flowers or of an artistically trimmed hedge always caught his interested attention. He started out to count the houses and the barns that had collapsed, but he gave over this task after he had counted 1,107.

With the many letters that Nutt received and De Foe's own observations in Kent, the latter wrote an excellent account of the storm, which appeared in July, 1704, and was favorably received by the public. It was his first bit of journalistic investigation; it was also his first attempt at a lengthy dissertation. With it his career as a journalist was definitely established.

In the first few months that followed his liberation, De Foe tried some new business deals, but he felt himself being drawn more and more to journalism; Harley's patronage made his success in this calling almost certain. Of course, for the next seven years, he would be, to a certain extent, limited in his expression by the terms of his sentence. He expressed his chagrin over this in an elegy to himself in which he ironically lamented the paradoxical situation of a poet condemned to silence. . . . "For to be dumb in poetry is death."

As a matter of fact he did not hesitate to continue bringing out pamphlets treating upon subjects of general interests; but he did not sign them, and he was rather less aggressive in his tactics; he did prudently avoid taking up those public topics upon which there was the most feeling. Occasionally he had the opportunity to put his pen to the service of some disgruntled citizen who had a complaint to make concerning a piece of tyranny or a real abuse. He did not scorn this means of adding to his uncertain income. Though he had been announced "officially dead," his "resurrection" was effected by the publication of *Jure Divino* in July, 1706.

Harley, now awakened to his need for a publication to support his policies, furnished De Foe with the funds necessary to bring out a weekly paper. As a consequence, the *Review,* ostensibly an independent political organ, appeared February 26, 1704; it remained in regular circulation until June 11, 1713. De Foe was the sole editor; the tremendous task could have been carried only by one capable of his superhuman activity; he had, in addition, great ease at writing and inexhaustible energy, which enabled him to dash off, as easily as his pen moved over the paper, clear and interesting articles. The rough draft of one of the issues of his *Review* shows only two erasures.

The *Review* came out first once a week, printed on eight pages quarto, and sold for a penny. In the fifth number, the editor announced that, because he was not making expenses, the paper would be cut to four pages, but that there would be the same amount of reading matter, for he was having it printed in two columns of smaller type. Encouraged by the success that the paper met with in this form, De Foe began with the eighth number to issue it bi-weekly, on Tuesdays and Saturdays. The format was improved with each issue so that the *Review* became by far the best looking paper of the time. Each number featured a long article on either domestic or foreign politics which filled the first three pages. The fourth page was devoted to announcements and a lightly satirical section known as the "Mercure Scandale, or Advice from the Scandalous Club, being a weekly history of Nonsense, Impertinence, Vice and Debauchery."

This "Scandalous Club," was concocted by De Foe for the purpose of tactfully censoring public morals; betrayed husbands, ugly shrews, and drunken magistrates were here held up to ridicule. Sometimes the Club discussions were used to call attention to injustices, or to abuses, it was even used as a question and answer forum; often it pointed out errors or absurdities that fellow journalists had made in their publications during the preceding week, in such matters leading the way for the newspaper columnist of to-day. In the sixteenth number, De Foe introduced *Mr. Review* and asked him if he were not afraid of attacking so implacably the stupidity and the vice of the times; Mr. Review replied that:

"As to the danger, he professes himself perfectly unconcerned about it, and questions not but his hands will, according to their duty, defend his nose."

By August, 1704, De Foe had accumulated so much extra material of this type that he brought out a *Supplementary Journal to the Advice from the Scandal Club,* consisting of no less than twenty-eight pages dealing with a medley of all kinds of contributions . . . poetry, announcements, and notes from his readers. There were five numbers of the *Supplement;* then, with the one hundredth issue of the *Review,* in February, 1705, De Foe announced that he would have to discontinue his magazine publication altogether. He expressed his appreciation to his readers for the confidence that they had given him, and regretted that the financial returns of publishing did not justify the amount of time it required. That the move was simply a discreet appeal to Harley for a larger subsidy was made evident by the postscript to his notice in which he advertised two complementary issues to carry the hold-over from Number 100. He even goes on to suggest the solution of his difficulty by saying that:

"The generous offer of some gentlemen, tho' not yet performed, assuring him that he shall not be a loser by the charge of it, he has embark'd himself again." Not to take any chances, he ends by an appeal for subscriptions which, he says, may now be sent in to the editor.

As a matter of fact Harley could not afford to let the *Review* die, and De Foe knew that. A larger subsidy for the magazine was forthcoming at once, and the first number of the second volume appeared on schedule time; with the eighth issue the journal undertook to make one more appearance a week, on every Thursday. At this time the department which he called "News of the Scandal Club" was given over particularly to amusing comments on life and letters after the manner that was to delight the readers of the *Spectator* a few years later. But with the appearance of Number 31, De Foe discontinued this humorous section entirely, because, he said, he felt even four pages were scarcely enough for the proper discussion of his serious reading matter. But to take the place of this popular department, he promised to bring out twice a week a small pamphlet to be called *The Little Review, or an Inquisition of Scandal, consisting in answers of Questions and*

Doubts, Remarks, Observations and Reflections. There were twenty-three numbers of the *Little Review;* with it the light section of De Foe's magazine disappeared almost entirely. Yet he was able to add to his tri-weekly articles a Miscellaneous department into which he threw helter skelter everything that he could not fit into the rather circumscribed limits of his "editorial."

But the *Little Review* was really a plagiarizing of the *Monthly Oracle* in which De Foe's old friend, Dunton, was continuing the traditions of the *Athenian Gazette.* De Foe had the advantage in that his journal came out more often. The seekers for odd bits of information found that they could get the answers to their questions sooner from the *Little Review* than from the *Oracle;* the latter journal went under, at a loss to its editor of 200 pounds sterling. Dunton was indignant that his friend, Daniel, should play him such a scurvy trick as shamelessly to rob him of his own idea and then practically to force him out of competition. He attempted to get even with him by defiantly challenging him to answer some difficult questions, such as:

"Is there any such thing as a *genus epicoenum?*

"Have the Grecians a *casus sextus?*"

De Foe took good care not to receive this challenge.

Had Dunton been De Foe's worst enemy, the latter would have been able to live in peace. Unfortunately, he had drawn upon himself the antagonism of a number of informative journals, among which the *Daily Courant* was the most aggressive because of the malignancy with which De Foe delighted in pointing out its mistakes and misinformation. Furthermore, as an independent in party politics, De Foe had to stand the brunt of criticism from the two strong party organs, the *Observator,* edited by the Whig, Tutchin; and the *Rehearsal,* founded by Leslie, a high-flyer, whose avowed purpose was to combat the nefarious influence of De Foe. There was not a week in which the *Review* was not severely taken to task for some reason or other. But De Foe was all ready with beak and claws; he maintained his dominant position, exercising his journalistic talents to turn the tables to his advantage or at least to get in the last word.

De Foe's style was more oratorical than literary; his articles read like debatēs or sermons. He dealt almost exclusively with arguments that bore upon the problems of the middle class of English people. He knew how to present his material in such fashion as to convince those who were inclined to be prejudiced against him. He never lost that Olympic calm of his, even in the midst of the most belligerent war of words; and he affected a truly Christian humility that won him the approval of his public. Such tactics, however, drew down the scorn of his skeptical opponents. Leslie let loose a vindictive thrust at his rival in his *Rehearsal.*

"The insolence of the Review is intolerable! He studies to provoke in the most affronting manner he can think of. And then he cries: Peace and Union, Gentlemen, and lay aside your Heats!"

Since Harley had become all powerful as a minister, De Foe, sure now of impunity, gave free reign to his passion for paradox. The complete name of his magazine, *The Review of the Affairs of France,* was a lucky stroke. It caught public attention, and an explanation was sought from the editor, who explained that "the affairs of France were the affairs of all Europe." His fellow journalists thought to tickle the national pride by emphasizing the supremacy of Great Britain; De Foe, on the other hand, filled the columns of his *Review* with bombastic passages, lauding the power of France, her wealth, the activity of her government, and the success of her armies. To the accusation of disloyalty, he quickly replied that he showed the finer loyalty by awakening the public to its dangers than by letting it sleep in a sense of false security. De Foe argued that it would be necessary for the nation to put forth its best efforts in order to overthrow such a formidable enemy. He cleared up his paradoxes with such fascinating verve that he convinced his readers and amused them at the same time. De Foe sought for variety by choosing a different type of article for each successive issue of the *Review;* he selected, in turn, an enlightening explanation of some historical incident, an inspiring political discourse, a clear and precise business discussion, or even a dialogue upon some current event between *Mr. Review* and *A Fool;* the latter was supposed to stand for De Foe's opponents. The dialogue had been made popular by Sir Roger L'Estrange, the real founder of journalism in England. The political papers of the time were in the habit of presenting all of their arguments in this form, time-honored since the days of Plato; English journalists would employ the same set of characters in issue after issue, until they had built up what amounted to a series of short comedies. De Foe was, perhaps, the first to prove that the dialogue form was not necessary for the success of a political journal. He created the type known as the familiar essay, vibrant and humorous, a sort of detached monologue by a brilliant talker. Although De Foe was often dull when he wanted to please, he did lay the foundation upon which Steele in the *Tatler,* and Addison in the *Spectator* were to build almost at one stroke perfect examples of the intimate essay.

The energy and persistence required from one man to keep up his public's interest in a tri-weekly journal is almost beyond comprehension. True, he wrote quickly, too quickly, one judges, for his enemies were able to make a collection of blunders that had appeared in the *Review* from time to time and that, picked out for their absurdity, caused Londoners much amusement. When Daniel did not have the time to write his usual article, he was in the habit of going to his desk and drawing out from the bottom of the drawer an old political or religious treatise that had never appeared in print, or, perhaps, a poem of ancient vintage that required only general editing to make it presentable for the day's consumption. If he was out of London on a trip, he sent his copy regularly to his printer in Saint-John's Lane. If he was in the City, he took it there himself, stopping usually for a few minutes to watch the compositors at work; one of them was a deaf-mute with whom he was able to converse in the new sign language.

The *Review* came gradually to be the most popular publication in London. De Foe understood business management, and he handled his journal as if it were a business proposition. He knew that if he satisfied his clients . . . his readers . . . he would be able to guide their judgment without their even realizing that he was doing so. He set out, in the first place, to capture the small Non-Conformist tradesmen with whose psychology he was most familiar; he knew that they were primarily interested in the business and financial problems of the nation; and that they were also responsive to the old Puritan ideals that were so much a part of De Foe's own bringing up that he felt himself drawn to them more as he grew older. The one campaign that brought the *Review* the most publicity was directed against the theaters, those "nurseries of sin," as De Foe called them. He suggested that the Government start a big national drive for 100,000 pounds sterling in order to buy all the theaters and put them to honest uses. He vented his utmost wrath against the companies of players that visited the University towns. And how eloquently did he hold up to ridicule a London minister who had originated the "infernal" idea of raising enough money to rebuild his church by putting on a performance of *Hamlet*. Letters of approval and of encouragement for the courageous stand that he had taken in such a laudable campaign, poured in on De Foe from his pious readers. His reputation as a good man was so firmly established that he was frequently made the recipient of large sums of money that anonymous donors sent him to distribute at his own discretion among the poor.

The *Review* was such a popular success that its editor was frequently called upon to reprint certain favorite articles. His name alone was sufficient to sell any pamphlet; but the abuse of it, led him to demand the arrest of those book-sellers who, in order to sell their dullest pamphlets would declare that they were written by "the famous author of the Review." Since this paper was read everywhere its appearance was the cause for a general stir. The exasperated high-flyers had to sit in the coffee-houses and listen to the Puritans regaling each other with its contents, commenting upon the striking passages in the nasal tone of voice that distinguished them. It was not unlikely that these same high-flyers, fleeing from too close proximity to the obnoxious followers of one whom they hated, would run into a mob on the street that was gathered around some man, reading in a high pitched voice from a journal; coming nearer, they would find it to be a group of citizens who were unable to read, but who wished to learn the latest remarks on the questions of the day from the wizard of the *Review*. De Foe was proud of this influence that he exercised on public thought; it was more powerful than that of a minister of the gospel. Was he not guiding, in his own way, the judgment of the people? And were not the people of England the rulers of England?

VIII. DE FOE'S STAR IN THE ASCENDANCY

Daniel, conscious of the important place he now held in the political world, looked fondly for a return to the halcyon days of William III. His new patron, Robert Harley, treated him with tact and skill which showed a perfect understanding of human psychology. Instead of placing him under strict orders, he gave him a free hand with the *Review,* so that there might be no question as to its complete independence. But De Foe, who knew which side his bread was buttered on, did not neglect to seek Harley's advice before publishing an article or a pamphlet. In spite of all his precautions, there were times when the tone of the *Review* was displeasing to Harley. The minister never stooped to reprimand, and the poor journalist knew of his offense only when he was refused admittance at his patron's door; nor was he given an audience until he had written an abject apology with a plea for forgiveness. Without stopping to realize it, De Foe had become the quite docile instrument of a clever politician. He knew that he was not the confidant or friend to Harley that he had been to William . . . he was at most his employee and assistant.

By the eighteenth of May, 1704, Harley had played his careful game to a successful climax; he was made Secretary of State in place of Nottingham. He immediately resolved to make De Foe his secret agent and, in certain instances, even his adviser. He first set him the task of discreetly sounding out some influential men who might become troublesome to the administration. De Foe not only reported as to their political biases but also sought out and denounced some libelers. . . . His

125

journalistic contacts made the latter comparatively easy to do. Furthermore, he wormed his way into the confidence of the editors of certain papers that were opposed to the Government. He was even ready, at a pinch, to write articles against the Ministry in order to cement this editorial confidence and so to get hold of the names of their regular contributors and of the men who supplied them with funds.

De Foe was all ready to go, at Harley's command, as his secret ambassador either to the Court of Hanover or to join Marlborough in Holland. He had even been asked to name his own recompense and had spoken for a place in a branch of the Auditor's Office, for, as he wrote Harley, "Matters of account are my particular element, what I have always been master of. . . . It will be a certainty in which I may bring my sons up under me to be in time serviceable to their father's benefactor."

But Harley changed his mind at the last moment, kept putting De Foe off, evaded the matter of reward, and, at last, left matters with his henchmen in such a way that the latter had to be content with a pension that the minister paid him, irregularly enough, out of his own purse.

As a result Harley was the only minister to whom De Foe could look for support. Even Lord Treasurer Godolphin went through Harley to seek De Foe's aid in a service of common welfare which would draw the pamphleteer into closer relationship with leading politicians; De Foe loyally laid the whole plan before his chief, who was quite agreeable about the matter . . . as well he might be since he could turn to his own profit the information that his faithful servant gathered by this new arrangement. It opened up a correspondence between De Foe and Lord Halifax, one of the "Whig junto" who even subsidized the *Review* for a period of time.

By June, 1704, De Foe was in the southeastern counties, on

his first trip as a political organizer, for it was more than likely that he was arranging with certain individuals to keep the government informed regarding the changes in public opinion in the main cities of the section. But the trip was spoiled for him by a quite disagreeable affair. The police had been looking for the author of a libel, entitled *Legion's Address to the Lords,* in which the Commons, with the high-flyers in the majority, was severely taken to task. It did not take the authorities long to reach the conclusion that De Foe was the one guilty of writing it. If Harley had not stepped in quickly to hush up the whole affair, De Foe might have had to repeat his term in prison and at the pillory.

Harley's next move was to set on foot a vast investigation concerning the state of mind of the people of England outside London, in order to modify, if need be, the policy of the administration. In conformity with this plan, De Foe started out, the first of August, 1704, with one of his best friends, Christopher Hurst, a custom-house employee. He began his careful sifting of opinions in the eastern counties, drawing in reliable agents in each of the larger cities, who were to send him political views from time to time. With this feeling-out process, there was employed also some tactfully pushed government propaganda. But he was not to escape his watchful enemies so easily. His wife wrote him that, shortly after he left London, an officer of the guards, Robert Stephens, had called for him. When he found that Daniel was out of the City, he managed to spread it about the neighborhood that he had an order for the arrest of one Daniel De Foe, who was to be taken at any price. The latter was furious at this trick to injure his good name, especially among the people he was trying to impress with "principles of moderation and peace." He returned at once to London to hunt up Stephens and force him publicly to retract his charges and to sign a statement that there was really no order out against De Foe. He settled the matter in two days and was back in the provinces with little time lost. But the Tories were hot on his trail; they sent after him a man named Toke, who challenged him to a duel; De Foe had no difficulty in overcoming this hireling and was off at once for Cambridge and Norwich.

At Bury Saint-Edmund he learned some disagreeable news; the papers there announced that there was an order for his arrest for having boldly attacked a Tory admiral, Sir George Rooke; but, fortunately, he received word from Harley, calming his fears and assuring him, henceforth, of complete government protection. Set at rest on this point, he was able to make a detailed survey of Suffolk and Essex before returning to London about the middle of October.

As soon as he arrived, he turned over to Harley a comprehensive chart, giving the party distributions in the eastern counties and confidential reports concerning local clubs and individual politicians who were worth watching. Since the rumor of his arrest had not yet died down, he indignantly denounced in his *Review* the trickery that had been used against him while he had been "traveling in the provinces upon business;" he offered the sum of twenty pounds to any one who could give him information with regard to the newsmongers who had started the false reports about him. He even found it necessary to show himself in all the public places to refute the slanders about him and to show that he was not afraid of any one.

The elections took place in May, 1705. Daniel, like a good general, visited the weakest points in his line of defense. Coventry was, of all the towns in England, the one in which political feeling ran highest; the high-flyers were in the majority there, and they did not scruple to mishandle the balloting to their own gain. De Foe, sent by Harley to make a

DE FOE'S HOUSE AT BURY ST. EDMUNDS

thorough investigation of conditions in this town, was a witness to the riotous scenes which accompanied the election. He testified to the attempts at corruption and intimidation which were easily carried out because of lack of system in the registering and the indifference of the Tory magistrates. De Foe denounced the scandal to Harley and exposed it in an issue of his *Review,* coming back to the same thing in the succeeding number in which he used Coventry as an example of what would happen to all of England if the High church party came into power.

Since the fine weather of early summer had now set in, it was almost impossible for one who enjoyed horseback riding as much as De Foe did to resist the appeal of the highways. As a further spur, there was Mrs. De Foe, demanding money for the household expenses. De Foe got permission from Harley to repeat his successful work as a propagandist in the western counties. With his faithful friend Hurst along he mounted his horse and crossed the barrier of the Temple. Thrilled by the sense of space, he set off at a gallop on the first twenty miles of his projected journey. *Westward Ho!* And a sense of elation! He could not deceive himself that he had an easy task before him. Sir Edward Seymour, a formidable enemy of the government, had practically made this whole region into an electoral fief for his own party.

In the beginning all went well. The one surprise was that, upon arriving at Dorchester, he found its citizens in a state of political indifference. They had so little of the spirit of partisanship that he himself witnessed the extraordinary spectacle . . . of an Anglican priest and a Non-Conformist minister amicably taking tea together.

But at Weymouth difficulties began. He had arranged to have his letters addressed to him under the assumed name, Alexander Goldsmith, and sent to the leading cities of the

West in care of certain friends upon whom he knew that he
could count. The one at Weymouth was called Captain Turner, but there was also in the same town another man named
Turner, the Captain of a Guernesey rover, into whose hands
some of the letters meant for De Foe were mistakenly placed.
As the letters were written in cipher, he could make nothing
of them, and, after trying all over town to find help he finally
handed them over to the other Turner, who delivered them to
De Foe when the latter reached Weymouth.

But the incident did not stop there. It had created quite a
little stir in the town so that the mayor of Weymouth began
to smell a plot. He ordered the captain of the rover to be
brought before him; the latter's ignorance expressed itself in
a confusion that only confirmed the suspicions of the mayor.
Everyone with whom De Foe had talked during his stay in
the town had to be questioned; but nothing could be proved
against any of them. Nevertheless, the rumor spread that there
was a dangerous spy in the district; and the Tories put themselves on guard.

In the meantime, De Foe went tranquilly on his way to
Exeter; making this town his headquarters, he prepared to
start on a wide circuit into the interior. The excessive heat
caused him to stop for a few days at Crediton. The high-flyers
at Exeter, believing he had left for good, plucked up courage
and boasted that this invincible pamphleteer had fled before
them. One of the city councilors was known to have said that
he regretted not having forced him to join the infantry. But
July the thirty-first De Foe showed up again on the streets of
Exeter smiling nonchalantly and making quite a stir in the
coffee-houses, mingling ostensibly with the leading citizens.
Here, as elsewhere, he put his finger to the political pulse of
the town and recorded its temperature. His dose of medicine
consisted of an assortment of tracts advocating the pacifist

policy of his patron, Harley. Having performed these duties, he took an unhurried leave and went on his way.

He had an interesting diversion at Dartmouth; he called the attention of the fishermen there to a large school of sardine in the harbor and later made a good meal upon their catch which cost him, all told, a penny and a half. And the good-sized lobster upon which he lunched the next day cost him six pence whereas it would have been at least three shillings in London. He would have enjoyed lingering in this land of milk and honey, but duty drew him on to Plymouth. He appeared to bring bad luck to this town, however, for on the very night that he arrived a severe storm scattered and destroyed a fleet of ten ships at anchor in the harbor. These ships, just back from the Barbadoes with cargoes of merchandise, represented a sorry loss in the eyes of a tradesman; but De Foe could not tarry to waste his own time in fruitless pity. Without pausing, he passed on westward, noting, on his way, traces of the havoc caused by the heavy storm of November, 1703.

While he was making his methodical survey of Devonshire, the high-flyers were busily engaged against him. The justice of peace at Crediton, whose name was Hugh Stafford, after due consideration, decided to issue an order for the arrest of De Foe and even went to the home of the Dissenting minister of the town, expecting to find him there; but De Foe had left Crediton more than a week before and was by that time on his way to Launceston. Stafford, not to be outdone, sent copies of the warrant for his arrest in all directions. At Bideford De Foe was taken and brought before the judge, who was, happily, a friend of his and hurried to protect him from the enmity of the Tories in the place.

Disheartened by all this persecution, De Foe wrote, on the fourteenth of August, to Harley, asking him for money and complaining that he had been tracked from place to place as if he were a wild beast. By the same messenger he sent a most unceremonious letter, filled with insulting terms and half-veiled threats, to Stafford; Stafford shriveled like a leaf in the hot sun of De Foe's scorn and trembled at the thought of the storm that might overtake him; all of the information he was able to get but confirmed him in the belief that this man was a conspirator against the government. Did he not always speak of the Tories in parliament as drunkards and incompetents, and had he not held long conferences in secret with the Non-Conformist ministers in each of the towns in which he stopped! Stafford wrote to headquarters for instructions as to how to proceed . . . either he received no reply or he was censored for acting too impetuously.

It was, indeed, high time that De Foe left Devonshire. Like all Englishmen of position, he took the waters at Bath, where the bathing places, so famous throughout all the country, were a great disappointment to him; he criticized the place severely:

"It is more like a prison than a place of diversion, scarce gives the company room to converse out of the smell of their own excrements, and the very city itself may be said to stink like a general common-shore."

There at Bath De Foe was to meet his brother-in-law, Robert Davis; for Hurst, his usual companion, was forced to return to his work in London. Since Davis had not yet arrived, De Foe, who hated inactivity and took but little pleasure in the attractions of the dirty watering-place, decided to explore the neighboring towns. He was pleased, upon his return to Bath, to find that Davis had come, bringing with him an encouraging note from Harley and enough money to pay their expenses on the rest of the trip.

The weather had now become so warm that De Foe decided to try the counties in the middle of England and to the north.

Davis made an ideal traveling companion, for he was intelligent, clever, and, like Daniel, given to working out fine projects; he had invented an ingenious apparatus for a diver's outfit and had dreamed of bringing up vast treasures buried in the deep; but he had been forced to give up his ambition because his wife, fearful of the danger attached to such an undertaking, had urged him to sell his diving outfit.

There was nothing very exciting about this trip into the heart of England. Here was a warm welcome for De Foe in every town in which he stopped because there were many Dissenters in this locality, and all were eager to aid him in his investigation. He passed rapidly through the Puritan cities near the Welsh border, and, by the twelfth of September, was already at Chester. He surveyed the Wirral peninsula and took the ferry to Liverpool; as the water was low, he finished crossing the Mersey on the back of a strong peasant of Lancashire. The man's jolting progress made De Foe long in preference for the roughest horse trot that he had ever experienced. After resting for three days at Liverpool, Daniel spent the second fortnight in September, visiting the new industrial towns of that district: Manchester, Halifax, Leeds, and Sheffield. These recently incorporated towns did not return members to parliament; De Foe intimated that, as a consequence, their citizens were more peaceable and more agreeable than those of the older boroughs.

The two travelers turned, the first of October, towards London. But the autumn days were perfect, the roads were still dry. . . . It would have been a pity not to have made use of this last fine weather to round up their work. De Foe decided to go back to the eastern counties in order to make some additional inquiries and to encourage the men whom he had appointed his agents. He did not get back to London until November 6, 1705.

He felt proud of what he had done, and he was justified in feeling so; his wide circuit, totaling 1,100 miles on the highways had not been in vain. He had made an almost complete chart of the politics of the people throughout the country. Nor had he wholly neglected his own affairs; he had had many opportunities in the taverns of the small towns, while he was seated before a bottle of wine, to impress upon the citizens gathered there that the *Review* was the best journal published in London. He had even added a number of new subscribers to his list. He had also found the means to conclude some successful speculations in woollen goods. But there was even more gain than all this; his long trips had offered him many new sights and had given him much to muse upon; he had stored up a wealth of experience and had ripened under adversity. All of this knowledge was by way of foundation for the superstructure that was to come later . . . his novels.

He felt now, however, that he had earned a rest and a reward; since his traveling about had been of much profit to his chief, he looked for a permanent post with a good salary attached to it. But he looked in vain; it was a wish he was never to have granted him. Once caught up in the maelstrom of politics, there was not an instant's rest or peace for him; it is a conflict that knows neither truce nor mercy. His enemies did not give him a single inactive moment; they would steal copies of the *Review* in the coffee-houses so that other patrons could not read it; they even bought up the whole stock of the street sellers and destroyed them so that they could not be read. Unscrupulous book-sellers bribed the printer of his long philosophical poem, *Jure Divino,* to send them the first proofs of the best pages; then they brought out a cheap, pirated edition which bore on the first page the insulting notice, "Sold for the benefit of the author." Some papers of the day called his attention to threats of a whipping; but apparently no paid sluggers could be hired to undertake a personal combat with this broad-shouldered man, who carried himself with such an air of assurance. He was extremely annoyed, however, "from the immediate fury of five or six unreasonable creditors." It reached the point where he did not dare step out for fear of being followed and having his way blocked by these insulting wretches. He turned to Harley, who never failed to get him out of a tight place.

There is no indication that De Foe ever shunned work. . . . It seemed, indeed, impossible for him to remain inactive and unproductive. During the two years, 1705 and 1706, he not only continued getting out his *Review* by himself, keeping up his correspondence with his agents in the provinces, undertaking some new business enterprises, and helping Harley draw up some important bills, but he also found the time to write many poems and timely pamphlets, as well as a long prose satire, called *The Consolidator: or Memoirs of Sundry Transactions from the World of the Moon.* This last piece, in spite of some delightful bits of keen humor, is much too long and too poorly written to take the place in literature that *Gulliver's Travels* takes; yet it did very evidently inspire that immortal work by Jonathan Swift. It, too, is a humorous take-off on English politics, which De Foe presented in the guise of an elaborate history of the kingdom of the moon. There is one detail of significance in any discussion of the psychology of its author . . . that is, the particular description he gives of various strange instruments used on the moon; there is, for example, a "cogitator, or chair of reflection," which he defines as a machine to make one think; and a "concionazimir," a kind of ecclesiastical engine, like that employed by the High church ministers to sound an alarm in case of danger.

To his abilities as a writer, De Foe added those of a reporter. Early in the year 1706, he made a special trip to Canterbury in order to investigate a story about ghosts that had reached him. He talked to the people connected with the incident, took careful notes of all the details they gave him, and, little by little, built up the story, pruning it of all irrelevancies. Published upon his return to London under the title, the *Apparition of Mrs. Veal,* it was a great success. Sir Walter Scott gave it his warmest admiration as an invention of realistic detail; later research brought out the fact that it was, instead, an excellent piece of that sort of reportorial work at which De Foe was adept.

The union between England and Scotland, that had been so fondly projected by William of Orange, was again brought up for consideration. When it was fully decided to attempt it, Harley made up his mind to send De Foe into Scotland to keep an eye on the progress of events and to be ready to aid and advise the English Commissioners who were negotiating the treaty. It was arranged for Daniel to leave London early in September, 1706, and he left with the understanding that, upon his return, he would be recommended for a regular government pension. Before he left he was given the honor of kissing the Queen's hand; Harley knew his servant well enough to know that this contact with royalty would be enough to inspire him with loyal zeal for the undertaking. Since it was to be a secret mission, De Foe took care to spread the rumor among his associates that he was going to Scotland upon a matter of business; dressed up in a splendid new outfit, he set off, taking the most roundabout way to his destination. He made but slow progress for several days because the ground, being damp and sandy, offered much difficulty to his horse. After he crossed the Trent at Nottingham, he found the road much harder. He arrived at Newcastle, September the thirtieth and went at once to the postmaster, John Bell, who, Harley had told him, would furnish him with money and horses during his stay in Scotland. Bell was also the source of supplies to another secret service man, named Fearns, whom Harley had sent to Edinburgh to keep a check upon De Foe; the wily minister saw to it that there was no chance for double-crossing.

Bell did not yet know exactly what De Foe, who traveled under the name of Goldsmith, was going to do in Scotland, and De Foe took little pains to inform him. But an accident to one of the two horses that De Foe had with him made it necessary for him to stop over in Newcastle long enough to buy another one. The delay threw him into Bell's company the greater part of two or three days; and the two had plenty of time for conversation as they sat over their bottles of wine. Bell soon made out that his companion was no other than the editor of the *Review*. That he was an impressive personality, Bell bore witness to in his letter the next week to Harley in which he told the circumstances of De Foe's sojourn in Newcastle . . . fortunate, he accounted them, because they gave him the chance to become acquainted with such an admirable man. The poor provincial was quite dazzled by the attention shown him by this great London writer.

De Foe reached Edinburgh before the end of the second week in October. From then on he continued to send Harley regular accounts of the political situation in Scotland . . . the intrigues of the clans who were opposed to the union and the state of mind of the Presbyterians who had received him as one of themselves. The Jacobites were furious at the idea of union; they vented their wrath upon the leader of the English Commission, the Duke of Queensbury, who had to take care in order to escape death at the hands of twenty-four young Scotch patriots, sworn to assassinate him; their formal oath showed each one's signature written in his own blood.

There was a particularly violent mob the last of October.

De Foe had had to keep to his room for some time because of a severe cold, and he had been warned that he had better not go out on the streets since a demonstration had just started. But his curiosity and his desire to get out overruled his good judgment. He entered a coach to go and call upon a friend, but he was at once recognized and followed as one of those "English dogs;" in escaping pursuit, he lost his way and arrived at his friend's home much the worse for his imprudence; he resolved to stay within doors until after dark. When he did return to his lodging, he listened to the uproar in the street but did not dare to look out very often, for he knew that the rioters would hurl stones at any one they noticed watching them . . . a precaution on their part to prevent their being identified later before a justice. It was not long until the report got out through the crowd that De Foe lived in that house; a mistake as to the floor that he was on saved the windows of his own apartment from being broken. Within a short time after this attack, De Foe looked on helplessly while an English gentleman of his acquaintance encountered a part of the mob who immediately attacked him. He defended himself bravely and called out to the guard who arrived on the scene to rescue the gentleman and put the attackers to flight. De Foe sat down without delay to write Harley a dramatic account of the whole affair, not neglecting to emphasize the dangers he had run and the peril he had just escaped.

Upon the whole, he could be satisfied with the way things were going; he himself had succeeded in working his way into the good graces of the Scotch people in spite of their difficult and suspicious natures. He had to play a double rôle at Edinburgh: part of his work was to keep an eye on the local journalists, picking out the agitators and seeing that their pamphlets, if they were dangerously anti-union, were suppressed at the printers; at the same time he was acting as technical adviser to the English Commissioners. He accepted it as a good augury that the first article of the union was adopted on November the fourth, the very day that William of Orange, the "savior of English freedom," had landed on English soil.

On November the thirteenth, Daniel warned Harley of his fear because of the presence in Edinburgh of so many Highlanders, all enemies to the treaty.

"They are formidable fellows," he wrote, "and I only wish Her Majesty had 25,000 of them in Spain, a nation equally proud and barbarous like themselves. They are all gentlemen . . . will take affront from no man, and insolent to the last degree. But certainly the absurdity is ridiculous to see a man in his mountain habit, armed with a broadsword, target, pistol, or perhaps two, at his girdle a dagger, and staff walking down the street as upright and haughty as if he were a lord . . . and withal driving a cow!"

In no time at all, De Foe became the undisputed king of Scotch journalists, holding his place by his verve, his talent, and his experience, as well as because he had the funds to get his prose circulated in all the towns of the country; but he was very careful to keep under cover his real reason for being in Scotland, whose people have little liking for spies. He had a different story for each group: to the business man he had come to Edinburgh to set up as a shipbuilder; to the lawyer, he was looking around for an estate that he might buy and then bring on his family; one day he would announce that he was going to establish a glass-works in partnership with a lord; the next day he spread the rumor that he was thinking of developing some salt mines. He had already laid his plans for making a tour of investigation across Scotland; at Glasgow, he would pass as a fish merchant; at Aberdeen, as a woollen merchant; at Perth, as a linen-draper . . . always an actor and

child-like in his delight in make-believe, he fitted admirably
into each rôle that he created for himself. But while he was
talking ships or shops; salt mines or glass-works; fish, wool,
or linens, he was casually turning the conversation upon that
topic of general interest . . . the union, adding sly bits of ridicule against them who set themselves against the Ministry.

De Foe was leading the active life he loved. He would have
been perfectly happy if his private affairs had not been under
such a cloud; Harley had given his word that he would take
care of the needs of De Foe's family during the latter's absence;
but, the last of November, Mrs. De Foe wrote her husband that
she had not had a penny for the last ten days. De Foe at once
wrote Harley, expostulating with him for his neglect. The
latter admitted his error and made good his promises. But
what hours of agony during the long days that elapsed between the demand and the response. Daniel had scarcely
calmed down from this experience when he had news of the
death of his old father. This came December the twenty-fourth
to sadden his Christmas and make him long to return to London. Such a move become almost imperative when he learned
that he had been named his father's sole executor. He felt,
besides, that there was little to hold him in Scotland . . . the
vote for the treaty of union had been obtained. But Harley
felt it was absolutely necessary for De Foe to remain there since
he would know how to cope with the many practical difficulties that the application of the treaty terms would give
rise to.

Daniel gave himself up, then, to quieting the suspicions of
the people in Edinburgh who questioned his prolonged stay
in their city. He first let the rumor that he had fled from
London to avoid paying his debts run its course; then he enjoyed baffling public opinion by starting a series of half-truths
that were so plausible they could not but get a hearing. Some

he told of his contemplated work, *The History of the Union,* for which he had just opened subscriptions and which would require at least a year's research in the registers and parliament books of Edinburgh. Others he informed that the Queen's Commissioners had arranged with him to write a new version of the Psalms for which performance he intended "to lock myself in the College for 2 years." A third group received the news that a weaving factory he was planning on establishing made his presence necessary.

In May, 1707, he started on his projected trip to all of the large cities of Scotland to educate the citizens to the practicality of the union. The fine weather made the trip particularly enjoyable. De Foe, always alive to new and strange sights, took in everything from the great bridge between Glasgow and Sterling, thrown over a dry river bed, to the porpoises that the fishermen of Kinghorn killed with a blow on the head; from the condition of the peasant class to the various horse races. He did avoid crossing the Highlands since to do so would have meant carrying a tent and camping overnight in the inhospitable mountains which held no charm for a traveler who preferred to remain on level ground and sleep at night in a comfortable inn. Daniel was satisfied to gaze from afar at the pine covered peaks inhabited by those monstrous people . . . Papists and Jacobites. He did not return to Edinburgh until the middle of June.

Godolphin had planned a definite post for De Foe in Scotland, that of Commissioner of the custom-house, but Harley wished to keep him directly under his own orders; once more then were the minister's promises put off until to-morrow, and, in place of a permanent place, he would substitute a private allowance. But the outcome was neither money, place, nor even the order to return to London. He dared to express his disgruntlement in no uncertain terms in the *Review:*

"There are 5 or 6 persons in London, who can not only give a true account of my removal, but recall me from my banishment, if they had humanity in them a degree less than an African Lion."

Nothing came of that; then, in a letter, dated September the eleventh, he appealed to his patron on the score of his long fidelity and his loyal services to relieve him of his necessity. He wrote:

"It is now 5 months since you were pleased to withdraw your supply, and yet I had never your orders to return. . . . If you were to see me now entertained of courtesy without subsistence, almost grown shabby in clothes, dejected, etc., you would be moved to hasten my relief. . . . I was just on the brink of returning . . . When I received your last, with my Lord Treasurer's letter. But hitherto his Lordship's goodness to me seems like messages from an army to a town besieged, that relief is coming, which heartens and encourages the famished garrison, but does not feed them."

At last Harley came to a realization that too long a delay would alienate De Foe's sympathy. He sent him a hundred pounds sterling with which De Foe, early in December, 1707, started out joyfully on his way south. But it seems as if his regard for his family stopped with seeing it provided for. . . . He does not appear to have been so eager to see them all, for he took more than a month to make his way to London. But who, with a pocket full of money, would give up stopping a few days at the different inns in Bawtry where there was such good living to be had? And, as a historian, how could he cross Marston Moor without pausing to listen to a detailed account of the surprising events connected with that memorable battle there when Charles I's army was wiped out by parliamentarian troops. It was not until the first of the new year, 1708, that De Foe paced again the streets of his beloved City.

A man so well known as he was could not pace them long unnoted. On January the twenty-second a Tory journalist made an ill-humored comment upon his return:

"He is come out of Scotland to shame us again as he used to do!"

De Foe relished this bit of spite and prepared to give an energetic tussle to all who sought it. He had a long account to settle with some of them . . . those who had tried to calumniate him and to tear up his pathway. They had made some of his imprudent articles in the *Review* a pretext for complaint, and had endeavored to have him arrested on the complaint first of the Lord-Chief Justice, then of the Swedish ambassador, finally of the Muscovite ambassador. It was Harley again who stepped in to save him from the terrors of prison.

Just after his return his enemies made use of a piece of information to instigate a subtile piece of scurrility against him. It seems De Foe had purchased some beautiful hair of a peasant in order to have a new periwig made for himself. The muckrakers twisted the story and reported that that "powdered ape" of a De Foe had knocked down a young girl and stolen her hair. Daniel was vexed and indignant, but he had the wisdom to make no reply. He did announce for all England to read that "the champion of Peace and the Union" hurled a new defiance to "Tyranny, Ignorance, and Intolerance." . . . The groups of idlers gathered around in a circle to look on and count the knockout blows.

An unforeseen event occurred to turn Daniel's joy to anxiety; Harley's private secretary was convicted of high treason. It was a rare bit of scandal that the Whigs knew how to make the most of, particularly since public opinion was already predisposed against the Ministry, as it now stood. Lord Treasurer Godolphin, in the name of the moderate Tories, asked for Harley's dismissal.

This turn of events sent De Foe to his patron for advice as to his own disposal. Harley, without hesitation, urged him to continue his work under the direction of those in power.

"My Lord Treasurer," he said, "will employ you in nothing but what is for the public service, and agreeably to your own sentiments of things; and besides, it is the Queen you are serving, who has been very good to you. Pray, apply yourself as you used to do; I shall not take it ill from you in the least."

Following this direction, De Foe presented himself to Godolphin, who asked for no explanation, but smilingly complained that he had not seen him for several weeks. Then he took him to the Queen; for the second time De Foe was allowed to kiss the hand of his sovereign. Her Majesty expressed her satisfaction with his past services and let him know that the Lord Treasurer was going to send him on another mission in which she hoped he would distinguish himself as he had done heretofore. Godolphin, accordingly, took De Foe off to his study and unfolded to him his plan for sending him into Scotland to watch over the menacing Jacobites.

De Foe set out with his brother-in-law, Davis, for a companion. But the latter's horse began to limp at Coventry. They stopped there and hired another to carry them on into Scotland. Arrived there, they decided to keep the horse, sending the owner of it back what they estimated would be enough money to pay for it. But the owner was not satisfied; he sent the money back and demanded either his horse or more money. The two parties finally reached an agreement after much argument back and forth. De Foe considered the incident closed and was surprised and extremely annoyed to have the whole story with its petty details grossly exaggerated, revived three years later in a pamphlet called, *The Hue and*

Cry after Daniel Foe and his Coventry-beast. This infamous libel was widely circulated by his enemies; it told how De Foe, passing through Coventry, had borrowed from one of "those Brethren whose good graces and Pockets he insinuated himself into," an excellent saddle-horse which he had kept and had entirely forgotten to pay for. This calumny, based upon a half-truth, did De Foe more damage than did all the violent attacks of the high-flyers; in spite of all his efforts to deny the accusation and explain the matter, it was this damaging pamphlet that was a big factor in making him lose caste with his British public.

Beginning with the middle of February, 1708, De Foe became quite active at Edinburgh. He sent reports upon the situation in Scotland to the two ministers, Godolphin and the Count of Sunderland, without letting either one know of his service to the other. The Duke of Queensbury invited De Foe to visit his splendid estate of Drumlanrig and asked his opinion about improving the landscape gardening and the general design of the park grounds. De Foe spent a good deal of time riding about the estate and even ran across some lead mines among the neighboring hills; he succeeded in interesting Queensbury in their development, but the project fell through with upon the death of the Duke a few years later.

De Foe listened to an old Cameronite preach for seven hours to a congregation of seven thousand, many of whom had come from distant villages on foot. The crowd, seated upon a hill, listened to him spellbound. De Foe could not but admire these Scotch Puritans . . . their detestation of swearing and their strict observance of the Sabbath struck an answering chord in his own heart. He made one trip to the Enterkin pass, the most dangerous one in Scotland. Imbedded in the high precipices that hemmed in the narrow way, he saw the bones of horses. Ordinarily, he might have drawn back from so difficult

a passage, but, fearing the scorn of the bold and brave moun-
taineers with whom he traveled, he went on, marveling the
while at his own intrepidity.

He was back home with his family by the last of December,
busy getting them all settled in a comfortable house at Stoke-
Newington, a charming little town to the north of London.
But he was soon called upon again by the Ministry to study the
perplexing question of what to do with the unfortunate
Palatins, who, leaving their country after it had been ravaged
by the armies of Louis XIV, had come to seek a refuge in
England. More than two thousand of them had already arrived by the middle of June, 1709, and each day saw an additional influx of them. One group in a particularly wretched
condition was taken care of in tents at Stoke-Newington,
where the De Foes did all they could to relieve the want and
necessity of the poor refugees. The haphazard method of
distributing them seemed to Daniel a pity; they were frequently quartered upon towns that were already overcrowded
with dependents of their own. He suggested a detailed plan
by which the Palatins would be given the New-Forest to clear
and then to build upon for a model town of their own. But
the idea was never carried out as more serious problems arose
to claim the attention of the Ministry.

In August, Godolphin, disturbed by the increasing activity
of the Jacobites, sent De Foe back into Scotland. He went on
his way in a joyful mood, stopping over for the horse races at
Pontefract and at Nottingham and joining a group of friends
for a trip into the Cheviot hills; but the slippery rocks and the
loose stones they traveled over quite upset him. . . . He imagined that he just escaped the peril of his life.

He stayed at Edinburgh until the beginning of February,
1710, studying business conditions in Scotland and the opportunities for British development there. It seemed to him the

Firth of Forth might be made into a better base of supplies in case of an attack from the sea than was Leith. He even began to be more interested in the Highlands, although it was not an interest based upon the picturesque appeal of the scenery . . . it was curiosity concerning the strange people there, who were said, by their credulous neighbors, to possess the gift of second sight. De Foe would have liked to look into this.

But disturbing news from London brought him home in a hurry. His old enemy, Doctor Sacheverell, had raised anew "the bloody flag of defiance," and had preached against the Ministry in terms that Godolphin declared were malicious, scandalous, and seditious. The latter demanded that the House of Lords impeach the libelous clergyman, whose trial, as a consequence, began February 27, 1710, at Westminster Hall. Sacheverell's advocate attempted to prove that the Dissenters were a menace to the Established church; in his speech for the defense he quoted distorted and garbled passages from the *Review*. As it happened, the London crowd, exhibiting its customary habit of jumping from one side to the other, took the part of the high-flyers this time against the government. The crowds even stopped the Queen's carriage one day, crying out:

"God bless your Majesty and the Church! We hope your Majesty is for Doctor Sacheverell!"

Sacheverell, on his way to Westminster or returning to his home in London, was always escorted by an enthusiastic crowd. The people shouted his praises for hours in front of his residence so that he had to appear at frequent intervals at his window to quiet them. They expressed their devotion to him by destroying the Dissenters' meeting houses, by scattering pamphlets and singing songs that glorified him and called down confusion upon his enemies. One odd pamphlet pre-

tended to give an account of a recent invention of the philosophic Doctor's which would enable the blind to recover their
sight and become good Christians again. It read as follows:

Take 3 drachms of Godly Zeal, 6 oz. of Plain-Dealing, mixed
together with some Spirit of Boldness, in the White Pot of Inno-
cency, and being made warm over a gentle Fire of Holy Prudence,
with 4 oz. of Mercy, and the like quantity of Christian Charity,
adding a sufficient quantity of Honesty and Sincerity to all these in-
gredients; being well incorporated together, make it plaister-wise
with the Doctrine of Passive-Obedience and Non-Resistance. And
when your eyes begin to dim, apply this plaister to your heart, and
some of it to your ears morning and evening, and by God's blessing
you will recover your sight. *Probatum est.*

De Foe made humorous comments in his *Review* upon Sacheverell's extraordinary popularity and did his utmost to ridicule this idol of the moment, pretending that he was only the
passing infatuation of a few brainless women. He wrote:

The Women lay aside their tea and chocolate, leave off visiting
after dinner, and forming themselves into cabals, turn privy-council-
lors, and settle the affairs of state. . . . Indeed they have hardly
leisure to live, little time to eat and sleep, and none at all to say
their prayers. If you turn your eye to the Park, the ladies are not
there; even the church is thinner than usual; for, you know, the
mode is for privy-councils to meet on Sundays. . . . Even the little
boys and girls talk politics. Little miss has Dr. Sacheverell's picture
put into her prayer-book, that God and the Doctor may take her up
in the morning before breakfast; and all manner of discourse among
the women runs now upon war and government. Tattling nonsense
and slander is transferred to the males, and adjourned from the
toilet to the coffee-houses and groom-porters. . . . This new invasion of the politician's province in an eminent demonstration of
the sympathetic influence of the clergy upon the sex, and the near
affinity between the gown and the petticoat; since all the errors of

our present or past administrators . . . could never embark the
ladies till you fell upon the clergy. But, as soon as you pinch the
parson, he holds out his hand to the ladies for assistance, and they
appear as one woman in his defence.

De Foe boasted of never having criticized the private life of
his adversaries. He accused Sacheverell of supporting the Pope
and the Devil, but he made it a point to attack the nefarious
ideas and not the personality of the Doctor. Nevertheless, without telling any one, he did send to General Stanhope, a member of the Committee of Impeachment against Sacheverell, a
long letter in which he named a number of jolly fellows in
the General's own House who could not deny having been
on many a drinking bout with the worthy Doctor; he also
declared that Sacheverell had drunk, kneeling, to the health
of the Pretender and that he had spoken scandalously against
the Queen.

This secret attack gained nothing. The Lords could scarcely
have passed a more lenient sentence. He was merely prohibited
from preaching for the ensuing three years. It was equal to an
acquittal in the eyes of the crowd which at once organized
public rejoicings for the justification of the popular Doctor.

De Foe struggled as hard as he could to prevent the Ministry
from slumping in public esteem. He made the *Review* into a
great political organ, and established regular centers for its
distribution in all the large cities of England. In March, 1709,
he began issuing from Edinburgh a special edition of the *Review* which appeared there at the same time the regular edition
came out in London and was distributed from there to all the
counties to the north and even into Ireland. This was a long
reach towards modern journalistic methods of circulation, especially when one considers the extreme handicaps under
which De Foe labored.

At about this same time De Foe extended his influence still

further by becoming the owner of the *Edinburgh Courier* whose editor had died in January, 1710. Profiting by his influence with the Ministry, he saw to it that his fellow journalists were no better informed than he . . . going so far as to stipulate that other papers should not be allowed to print original translations from foreign sources if such matter contradicted what De Foe was allowed to publish in the *Review*. As a further measure of protection, he made a reciprocal treaty with his most formidable opponent, the journalist, Dyer, to make no personal attacks upon each other.

The Jacobites and the high-flyers did all in their power to kill the *Review*. They so seriously threatened its printer, Morphew, that he gave up the publishing of the journal; but De Foe got another printer, Baker, who was used to handling even libelous matter so that he only laughed at all their threats. The attacks were then turned against De Foe himself; he was several times drawn into encounters from which only his daring effrontery saved him. He tells how one day he bravely entered a room in which five men sat, plotting his death. His appearance, calm and self-assured, turned them all from blustering homicides to fawning servants. A group of religious zealots once notified him of the day and the hour they proposed to sacrifice him for the welfare of the Anglican religion. He answered them openly in the columns of the *Review* by stating that he never went out after nightfall and that he wore a coat of mail to protect his back in the daytime.

He was never ruffled in debate. That gave him the superiority over the hot-headed.

"Man of great rashness and impudence, mean mercenarie prostitute, state mountebank, Hackney tool, scandalous pen, foul-mouthed mongrel," were the heated epithets hurled at him by a Glasgow clergyman, named Clarke, who had believed himself attacked in one of the chapters of the *History of the*

Union. Did De Foe become angry and seek justice from these libelous statements by this unchristian gentleman? He did not. He calmly replied:

"Mr. De Foe whose writings made him famous, since in them is conspicuously to be seen Eminency of Gifts, Humility of Spirit, Elegancy of Style, Solidity of Matter, Height of Fancy, Depth of Judgment, Clearness of Apprehension, Strength of Reason and Ardent Zeal for Truth. . . . To rail on and reproach such a phœnix of his Age, such a rare and precious gentleman, the Envy and Glory of his sex is a sort of Indiscretion (not to call it worse) that none would have thought Mr. Clark capable of."

This did not put Mr. Clarke in the best possible light; in fact, it left the impression that De Foe was too big to be much disturbed by petty backbiting.

But there was one man De Foe could not put down, against whom he held a lasting dislike . . . that was the celebrated Doctor Swift, who had touched upon the one weak spot in De Foe's armor . . . his literary vanity. Speaking of the Whig journalists, Swift said one day,

"One of those authors (the fellow who was pilloried, I have forgot his name) is indeed so grave, sententious, dogmatical a rogue, that there is no enduring him."

De Foe took pride in being hated or admired, but he could not stand being contemptuously ignored. He found his most insulting words to characterize the man who had so scorned him; called him: "Cynic in behavior, fury in temper, unpolite in conversation, abusive and scurrilous in language, and ungovernable in passion."

Although these two powerful figures were later united in serving the same patron, their hatred of each other kept them forever apart. It was a pity, for had they only reached an understanding, together they could have molded English thought at their will.

IX. ROBERT HARLEY'S TOOL

THE Whig Ministry was overthrown when the Queen replaced her former favorite, the tyrannical Duchess of Marlborough, with a new confidant, Mrs. Masham. Mrs. Masham was related to Harley, who had been for months carefully and shrewdly laying his plans to return to power. He had just gone over, bag and baggage, to the Tory camp where he had been received with open arms. On June 13, 1710, the Earl of Sunderland was removed from the government. This news warned De Foe of the way the wind was blowing. . . . His ardor in Godolphin's service had cooled quite a bit as he found his abilities were not being rated at their full value and that his pay was not forthcoming at regular intervals.[1] The moment seemed a favorable one to approach again his old patron.

On the seventeenth of July, De Foe took up his interrupted correspondence with Harley, begging permission to call upon him in order to give him, as he had given him in the past, some secret reports. These, he felt, should be in the minister's possession . . . not for any personal gain to De Foe, but for the common good. Harley was not misled by this pretense of self-effacement; he granted De Foe the interview he sought, accepted what he had to offer him, and put him to work on one of his political schemes. All of the time, however, he was keeping quiet about his alliance with the Jacobites, for he

---

[1] Long after the fall of the Whig Ministry, De Foe received some of his back pay from Godolphin, thus giving his enemies the chance to say that he received money from both parties.

knew that De Foe's hatred of the Pretender was deep-seated. As a consequence of this interview, De Foe became actively engaged in advancing the interests of his old patron and also of the Duke of Shrewsbury, whom Harley had succeeded in attaching to his cause. On August the eighth, the Queen asked Godolphin to resign. De Foe had the effrontery to present himself humbly before the fallen minister, to whose downfall he had contributed, and asked his advice as to what he should do. Godolphin assured him, as Harley had once before, that he was really in the service of the Queen and not that of any one minister. He told him that, consequently, it was his duty to serve under any government which followed English laws and respected English freedom. It was exactly the answer De Foe had hoped for; it justified his acceptance of Harley's orders and allowed him to proclaim his own independence from the rule of any master. That he served the nation alone was his fond delusion; in reality, he was a blind tool in Harley's hands from 1710 to 1714 . . . following his patron's devious ways, though always unaware of the latter's secret dealings with the Pretender. De Foe took every opportunity to deny that he had ever been given orders from Harley as to what he should publish in his journal or his pamphlets; yet his correspondence shows that he never let up seeking Harley's advice and obediently following it . . . content that it was always given discreetly so as not to offend his independent pride.

On August the twelfth, De Foe wrote Harley a long letter, congratulating him upon his being named Chancellor of the Exchequer and assuring him of his fidelity, for, he added, "it was always with regret that . . . I found myself obliged by circumstances to continue in the service of your enemies."

Harley promised to bring De Foe to the Queen's attention, assuring him that she would not cut off the pension due to

so zealous a servant as he was. Taking advantage of this attitude, Daniel asked for money for his political information
bureau, which was in danger of falling through for the lack of
support. As the elections were close at hand, he suggested that
he would go into the provinces to check the report spread by
the Whigs that the Ministry was Jacobite, but Harley thought
he might be more useful in Scotland. Daniel could not ask
for anything better; he was always ready for the activity of the
open road. By the twenty-first of October, he was off on horseback, taking the highway to the north. He had received exact
instructions as to how he should proceed, had arranged for a
code in which to carry on his correspondence, and had taken
a new pseudonym, Claude Guilot. At Newcastle he got some
money, upon Harley's credit, from his old acquaintance, the
Postmaster Bell. But Bell, who had followed in Harley's political footsteps and who believed that De Foe had been sent
into Scotland by Godolphin for the Whig cause, thought to
hamper him by telling everyone in town of his presence and
of the object of his visit.

What annoyed De Foe the most was that he could not count
upon Bell to handle his letters for him. All of the time he was
in Scotland, he had to resort to the most complicated of
subterfuges in order to keep up his correspondence with Harley; he disguised his handwriting and, further to baffle suspicion, had his mail sent through a number of different addresses; such as, "Mr. William Clift, to Mr. Walter Ross, in
care of Mr. David Monroe." In spite of all this, he was never
sure whether or not his letters were properly forwarded and
safely arrived.

At Edinburgh where he stayed until the middle of November, he spent the greater part of his time fighting the Jacobite
influence of the Episcopalian church and bringing pressure
to bear upon the electors, urging them to vote for the mod-

erate Tories who were pledged to support the new Ministry. He was ready to return to London on December the eighteenth, but storms and flood prevented his departure. He put in the extra time that the delay gave him preparing some pamphlets on financial subjects. His satiric verve led him also into a dangerous undertaking; he helped to get out a libelous burlesque something like the *Consolidator*, entitled *Atalantis Major*, in which a number of Jacobite lords, all friends of Harley's, were variously lampooned. Harley resented the paper and wrote about it to De Foe, who had his story all ready; he replied that he did not know who wrote *Atalantis Major*, that a number of persons had spoken to him about this work, that he had encouraged them to publish it, but that he had done so only to gain their confidence, hoping that they would put the manuscript into his hands and so enable him to prevent its coming out. Unfortunately, it had not been possible for him to do that. In this way did De Foe turn suspicion aside and get himself out of what might have become a most disagreeable situation . . . but Harley was beginning to look a bit askance upon his faithful henchman and to regard his professed devotion with some misgivings.

As the weather improved by the middle of January, 1711, De Foe set out on his return trip to London. He passed by way of Newcastle, stopping there long enough to have printed a small book of prophecies, somewhat like an astrologer's almanac, but with a political purpose; he called it *The British Visions: or Isaac Bickerstaff's 12 Prophecies for the year 1711*. The book was announced in the *Review* and attained such success that De Foe brought out similar volumes in the succeeding years.

Harley was only too glad to have De Foe's advice in matters pertaining to business and trade. He could not but acknowledge that this talented writer had initiative and industry, was full of good ideas and easy to please; the least extra consideration overjoyed him. Harley could not say so much for his other political adviser, Jonathan Swift, who was whimsical and exacting . . . he once returned a fifty-pound note, saying that it was not sufficient. The historian, Oldmixon, however, does make the statement that Harley paid De Foe much better than he did Swift, but De Foe was undoubtedly a more active and a more useful servant than was Swift.

On March 8, 1711, Harley was stabbed at an open meeting of the Council by the French spy, the Marquis de Guiscard, who had been brought before the ministers on the charge of treason. Harley became at once a hero and a martyr in the eyes of the crowd. As soon as he was recovered, the Queen made him Count of Oxford and conferred upon him the Order of the Garter; later he was appointed Lord High Treasurer of Great Britain, distinctions that set him above his colleagues.

De Foe was proud of being in the confidence of such a great man, especially since it led the highest lords of the realm to seek his favor. He himself tells of how Lord Buchan solicited his influence in order to get a hearing with Harley. Buchan backed his solicitation with a generous gift of money, a practice that was not regarded as so reprehensible in those days. It is quite certain that De Foe undertook such a trust with the same seriousness with which he would have undertaken a business deal in merchandise.

The renewed alliance between Harley and De Foe did not proceed without some jolts; there were quarrels from time to time that separated the two men either because Harley was displeased with some article in the *Review* or because De Foe grew bitterly vindictive at insufficient or irregular pay. For example, on June 19, 1711, De Foe, who had been several times repulsed when he had asked for admission at his patron's

door, wrote both humbly and boldly under his pseudonym of
Goldsmith:

"God is my witness if I knew anything in which I should
displease you, I would avoid it dilligently." Then came thinly
veiled reproaches:

"Your Lordship knows, and I presume remembers, that
when you honoured me with your recommendation to the
late Lord Treasurer [Godolphin], my Lord offered me a very
good post in Scotland, and afterwards offered me to be commissioner of the Customs there, and that I did not refuse
those offers; but it being your opinion, as well as his Lordship's, that I might be more serviceable in a private capacity,
I chose rather to depend upon Her Majesty's goodness. . . .
Had I not the importuning circumstance of a large family, a
wife and six children, I could serve Your Lordship 20 years
without the least supply, rather than thus press upon your
goodness. But my weakness permits me to say no more, a
family often ruined and now depending upon Your Lordship's goodness presses me beyond measure. I humbly ask your
pardon for it."

Then came the last little touch, scarcely accusatory, but
neatly suggestive and skilfully insistent. De Foe urged the importance of a hearing . . . not to pour out his own troubles,
but to tell Harley of a serious revolutionary movement which
threatened to cause an upheaval in Scotland.

Differences between the two were of short duration; De Foe
was again received by his patron on June the twenty-sixth and,
on July the thirteenth, acknowledged the receipt of a generous
allowance of money. Harley seemed to enjoy letting his too
presumptuous assistant cool his heels awhile on his doorstep,
and then he was ready to receive him, a repentant sinner. His
need for the kind of aid De Foe could give him was too imperative to be set aside for long. There was a double task now

for which De Foe was peculiarly fitted; Harley wished to fill
the depleted coffers of the British treasury and to make peace
with France. With the aid of his trusty counselor, he worked
out his great financial scheme . . . the organization of the
South Sea company whose activities were to aid in wiping out
the public debt. It was a bold enterprise, but it succeeded, in
part at least, although it led to a dangerous fever of speculation
that spread over England and from there to all of Europe.
De Foe entered into the situation and brought up again his old
project of establishing some English colonies in South America; the idea interested Harley. . . . It would give him the
chance to meet the Spaniards in the matter of gold competition right on their own ground, but he kept putting off the
actual carrying out of the scheme and finally ceased speaking
of it.

Meanwhile, Scotland was quite stirred up about the new
methods being employed in the Customs. The agitation was
kept alive by the Jacobites, who had never accepted the idea of
the union with England, and also by the Squadroni, fanatic
Presbyterians who believed that the English ministry was
backing the Pretender. De Foe offered to go north again and
make a careful investigation, doing what he could to quiet the
fears of those whose service to the government could be relied
upon. He did not add to his offer the information that his own
business affairs made a trip into Scotland almost necessary.
He had just become a partner in a weaving factory there and
wanted to settle everything with his partner. Harley agreed to
the trip, and De Foe made his preparations to leave; but when
he announced, early in September, that he was all ready to
jump on his horse, the order to depart did not come.

Harley had changed his mind again at the very last minute.
The preliminaries of the treaty of Utrecht had just been
signed; Harley foresaw that this measure would give rise

to a furious outcry from the Whigs and that all of De Foe's arguments would be extremely useful to calm the tempest and reassure moderate opinion. Therefore, he gave De Foe the task of convincing his reading public that the treaty would be a real gain from the business point of view; Swift was called upon to explain the political advantages. De Foe's pamphlet, *Reasons why this nation ought to put a Speedy End to this Expensive War,* gave much satisfaction to a secret envoy of Louis XIV's, Monsieur Mesnager,[1] who wished to translate it for circulation in France. He was resolved, also, to engage for his own purposes this writer who upheld so eloquently a measure dear to His Most Christian Majesty. He had sent to De Foe a hundred pistoles, but he was able to get no further with his designs because De Foe, guessing at their source, denounced Mesnager to the Queen. Daniel did quietly pocket the hundred pistoles, but his pamphlet was well worth that to Mesnager and to all of France, since it favored free trade, a measure that appeared as a salvation to that country, now almost at the end of her string. The French ambassador said nothing about it, particularly as he had learned, in the meantime, that De Foe was "Harley's tool;" for De Foe, really a protectionist, as were all Whigs at that time, had, at Harley's instigation, forsworn himself to write against his own political and even against his own religious convictions.

He had become an opportunist . . . one by one his earnest beliefs had been undermined. He even defended the Administration in its persecution of Dissenters, trying to cover up with his skillful rhetoric the injustice and the cruelty of the measures adopted to restrain their freedom. The Non-Conformists of the City were united in treating him as a renegade, and they sought by every means in their power to undo him.

[1] Cf. article by Paul G. Dottin in *Revue Germanique,* July, 1923, entitled, "Daniel De Foe, mystificateur."

He had again to suffer the humiliation of having his door besieged by urgent creditors, demanding immediate payment of old bills. Insulted in the streets, villified in the papers, he begged Harley in February, 1712, to let him leave for Scotland. But the government had need for all its clever and energetic writers in this impending war of words. The premature peace was harshly criticized by the Whig journalists. De Foe every day called the attention of the Ministry to seditious articles and attempted to answer all its opponents' arguments with even better ones. When he had occasion to see Harley, he went now at night to avoid attracting too much attention. In the midst of all this overwhelming work, he did not neglect either his business or his diversions; he managed to find the time that summer to attend the races of Aylesbury where he saw the Duke of Marlborough, ready to leave on his exile to the Continent, having chosen that rather than remain at the mercy of a Tory government.

But the too-strenuous program De Foe was following began to take its toll of his health. The doctors advised him to take a cure at some watering-place; furthermore, his business interests called him even more imperatively than ever into other cities. He took the whole matter to Harley, asking permission to spend a fortnight at the baths of Buxton, suggesting that he would make the trip incognito as far as Edinburgh. Harley yielded to De Foe's importunities; early in September, Daniel was far from London, breathing the fresh country air and drawing in new health and vigor with each breath.

Business first! That was always De Foe's motto, and seldom did he veer from it. He attended the great fair at Stourbridge where he put through a good deal in wool and cloth. Next he looked up a hosier of Coteshill in Warwick by the name of Ward with whom he undertook some speculations that after-

wards turned out rather badly. Another invitation that seemed
to offer him some pecuniary advantage led him to diverge
from his northern route to the east as far as Lynn. As he was
unknown in this town, he was able to get an unbiased political
opinion there which was decidedly unfavorable to the government. The people of Lynn accused the Queen of having
Jacobite leanings and the Ministry of being in the pay of
Louis XIV.

From here De Foe went on his way to Lincoln, reaching
there September the twentieth; his next stop was at York.
He attended the races at Hambleton Down where he
was impressed by the northern women whose beauty he describes like a connoisseur. He probably viewed once more the
famous battle field, Marston Moor. By October the third,
"Claude Guilot" was in Newcastle, where some heavy rains
held him for several days. He passed the time getting information as to the politics of the principal people in the city.
As soon as he could, he went on into Scotland, but he confined himself to a short excursion into the Border counties
to look after his own affairs and to pick up the exact details
concerning the religious conflicts that were tearing up the
country. He was soon on his way home, stopping, however,
for a few weeks' complete rest at Halifax with two good
friends of his, the minister, Priestley, and the physician, Nettle-
ton. Finally, he went on to the baths at Buxton where he
took the waters, wrote some verse, and made a number of
excursions into the picturesque region of the Peak. But he
grew weary of the monotony of the place, found the cure too
long drawn out, and returned to London early in the year,
1713.

Immediately after his arrival in the City, on January the
seventh, he asked for an audience with Harley in order to
make an oral report of his trip and to put before him a petition

from a brass company that wished to supply the government with copper coins. De Foe had, for a certain sum, assured them of his support and aid; but Harley was ill and would see no one. De Foe was disturbed; he had been meeting with coldness now for some time whenever he went to call upon his patron ... perhaps, he was not too easy in his own conscience, for he had written some articles for the *Protestant Post-Boy,* a paper which was violently opposed to the Administration. The situation had evidently got on his nerves, for he wrote Harley in a tone that bordered on impudence:

"I had not given you the trouble of my calling last night, but (as I understood your servant) by your command and ask pardon for the mistake."

The comedy had the usual ending. He was back again before the end of the month, making his regular nightly calls. Next De Foe started legal action against the *Flying Post,* a journal which had attacked him with rash obstinacy; to back his suit, he made use of a letter from his agent in Lincoln which showed the harm caused in that county by the articles published in this antagonistic journal. It seemed that he was not able to make a case out of it, however, for Harley frequently refused to support his myrmidon's personal quarrels.

Throughout this period of personal and political conflict, the *Review* continued to sow the seeds of doubt and confusion in the ranks of the more fanatic members of the different factions. De Foe was quite effective at grafting some new alarms upon the plotting Jacobites, as, for example, suggesting the possible return of the plague. He made an art of spreading a panic, maintaining an attitude of studied calm even while he was lavishing consolation upon others for what was sure to come upon them. The result was just what he desired ... the prophesied disaster became the talk of the country so that everybody must buy the next issue of the *Review* and learn the last word about it.

De Foe attempted to meet the tastes of his public; he wrote, after the manner of *Spectator,* recounting trivial personal incidents in a light and humorous vein that captivated his readers. Such matter as his observations while he was walking one summer evening in 1712 in the fishmarket district of London. He happened to be a disinterested onlooker at the breaking out of a fire in one of the buildings in the district and noticed that the women in the nearby houses, instead of thinking of their children, were first concerned with the salvage of their clothes and their ornaments. Starting with this observation, he was off on a long tirade against the frivolity of the fair sex which appeared in the pages of the *Review.* Addison, who had set the fashion for misogyny, would not have refused credit for the authorship of the article.

On the whole, however, the *Review* remained essentially a political organ; almost every anecdote De Foe saw fit to include in his columns tended to strengthen its anti-Jacobite bias. When he told a story about a home ruined because husband and wife held different religious beliefs, he did not fail to point the analogy to the State where discord would be sure to follow the marrying of Protestant England to a Catholic ruler like the Pretender, James Stuart. The *Review* was still Whig on the surface; it was ostensibly at odds with the government. In that way did Harley, who had often been alarmed by the violence of his Tory colleagues, keep in touch with moderate Whig opinion. The *Review* became more and more specialized in its study of political questions; as a consequence, a great number of its subscribers, whose interests lay more in trade, became dissatisfied with it. To meet their needs De Foe proposed to divide his journal and put out an issue wholly devoted to business discussions. This project fell through with when the government instituted a reactionary measure that called for a tax of a half-penny on every copy of periodicals circulated in the realm. It was a heavy blow and did a great deal to cut down the sale of the *Review* which, to meet the exigency, appeared now as a single sheet, printed in two columns. De Foe took the blow smiling; he declared that the *Review* had never made him a penny anyway. Also his new work was beginning to call forth the appreciation of Lord Bolingbroke, the learned minister, a friend and teacher of Voltaire's.

All this time De Foe was not limiting his activity to the *Review.* He continued to direct from afar the policy of the *Edinburgh Courier.* He planned, as early as December, 1710, to start in Scotland another journal dealing with current events to be called the *Postman;* he had even arranged to handle it in partnership with his erstwhile associate, the political spy, Fearns, who had become a lawyer in Edinburgh. But this was one other of the many outcroppings of De Foe's fertile brain that did not develop. It is true that all of his time was taken, editing the numerous pamphlets in which he presented the economic consequences of the peace treaty.

Perhaps the peace has not been handled in the very best fashion, he once admitted to the Whigs in the *Review,* but added that one cannot expect to gain everything; it is better to put up a good face and look for the best side of a bad treaty.

In his unsigned pamphlets he employed other tactics, praising the benefits to be gained from the treaty made by the Ministry and pointing out all the advantageous angles of it. It is almost certain that Harley went very carefully over these pamphlets, which must have been written at his command; he may even have revised some of them. Their success led De Foe to project a work of considerable importance, he thought, entitled *A General History of Trade.* Only two parts of it appeared because he was called upon to meet more urgent demands. About this time he began a series of pamphlets in which he commented upon events of the day in the phraseology of the Quakers. His imitation of the biblical style of the "Friends" was so exact that responsible members of the sect felt it necessary to make a printed statement denying that any of their society had written these "sacrilegious pamphlets."

De Foe must certainly have had his flair for paradox satisfied by the equivocal position he held at this time in the midst of the political parties of England. He was, in the first instance, a Non-Conformist Whig pamphleteer; but he was in the service of a moderate Tory ministry that, in turn, operated with a parliament composed, in the majority, of high-flyers. To offset the general hatred that these conflicting forces brought upon him, he held up as an ideal the pacific union of all parties. At one time he sought to create a great central party, opposed to the Jacobites, to be made up of Dissenters and Low church followers; but the Dissenters had already formed an alliance with the extreme Whigs against the Administration, and they had only the utmost contempt for De Foe. To spite them, De Foe strove to spread panic in their ranks and to force them by threats to support the government. He succeeded only in arousing their hatred against him at the very time the high-flyers started renewing their attacks against him. He wrote in the *Review:*

"It was but two days ago, that I received at one and the same time a Letter from a passionate Whig, and another from a furious Jacobite, the one threatening me with the gallows when their party gets up again, and the other with assassination immediately, after the manner of John Tutchin."

He collected the most insulting of these letters and published them, selecting the ones that, by their violent language and their poverty of argument, would best serve his purposes. The following letter from the "furious Jacobite," written in bad French, is, perhaps the most typical of all these anonymous missives:

De Foe, quelle furie infernale et quel démon t'ont inspiré le poizon du mensonge que tu vomit aujourd'huy contre la pierre que les ouvriers ont rejettée; souvien toy Esprit Malin que cette pierre sera un jour la clef du cintre? La Sédition que tu publie tous les jours te causerie un chastiment, quel te souvien de ton prédécesseur Tutchin come il fut bastoné pour ses infâmes libelles; engense de vipaire, quant cesseras to d'insulter les Tests couronnée dont tu est esnemy mortel; ausy bien que ceux dont tu espouse le party? Tu est un misérable chien quy ne fait que hurler. *Nigro.*

There were times when De Foe's enemies did not stop with words, but carried their enmity into deeds. For example, a bandmaster of the City who had been taken to task in the *Review* for having allowed his orchestra to play a Jacobite hymn, once encountered Daniel's brother-in-law, Samuel Tuffley, as he was leaving a tavern. The irate bandmaster followed Tuffley, struck him in the face, and forced him to fight a duel, in which the musician disarmed this near relative of the man who had criticised him. Tuffley asked for his sword, but was refused; this insult so angered him that he leaped upon his adversary and engaged in a fist fight with him. Which one came out the victor will never be known, for the high-flyer journals declared that "De Foe's pious brother-in-law" had been thrashed unmercifully, while the Whig papers were equally emphatic in proclaiming that the bandmaster had been half killed by Tuffley's blows. Whichever way it was, it was made evident that it was not always pleasant to be accounted a near relative to Daniel De Foe.

They took different tactics with De Foe himself, employing the old device of hounding him with pretended agents, bear-

ing forged warrants for his arrest from old creditors. At first he
was not aware of the deception and, to gain his freedom, paid
the sums asked by these self-styled officers of justice to satisfy
mythical creditors and hush up matters. But when he did get
at the truth of affairs, he charged these agents who came
threatening him with blackmail, had them arrested, and forced
them to acknowledge their trickery before a judge. But when
the judge learned that the plaintiff was none other than the
editor of the *Review,* he ordered the prisoner released, declaring that his accuser was a much worse rogue than he. As a
further indication of De Foe's slump in public esteem, there is
the incident of the Whig shipowner; when he found that he
had merchandise belonging to Daniel De Foe, he refused to
allow it put off at London, commanding that it be returned
to the country from which it was brought because, he said, a
pamphleteer whose writings had caused so much trouble to
British commerce, should not be allowed to make profitable
deals through honest merchants. What had become now of
crowds that had once drunk to the health of the pilloried
Daniel and had decked their hero with flowers?

The irony in the situation is that De Foe, repudiated, not
without reason by the Whigs, was also villified by the mass of
Tories, who still classed him with the Whigs, for they were
ignorant of his relations with Harley and believed that he
must be caught under in Godolphin's fall. They expressed
their hopes for such an outcome in some crude verses [1] that
took the fancy of the crowd:

> Now Daniel De Foe, now run for thy life,
> For Robin-Hog swears by's old grunting wife,
> He'll end all your Gov. . . t. quarr'ls and strife.

[1] *A Hue and Cry after Daniel De Foe for Denying the Queen's Hereditary Right.*
By Robin Hog (broadsheet, 1 d., 1711).

He's hard at your heels and has you in view,
And tho' he is lame, he'll closely pursue,
Soon find you without Ariadne's long clew.

He'll hunt you thro' all the Fantastical-race,
Throw salt in your breech, lest you stink in the chace,
You'll hardly have time to Calves-Head say grace.

Be jovial and brisk then, liquor your tripes,
Justice has said you deserve many stripes,
And nothing can save you but Middleton's pipes. . . ."

It became almost impossible for him to answer all the
charges against him. Ridpath, a Whig journalist, made the
defamatory statement that no one dared trust the editor of the
Review with a shilling. Swift, in the *Examiner,* a Tory organ,
made his insulting remark concerning that "individual whose
name he forgot." Gay, Swift's friend, departed from his usual
moderation to write:

"The poor *Review* is quite exhausted, and grown so very
contemptible, that though he has provoked all his Brothers
of the Quill round, none of them will enter into a controversy
with him. This fellow, who had excellent natural parts, but
wanted a foundation of learning, is a lively instance of those
wits who, as an ingenious author says, 'will endure but one
skimming.' "

What could De Foe do? Protest? He could not very well do
otherwise! But his protestations made his slanderers only the
more wrathy in their retorts. If a seditious pamphlet appeared,
as quickly as rumor could carry it, it was noised about that
De Foe was the author. When the Mohawks, those elusive
roustabouts that terrorized the people of London at night were
about their deviltry . . . beating the watch, cutting off the
noses of belated passers-by, rolling stray females in barrels
it was at once reported in the papers that De Foe was a member

of the unruly band. He denied it, protested his innocence, presented convincing alibis in the *Review* . . . the people only shook their heads incredulously. He, who had molded public opinion to his own ends, was now a victim of the same machinery. Worn out by the warfare, De Foe quit fighting and assumed his favorite attitude of martyrdom, viewing himself as a victim of the spitefulness of human nature. He piously lamented the vices of the century in the columns of his journal:

One author was such an unfashionable Wretch, that he set Truth and Honesty upon his Frontispiece and pretended to keep to his title. But what was the consequence? Alas, what could be the consequence? Why, the Man broke: what could you expect from one that had no more wit than to be dress'd quite out of Fashion.

Giving in to self-pity, he proclaimed: "I am now hunted with a full cry, Aceton like, by my own friends."
And again:

I have been fed more by miracle than Elijah, when the ravens were his purveyors. . . . In the school of affliction I have learnt more philosophy than at the academy and more divinity than from the pulpit; in prison I have learnt to know that liberty does not consist in open doors. . . . I have seen the rough side of the world as well as the smooth. . . . I have suffered deeply for cleaving to my principles. . . . The immediate causes of my suffering have been the being betrayed by those I have trusted, and scorning to betray those who trusted me. To the honour of English gratitude, I have this remarkable truth to leave behind me—that I was never so basely treated as by those I starved my own family to preserve. . . . And now I live under universal contempt, which contempt I have learned to contemn, and have an uninterrupted joy in my soul: not at my being contemned, but that no crime can be laid to my charge, to make that contempt my due. . . . I have a large family, a wife and 6 children, who never want what they should enjoy,

or spend what they ought to save. Under all these circumstances
. . . my only happiness is this: I have always been kept cheerful,
easy, and quiet, enjoying a perfect calm of mind, clearness of
thought, and satisfaction not to be broken in upon by whatever may
happen to me. If any man ask me how I arrived to it? I answer
him, in short, by a constant, serious application to the great, solemn,
and weighty work of resignation to the will of heaven.

Noble words, inspired by the most sincere Christianity!
Robinson Crusoe on his lonely island reached the same conclusions that De Foe did, isolated in the midst of his fellow
citizens. How was it possible for him to make such a noble
profession of faith at the very time that he was involved
in acts questionable to his honor so that one is tempted to cry,
Hypocrite! One can scarcely reproach him for his open attacks against his old enemy, the Earl of Nottingham, who had
threatened him with imprisonment. But to lambast a political
opponent in the columns of the *Review* or in the pages of his
printed pamphlets was a different matter from secretly turning
the Ministry against one of his rival journalists. It was just a
couple of days after he had expressed the preceding sentiments
of Christian resignation that he was guilty of such underhand
work, even against Richard Steele, who had never said one
word against him. De Foe had painstakingly made from
Steele's printed articles a collection of clippings which seemed
to him compromising in their nature; he sent them to Harley,
insisting that this Whig journalist should be found guilty of
high treason. He continued to push the matter, urging Steele's
culpability upon the government, until at last he had the satisfaction of seeing his rival unjustly expelled from the House
of Commons. As the curtain fell, the figure of the "martyr"
took on the aspects of a "persecutor;" so that one can understand why his contemporaries, who suspected him of under-

hand dealings, evidenced such blind fury whenever his name was mentioned.

The Whig offensive against De Foe opened vigorously in April, 1713. By a strange irony it was directed against the three of his pamphlets which best served the Whig cause. De Foe had apparently forgotten the consequences of his earlier hoax, *The Shortest Way with Dissenters,* because he again employed the same method of attracting attention and of selling his pamphlets among the Jacobites, giving them the equivocal titles:

Reasons against the Succession of the House of Hanover;

And What if the Pretender should come? or more Considerations of the Advantages and Real Consequences of the Pretender's possessing the Crown of Great Britain;

and

An Answer to a Question that nobody thinks of, viz. What if the Queen should die?

The author started each of these three papers in a restrained manner, discreetly examining the actual evidence in each case as far as he could get hold of it. Then, toying with his ideas, he began to unravel his paradoxes, until he had clearly revealed his objectives. It would be good for the nation, he said, to submit, for a period of time, to an absolute Papist government, as a sort of a purgative. . . . A dose of this medicine would leave the country free to appreciate the advantages of constitutional government. He pointed out that the coming of the Pretender would, moreover, ward off all danger of a new war with France. During his reign England would live quietly under the proud protection of Louis XIV. . . . There would be no arguments, no journals, no oral discussions, no parliament; it would mean a Roman peace throughout the country. Coming to serious thoughts upon this important question of succession to the throne of England, De Foe concluded that, without doubt, our individual liberty, our property, and even our lives could be snatched from us by our weakly allowing the Pretender to assume the power.

The Whigs were not at once taken in by this artfulness; they wished to take their revenge against Harley whose political maneuvers had brought about the downfall of the minister Godolphin; and they looked upon De Foe as a double-crossing journalist who had spread trouble in their ranks. They grabbed at any pretext, no matter how trivial it might be, if it would but lead to the ruin of these two hated enemies of theirs. By accusing De Foe of high treason for writing these Jacobite pamphlets, the Whigs hoped to strike a double blow; they counted upon Harley's coming to the aid of his assistant; that would give them proof of the relationship between the Tory minister and the Whig politician. Harley's Tory colleagues would look askance upon his dealings with a Whig pamphleteer; the still credulous Whigs could no longer doubt the perfidy of a Whig writer in the pay of a Tory minister. It was an adroit scheme, and it was so well plotted that there seemed to be every chance for it to succeed.

It was necessary, first of all, to be sure that De Foe would be at home when they came to arrest him. To make certain of this, the Whigs ran down an old creditor at Yarmouth who had not been heard of for ten years; they bought up the note in his possession and presented it to De Foe one evening just as he was getting ready to leave Stoke Newington to come to London to call upon Harley. Daniel did not have enough money to pay the note and, for fear of being arrested upon the demand of the creditor, he had to stay inside until he could get it. That was exactly what his enemies had counted upon to develop their attack.

De Foe's first move was to send one of his sons with a letter to Harley, asking for his back pension, which he must have

DE FOE'S HOUSE AT STOKE NEWINGTON

His refuge outside of London to which he retired during political storms.

at once in order to meet the demands of an importunate creditor. This was the first of April, 1713, but before Harley could
get around to taking care of De Foe's demand, the Whigs had
been making every minute count. Their leader was a deputy
named Benson; he had been convicted of libel by the Ministry, but he held De Foe responsible and was implacably bent
upon undoing him. Benson had gone to Janeway, the printer
of the three pamphlets and had got his attention upon the
pretext of leaving an order with him; then he had used intimidation to force him to hand over the three manuscripts. But a
new difficulty arose; all three of the manuscripts were in different handwritings. Benson did not give up; he held before
the terrified eyes of the printer and his associates the specter
of high treason until he had extorted from them admissions
that De Foe was really the author of the incriminating works.
The triumphant Benson took his trophies to Chief Justice
Parker, pointing out to him that, in the first place, the titles
were seditious, that treason was openly preached throughout
the text, and that the irony detected in certain passages was
only a veil cleverly thrown over the author's criminal inten-
tions. Parker was only too ready to be convinced.

"Those are not subjects to be trifled with," he said, after carefully examining the manuscripts. Straightway he issued warrants for the arrest of De Foe, Janeway, and Baker, the author,
the printer, and the editor of the three pamphlets, basing his
action upon the fact that those responsible for the writing and
circulating of such articles must be regarded as agitators working against the peace of the loyal subjects of her Majesty. On
Friday, April the tenth, just at nightfall, Janeway's young
apprentice came to call De Foe upon some pretext or other. In
reality he was sent by the constable, who had just reached
Stoke Newington and who wished to be sure to find his bird
in its nest. The night was given over by the plotters to setting

the stage for the dramatic arrest which took place in the morning at about eleven o'clock. It started with a whole flock of bailiffs settling down upon De Foe's home in order to make sure that he and all of the manuscripts he might have in his possession would be seized. The ordeal was carried out with as much noise and show as possible so that the entire village might be convinced that it was a dangerous criminal who was being taken. It is more than likely that De Foe actually made but little resistance since he was too prudently regardful of the law and was too familiar with its workings to oppose it; then, too, he had just received a letter from Harley, in which the latter assured him that he would stay by him whatever happened. But in spite of what must have been passive submission on De Foe's part, the Whig journalist, Ridpath, who had been one of the ringleaders in the conspiracy, brought back with him to London a sensational account of the taking of the editor of the *Review;* he told quite a story of how De Foe had barricaded his home against the police, of how the latter had had to lay regular siege to it, make a decisive assault, and take the place by storm before they could carry off their prisoner. All of De Foe's protestations that this was mere fabrication were of no avail; the gullible public preferred to believe the more fantastic version. Fantastic enough was the strange procession that brought the prisoner from Stoke Newington to London that Saturday in April. Across the fields came the long line, accommodating its progress to that of its leader, for De Foe, physically indisposed at the time, had been allowed to go on horseback. There was delightful humor of the very sort De Foe himself most appreciated, in the sight of the prisoner on horseback, leading the way to a straggling line of half drunken bailiffs, sent out to take him to prison. As soon as they reached London, he was taken to jail, where he had to spend the time until Monday morning before he could be allowed a hearing and the chance to be admitted to bail. Of course the Whigs had planned it just that way, knowing that, by timing their arrest for a Saturday morning, their victim would have to spend at least one full day in jail. De Foe put his time in on Sunday writing a long letter to Harley. He denounced as libelers the Whigs, Benson, Burnet, and Ridpath, who, he was convinced, made up the cabal against him; he begged Harley to do what he could to help him.

On Monday, April the thirteenth, De Foe was taken before Lord Chief-Justice Parker. He demanded his freedom, offering as his bail, the book-sellers, Grantham and Warner; each of these men agreed to be his bail to the extent of 400 pounds each; De Foe himself put up 800 pounds bail. His accusers cried out that this was not enough. But the state attorney, William Borrett, who had been coached by Harley, casually remarked that it was all that was legally necessary. This quieted De Foe; but Parker, slightly disturbed by Borrett's attitude, leaned over to ask him in a low voice if the State intended to prosecute the prisoner. Borrett feigned indifference, and Parker said that he would write to Lord Bolingbroke in order to make sure about the matter. This colloquy did not escape the attentive ears and observant eyes of the prisoner. He passed the information on to Harley, who at once took measures to see that his colleague, Bolingbroke, would not give the judge any inkling of the secret relationship between De Foe and the Ministry. Indeed not a hint of it did get out.

Daniel was back home by Tuesday with no worse effects than a severe cold which he had caught in his prison cell. The first thing he did was to write a lengthy epistle to Harley, thanking him for his intervention and begging him to extend once more a helping hand. As a matter of fact, the Whigs were not to be foiled; their journals gave much space to the story of De Foe's arrest; the rumor got out that he had been taken to Newgate, at which the crowd became delirious with joy. One pamphlet, *Judas discover'd and caught at last,* reveled in the most abusive terms it could find to cast upon De Foe's head. This paper, prepared for quick street sale, was eagerly bought by the crowd, avid for every fresh detail about one whom they now regarded with disfavor. The Whig chiefs were furious at having their prey just escape them. They took measures to see to it that, in the event of a trial, they would have the best legal aid available. Benson offered to pay ten guineas to a distinguished advocate, who agreed to take the case, although it promised to be a difficult one.

Meanwhile the prosecution had already started on its course. The Lord Chief-Justice ordered the employees of Janeway and Baker brought before him, and he himself took their depositions. The information gathered in this way is interesting because it shows how De Foe's manuscripts were handled. The first of the three pamphlets, *Reasons against the Succession of the House of Hanover,* had been edited by Janeway. De Foe had run across this printer, had spoken to him of the article he wished to write, and had given him an idea of it from the sensational title. Janeway, scenting a big success in the scandal, had bought the piece from the title alone, agreeing to give De Foe four guineas and twenty-five free copies out of the printing of a thousand.

The other two pamphlets had been printed by Baker, who paid De Foe two guineas for the 500 copies sold. Both manuscripts had been copied in part by De Foe himself and in part by his two sons, Daniel and Benjamin. It is not certain whether they wrote from their father's dictation, or merely made a good copy from his first rough one. Benjamin had the additional task of verifying the quotations that De Foe always wrote from memory. The employees of the printshop would bring the proofs either to De Foe in his Temple quarters in London, or they would bring them out to Stoke Newington; one of the two boys would meet the messenger at the door, and have him wait while he took the proofs to his father to correct or corrected them himself. De Foe's two sons made good "Fridays" to their father's "Crusoe." By relieving him of much of the humdrum and monotonous work of authorship, they left him free to pour out his inexhaustible and uninterrupted flow of words.

As the day for De Foe's trial approached, he became quite apprehensive of the outcome. But it was his own imprudence that caused the most trouble: in spite of the fact that, as he told Harley, he feared Parker, the Lord Chief-Justice was prejudiced against him, he had the audacity openly to question the honesty of his judges in the pages of the *Review* for April the sixteenth and the eighteenth. It was on April the twenty-second that the Court convened. De Foe had no difficulty, when he appeared with his two bails, in getting an extension of his freedom; but, just as he was leaving, well satisfied with this, the Lord Chief-Justice stopped him and questioned him about the authorship of the two articles reflecting upon him and his associates. De Foe hesitated, and then acknowledged them as his own. Parker declared they were insolent libels, but that, since he considered them a personal attack, he would leave the decision about them to two of his colleagues in attendance. The articles were read aloud and were condemned by the two justices as infamous insults leveled at the Lord Chief-Justice; they declared that the author of them must be regarded as having shown the utmost contempt for the Court and the laws of the land. De Foe was at once sentenced to be imprisoned in the Queen's Bench while the three pamphlets that had led to his prosecution were pronounced "scandalous, wicked, and treasonable libels." De Foe began to protest weakly that the papers had been written in an ironical vein, but he was cut short by the judge, named Powis, who, with a heavy display of judicial learning, showed that De Foe lied; he brought his arguments to a close with the awful pronouncement that, for such a crime, the prisoner could count upon being hanged and quartered alive. De Foe, dumbfounded, uttered not a word, but allowed himself to be led quietly away to prison.

There, once again shut within four confining walls, he gave in to deepest despair. But he was not left in this condition long; Harley advised him to ask for permission to make his apologies to the Court; then the minister brought enough pressure to bear upon the judges that they agreed to listen to him. On the second of May, he paid his respects and a fine of three shillings and six pence, as a matter of form. His apologies were accepted, and he was allowed his freedom upon a renewal of his bail.

This prompt ministerial succor was not wholly disinterested; there was great need for De Foe's services in getting out a new periodical which Bolingbroke proposed to launch in the interests of the government. As it was to present material of financial interest, Bolingbroke was eager to have a man as experienced as De Foe at the head of it. De Foe, grateful for the aid that had, he felt, practically saved him from hanging, abandoned the little political independence he had kept and went over completely into his patron's pay. It was not difficult to find a pretext for ending the *Review,* which had been at the point of death for more than a year now. He took the first step by announcing openly that it would be impossible for the *Review* to meet the competition offered by a new journal, the *Mercator,* a government subsidized paper, which would have the exclusive use of all official statistics on business and trade. He added that he had reluctantly decided to give over the publication of the *Review* and that, from now on, he would write no more but retire to the country. On the eleventh of June, he ended his regular contribution to his paper with the final words, *"Exit Review."* No doubt at the same time he breathed a sigh of relief, for it had been a tremendous task for one man alone to carry for a period of more than nine years. It is more than likely that some of the old subscribers of the *Review* swore at the *Mercator* as an intruder which had supplanted their favorite paper; they may even have paused to pity the poor journalist, who, by it, was being deprived of a livelihood, little thinking that this same "poor journalist" had become, at a liberal salary, the editor in chief of the new periodical whose advent he had made an excuse for discontinuing the journal they missed.

The *Mercator* came out three times a week and was printed in two columns. It was much the same sort of publication the *Review* had been, except that it emphasized the business rather than the political angle of affairs and was furnished with the current data from the Customs by the government. It showed a slight progress over the *Review* in that, at the head of each article, it presented a résumé of what followed, thus instituting the practice that has developed into the elaborate headline writing of to-day's press. It did not take the Whigs long to find out who was the real editor of the *Mercator,* and De Foe was subjected to the same kind of insults he had endured in the past.

The old matter of the three seditious pamphlets kept coming up to bother him; the more the Ministry endeavored to lay the ghost of it, the more Benson kept resurrecting it. Finally, in order to gain some peace of mind, De Foe wrote to Harley, October the ninth, asking him for a "royal pardon under the great Seal," the only means, the advocate general had told him, by which he might make an end of judicial proceedings

on that score. This pardon, signed by the Queen and counter-
signed by Bolingbroke, was granted to De Foe on November
20, 1713. Harley, at De Foe's suggestion, even paid all the chan-
cery costs. Free from all personal worry now, the new editor
could bring all his powers into play in this journalistic war,
which offered a broad scope for them.

At about this time, the lack of harmony between the two
leading ministers, Harley and Bolingbroke, reached the point
of open discord. Bolingbroke, whole-heartedly Jacobite, resented the evasive acts and the subterfuges of his chief in the
Council. The Queen was becoming more and more drawn
towards the cause of the Pretender and had begun to lend a
willing ear to Bolingbroke's suggestion that she cede the throne
to her younger brother. Harley, feeling he was beaten, lined
up with the House of Hanover. The Queen removed him on
the twenty-seventh of July, pretending that he had grown
insolent and negligent at his post. Bolingbroke's triumph was
of short duration, however, for the Queen was taken suddenly
ill; almost unconscious of what she was doing, she weakly
obeyed the last suggestion made to her and passed the staff
of power, not into Bolingbroke's hands, but into the hands
of the Duke of Shrewsbury, a moderate and a follower of
the Hanoverians.

Anne died on the first of August, leaving the Jacobites
wholly unprepared to meet the emergency; they had nothing
ready to oppose the legally established succession of the Hanoverian line. From beyond the grave the influence of De Foe's
great hero, William of Orange, was directing British destinies,
keeping England from falling into the hands of Catholic
and French dominance. While the country awaited the arrival of the new king, a Council of Regents, to which Harley
belonged by right, succeeded in handling the general run of
affairs.

As soon as these new arrangements were under way, De Foe wrote Harley to assure him of his faithful and devoted interest in his cause. It was an opportune step to take because it was not long until he was in need of Harley's powerful influence to help him out of another tight place. His intense hatred of the Jacobins led him to send a contribution to the *Post-Boy*, filled with insulting remarks about the high-flyers. Naturally a warrant for his arrest was the answer to it. But Harley intercepted that and killed it. At about the same time, Hurt, whom De Foe had put in charge of a journal he called the *Flying-Post*, in mimicry of a journal of the same name conducted by his enemy, Ridpath, sent his master a letter from a correspondent in which the Earl of Anglesey was accused of Jacobitism. This letter was a bit overdone, even for De Foe's purposes; so the latter modified it somewhat, copied it, and returned it to Hurt, who printed it in the issue of August the nineteenth. Two days later, upon the request of Anglesey, a member of the Council of Regents with Harley, Hurt and Baker, the latter the book-seller who handled the Flying-Post, were taken up for prosecution, but were allowed their freedom upon bail. All of their papers and letters were seized, however, and among them was the tell-tale letter in De Foe's handwriting. These circumstances led to the latter's arrest again on August the twenty-eighth; he also furnished security and was allowed provisional liberty. A few days later De Foe wrote Harley, begging him to use his personal influence to get Anglesey to withdraw his complaint; this Anglesey refused to do and the matter was allowed to stand, much to De Foe's chagrin.

Meanwhile George I, carried forward by a good "Protestant wind" landed on English soil and proceeded to London, making a solemn entry into the City on September the twentieth. His first act was to appoint an entire Whig ministry in which Lord Townshend soon took the lead. Now, if De Foe had only remained faithful to his early principles, he would have been able to salute the new king with the same enthusiasm with which he greeted the Revolution of 1688. But he was out of countenance and full of dark forebodings. He saw little promise for himself in the advent of this Hanoverian; true, Harley still maintained his prestige with the parliament he had helped to elect, but De Foe saw clearly that Townshend would not keep long a hostile House of Commons. Furthermore, Anglesey continued with pitiless persistence to demand that his trial against De Foe should go on; Harley made a second attempt, the last of September, to change him in the matter . . . it was futile. Anglesey was set upon having justice done him. And Daniel could only wonder, with superstitious alarm, if he would again have to greet the opening of a new reign from a cell in Newgate. It was the second time that he had just arrived at the highest honors, and, with the act of reaching out for more, had lost his equilibrium and fallen into an abyss. This time destiny had struck a decisive blow to his political ambitions, but, in the ruin of De Foe's hopes in 1714, lay the germs of development for *Robinson Crusoe* a few years later.

X. "BOWING IN THE HOUSE OF RIMMON"

T HE Whigs were thrice happy: they had a king all their own, a Ministry all their own, and they were getting ready to elect a parliament all their own. They at once began to exercise their supremacy by instituting judicial proceedings against the members of the fallen government and their satellites. De Foe thought to confuse them by bringing out a series of pamphlets which were intended to stir up a cloud of dust around the events of the last Administration in such a fashion that no one would be able to say what was true and what was false about them. He was particularly concerned with a denial of Harley's Jacobitism, but he made such a clumsy job of it that he completely alienated, for the time being, his erstwhile patron.

In spite of that rupture, however, De Foe continued to defend the policy of the preceding regime, perhaps mostly because it was his own best defense; that is, until the last few days of 1714, when he felt the time was ripe to make a clear presentation of the factors that had governed his own conduct in the past. He wrote his *Appeal to Honour and Justice,* in which he offered proof that he had always been independent and faithful to his first principles. He had just completed this piece of work when he had a light stroke of apoplexy from which he quickly recovered. But it gave him an idea which amounted to a stroke of genius; he sent his publisher a short note, which Baker published as a *Conclusion* to the book, saying that he was in a state of extreme weakness, and that his life was despaired of, since he could not long survive the persecutions

183

he had had to undergo. The stratagem worked; his enemies would not demean themselves to attack a dying opponent, and, besides, of what use would it be! Daniel, left in peace, turned out pamphlet after pamphlet which kept the public in a state of bewilderment, for they had no idea as to their authorship; they were wholly unsuspicious of De Foe, whom they believed to be quite out of the running; but he was, in reality, comfortably ensconced in his study at Stroke Newington where he could, uninterruptedly, fill one sheet after another; as quickly as each was filled, it was hurried straight off to the printer's.

How much better it would have been had he been able to maintain his independence from then on. But there was still the old matter of Lord Anglesey's prosecution against him which required his presence in court on July 12, 1715. He was declared guilty of having written a seditious libel, but the pronouncement of a sentence against him was put off until the next session. As a matter of fact, he did not appear again, and the whole thing was mysteriously hushed up.

What had taken place? De Foe himself explained it as an intervention of Providence in his behalf. He told how, frightened at the news of Harley's arrest, he had determined to flee when, one morning, his guiding spirit whispered distinctly in his ear several times: "Write to the judge! Write to the judge!" He said he at once seated himself at his desk and took up his pen; without any effort on his part, it had filled his letter paper with pathetic and eloquent phrases, addressed to the Lord Chief-Justice Parker. De Foe sent off his message, which had seemed to him dictated by a supernatural power, and which brought him an almost supernatural reply, for Parker informed him that all proceedings against him had been dropped. So did Daniel escape the greatest danger he had ever had to run. But the "divine inspiration" of his letter bears a

wholly mundane interpretation; De Foe had assured Parker
that his heart had always been with the Whigs and that, if
the present Ministry had any need for his services, he would be
glad to atone for all of his former "errors" by putting himself
entirely at its disposal.

Parker had already weighed De Foe; he considered him a
spy of remarkable talent and passed on his proposal to Lord
Townshend. Townshend responded with alacrity, sent for
De Foe at once, and laid before him a proposition that was
of great moment to his party administration. It involved De
Foe in a dangerous rôle, but he did not flinch at that sort of
thing; he was used to it. During the time that he had controlled a part of the Whig press in the interest of Harley's
Tory government, he had been accepted by the general public
as a Whig. When his connection with the fallen Ministry was
found out, he was then regarded as a Tory. Now he was being
asked to control the Tory press in the interests of Townshend's
Whig government. It was practically the same thing he had
been doing, in reverse. To the public, he was under the ban
of Ministerial disfavor; that gave him a footing among the
Tory journalists and aided him in getting hold of articles
opposing the present administration. He had no scruples in
summarily suppressing them.

His first step was to make a place for himself in the editorial
departments of the many Tory reviews; this gave him the
opportunity to take the sting out of many a sharp bit of satire
directed against the Ministry, and De Foe did it so cleverly that
no one was aware of the subtile touches which guided the
reader insensibly to a moderate point of view. A really brilliant stroke of his that succeeded was when he got Mist, the
director of a weekly journal with Jacobite tendencies, to take
him on as a translator of foreign news. Mist, quick to recognize
the talent of his new employee, unsuspectingly allowed him to

take a more and more important part in the editing of his journal, a paper that had been, heretofore, much feared by the government.

This clever bit of business won Daniel just the kind of recognition he needed; he knew the value, for one in his equivocal position, to stand well with the men at the top of things. He was grateful then to earn a pat of the back from Sunderland, the prime minister who had succeeded Townshend, and from Lord Stanhope, the secretary of state, who was particularly concerned with the kind of thing De Foe was doing. Regarding his own status, De Foe himself wrote:

"I am, Sir, for this Service, posted among Papists, Jacobites, and enraged High Tories . . . a generation who, I profess, my very Soul abhors; I am obliged to hear traitorous Expositions and outrageous Words against His Majesty's Person and Government, and his most faithful Servants, and smile at it all, as if I approved it; I am obliged to take all the scandalous and, indeed, villainous Papers that come, and keep them by me as if I would gather Materials from them to put them into the News; nay, I often venture to let things pass which are a little Shocking, that I may not render myself suspected."

But even all this was not enough to keep De Foe busy. He found the time to write a number of pamphlets in defense of Harley as well as of those who served under him. Harley's trial was scheduled to begin June 13, 1717, but, at the last minute, it was put off until the twenty-fourth. De Foe's object was to throw into the very midst of the arguments for and against Harley, a bomb that would, he hoped, create an upheaval in favor of the accused. The book that appeared on the seventeenth was quite the most provocative of all the hoaxes De Foe was guilty of. It claimed to be the actual *Memoirs* of the French ambassador, Mesnager, with whom De Foe had once had dealings. It pretended to relate the nego-

ciations that preceded the peace of Utrecht in such a way that
Harley stood out consistently for the very measures advocated
by the followers of George I. But, in his haste to get the work
out at just the right minute, De Foe had neglected to check it
over carefully; it is full of anachronisms and inaccuracies, but
it was unnecessary to change them then, for Harley was already accepted by the people as the champion of Protestantism,
the one incorruptible minister who had succeeded in frustrating the Jacobite designs of the Queen. His acquittal on July
the first was made the occasion for a triumphant celebration.
De Foe breathed a sigh of relief at one more narrow escape.

He seemed to be riding the crest of another small wave of
good fortune, and he made the most of it. He got in the last
word in a series of arguments he had with a radical Whig
journalist, named Boyer. Then, like a child amused with the
mechanism of a new toy, he played with the Quaker style,
which he imitated so successfully; it enabled him to state some
hard facts in such a way that no one could resent them. It
also gave him a chance to reach his old enemy Sacheverell
from a new and vulnerable angle. He addressed him thus:

"Verily, Henry, . . . thinkest thou that the Man George,
whom the Lord hath delighted in, and hath chosen to exalt,
and who the princes and great men of the Land have placed
upon the throne, even as the Lord hath commanded, thinkest
thou, I say, that he can ever be prevail'd with to receive into
his bosome any of those thy people who are called Tories?
Nay, Henry, but be thou not so vain, for this thing cannot
come to pass in the Land, seeing the King knoweth that they
are wicked Men and Sons of Belial, Men not fearing the Lord,
neither working the Thing which is right in the Land."

De Foe found this a rich vein, for such matter amused the
public and caused no hard feelings. A popular question was
the religious controversy that had brought the Reverend Snape

to blows with the Bishop of Bangor. De Foe, in the guise of a London Quaker, took one side of the debate, and, as a Turkish merchant at Amsterdam, took the other, turning off a great number of pamphlets which served as excellent training ground for his later impersonations as pirate, robber, and prostitute. This ability to throw himself utterly into the character he was portraying is one of the great artistic achievements in De Foe's creative prose. To all of this he added many works that were collections of historical data as well as others in the series of prophecies, supposedly uttered by a Scotch Highlander gifted with second sight. He revised and edited the memoirs left by the Dissenting minister, Williams, and even collaborated in writing *A Continuation of Letters Written by a Turkish Spy* in which, with the aid of contemporary journals and his own remembrance of what had occurred during the time involved, 1687 to 1693, he achieved a fairly vivid recreation of that period. It is easy to see that all this was merely hack work for the trade; almost any discussion on one of the leading topics of the day was salable.

The articles that De Foe published in the Tory journals he was directing,[1] clearly indicate that he was doing his best to avoid dangerous political controversy. It was he who started the fashion of *letters introductory* or "editorials" in the form of letters which were supposed to come from interested readers. De Foe succeeded in giving his letters a delightfully humorous and imaginative twist that suggested and, at times, equaled the light and playful touches of Addison's *Spectator*. De Foe was quickly recognized as a master of this type of writing, and his contributions were solicited by a number of magazine directors because they were especially pleasing to the

---

[1] He was called in these journals, the author, which, in those days, meant that he was responsible for the editing, under the orders of the owner or proprietor, who alone guided the paper's policy. The editor was more of a business administrator.

women of the middle class, who were just developing into magazine readers and who did not care for dull political debates. The demand fitted in exactly with De Foe's objective of "taking off the edge" of articles that were against the government. He set out to prepare a series of reports on the social problems of the day. He urged once more an improvement of conditions for the insolvent business man. He studied the problem of the unemployed weaver who had been turned out on the street when the women set the fashion for wearing calico prints imported from India. He described with verve the riotous scenes he had witnessed when these idle weavers, rebellious at their predicament, attacked the women on the streets, tearing at their calico dresses and besmattering them with mud. He directed one of his campaigns against the stock jobbers of the City; he made a humorous story of his visit to Exchange-Alley, but he seriously urged the suppression of a practice so detrimental to "honest business" and to the general financial equilibrium of the country. Measuring exactly the demands of public taste, he sought out the most unusual news from far distant countries and presented it in a sensational fashion. The English public has always been passionately avid for strange details and incidents on land and on sea. De Foe made good use of the queer story that reached London through a letter from the Barbadoes that the Island of Saint-Vincent had disappeared, following a frightful volcanic eruption. Daniel used his imagination and his knowledge of geography to prepare for *Mist's Journal* a long account of this unprecedented occurrence "the like of which never happened since the Creation, or at least, since the destruction of the Earth by Water in the general Deluge."

A subterranean fire, he believed, caused "the whole body of the Island" to be "raised so furiously, that the Earth was entirely separated into small particles like Dust; and as it rose to an immense Height, so it spread itself to an incredible Distance, and fell light and gradually, like a small but thick Mist . . . there appeared no Remains,—except 3 little Rocks—that such an Island had been there . . . on the contrary, in the place of it, the Sea was excessive deep, and no Bottom to be found, at 200 Fathom."

This sensational story created a huge demand for the paper in which it appeared. When the actual facts came to be known a few months later, Daniel had to stand a good bit of chaffing from his fellow journalists. It seemed his "scoop" was only a "false alarm," for the Island of Saint-Vincent was still standing, quite as usual; a slight volcanic eruption to which it was periodically subjected every twenty or thirty years was the only foundation for De Foe's lurid piece of journalism. But he refused to be put out of countenance about it; his only response was an unbelieving paragraph:

"They pretend to tell us a strange Story, viz. that the Island of St. Vincent is found again, and is turn'd into a Volcano, or burning Mountain; but we must acknowledge, we do not believe one word of it."

Of what consequence was it to him anyway? It had inspired him to satisfying self-expression and had contributed to the successful sale of the paper he controlled. A little chaffing did not bother him, who had been threatened with imprisonment and hanging.

Upon the whole Daniel would now have been able to pass his days in comparative quiet had he not had to edit certain papers whose opinions he must endeavor to keep moderate. It was *Mist's Journal* that caused him the most trouble. He had become connected with it in August, 1717, and had quickly made himself indispensable to its proprietor, who, by June, 1718, had given De Foe his word to keep it moderate in tone and not to print any articles without first getting De Foe's

advice upon them. Unfortunately, Mist's good resolutions were
not very long-lived; he quickly fell under the influence of his
Jacobite following and, ignoring De Foe's caution in his two
articles, signed Sir Timothy Caution, continued to print matter
offensive to the Administration. A letter he published over the
signature, Sir Andrew Politick, contained a biting criticism of
the conduct of the Spanish War and led to his arrest the last
of October. His shop was ransacked from top to bottom by
the police. Some seditious libels were discovered, hidden in
the rafters overhead. Warner, the editor of the *Journal,* was
also led before Lord Stanhope. Confused by Mist's declarations,
Warner testified that the letter, signed Sir Andrew Politick,
had come from a provincial correspondent; that De Foe, following instructions, had rewritten it, modifying its more violent expressions; but that Mist, before sending it to the
printer's, had gone over it again, adding the more disturbing
phrases. Warner really had little to do with the run of things,
but his deposition, full of interesting details, shows that he
was pretty well-informed about them. According to this information, De Foe had been paid in the beginning twenty shillings
a week for his collaboration on *Mist's Journal,* but his salary
had been since increased to forty shillings. It seems, too, that
De Foe prudently destroyed all manuscripts as soon as they
came back from the printer's. One little detail, supplied by
Warner, illustrates De Foe's methods of deception. The editor
met De Foe and told him of the fact that Mist had been arrested and would have to stand trial. Warner stated that De Foe
seemed much perturbed at the news and declared that, if the
government found out by chance of his collaboration on *Mist's
Journal,* it would mean he would have to leave England to
escape being hanged. All the time Warner was telling this,
De La Faye, Lord Stanhope's secretary, was having difficulty
repressing a smile. He had, in the drawer of his own desk, let-

ters of De Foe's giving the government information of all that took place at Mist's.

To protect their spy, the ministers dropped proceedings against Mist, but the two collaborators were left somewhat at odds with each other and so severed their relationship for a time. Mist soon came to realize, however, that his *Journal,* lacking De Foe's contributions, was losing many of its readers. He made the first move to a reconciliation, promising to be wiser in the conduct of his paper if De Foe would return to it. Beginning in January, 1719, De Foe was again overseeing the copy for Mist's paper. As long as the *Journal* held to a moderate tone, all went well; but, as the Jacobite influence gained ground, De Foe grew indifferent until an almost complete break followed upon an indiscretion of Mist's in July, 1720. From then on, De Foe's collaboration was only occasional.

His most serious opponent now was the Whig pamphleteer, Read, who chose to attack both De Foe and Mist in his periodical, the *Weekly Journal and British Gazetteer.* Read was bent on overthrowing Mist at any price, and he resolved to include De Foe, whom he considered dangerous for his two-faced attitude and his real talent as a journalist. Read, although he was ignorant of the exact rôle De Foe played, opened his campaign with an attempt to compromise the latter in the eyes of the government by associating him with Mist. He wrote, October 4, 1718:

"That notorious, insignificant animal Mist permits his scandalous Author, Daniel Foe, to take the Liberty at all times insipidly to ridicule and insult his Majesty's Friends and Allies with foolish comparisons and dull reflections."

A little later he printed an announcement that De Foe had hanged himself as "the shortest way to the devil," neglecting to correct the statement for several days. When he learned of

the first break between De Foe and Mist, his delight at the
news expressed itself in limping verse:

> What strange Adventures could untwist
> Such True-Born Knaves as Foe and Mist?
> They quarrel'd sure about the Pelf,
> For *Dan's* a needy, greedy Elf,
> And *Mist* has not much loin to spare
> If Colonel *Hepburn* [1] has his share.
> As Rats do run from falling Houses,
> So *Dan* another cause espouses;
> Leaves poor *Nat* [2] sinking in the Mire,
> Writes *Whitehall Evening Post* for hire.

De Foe would not have minded this attack if his mind had
been wholly free from worry; but his needs had forced him
to undertake some work which would have been regarded
with much disfavor by the government. Read's attack drew
public attention, in a most embarrassing fashion to matters
that had better have been left *sub rosa*. It did not look very
well to have it said that De Foe was collaborating with such a
Whig paper as the *Whitehall Evening Post* at the same time
that he was assisting Mist with his influential Tory *Journal.*
Read loomed up as the most impressive of his enemies, past
and present.

All of these trials and difficulties explain, to an extent, the
bitterness that crept into some of De Foe's last works. Added
to his public disgraces were domestic problems that gave him
a constant sense of being thwarted; his oldest son, after a
series of quarrels, left the family home in 1714 and set up as a
merchant in the City. Mrs. De Foe sided with her children
against her husband in his mania for speculation. He, accustomed to laying down the law at home, resented this re-

[1] A stockholder in *Mist's Journal.*
[2] Mist's first name was Nathaniel.

sistance to his authority which had been, hitherto, unquestioned. He was convinced that the only way to overcome bad fortune was to keep on trying, and it irritated him to be hindered by the family protests against his risking all his resources in one chance on the Exchange.

Of course, he was all the more obstinately set on following out his own ideas when his speculations proved successful. In March, 1719, he got some information that drew him to the stock market, and he sold his shares in the South Sea company just in time to come off with a neat margin of profit. At the same time, he had the wisdom to put some of his money into property; he rented a farm near London and put it in charge of a caretaker. This man was the cause of some trouble, though, and De Foe reproached him, not so much with dishonesty, it seems, as with coveting his neighbor's wife. This indicates the change in De Foe's morality which was more uncompromising than it had been a few years earlier. Age, misfortune, and sickness had drawn him back to the Puritanism of his youth. He had been influenced, too, by the Quakers who had come to console him when he was stricken with apoplexy in 1715; although he had smiled a little at their odd customs, he was moved to tears by their naïve goodness of heart; their quick sympathy seemed to him an ideal quality. He never joined the great Society of Friends, but he had always a sincere respect for its members; and, although he could poke a bit of fun at their peculiarities, he could also be generous towards any of them who needed his help. For example, when the Quaker book-seller, Keimer, was imprisoned in Gatehouse in 1717 upon a charge of libel, De Foe sent him a small gift of money and an offer to aid him, adding mysteriously that he had more power with the government than any one imagined him to have.

De Foe, during the long days that he lay sick, was filled with

horror about many details of his past life. The fever of ambition which had sapped so much of his energy now left him
filled with remorse that he had so often sacrificed his family
to his personal interests. He resolved to say his *mea-culpa* by
publishing a discussion on education in which he would offer
advice to fathers on how to bring up their children. This work,
The Family Instructor, appeared March 31, 1715; De Foe, suffering with a relapse of the gout, had been forced to give up
correcting the proofs and writing the preface; the editor had
called upon the Presbyterian minister, Wright, who prepared
a letter-preface in which he recommended the book to all
pious persons. The introduction, which De Foe wrote later,
contains two quite interesting details . . . one, revealing his
own state of mind, the other, revealing the state of mind of the
people of his time. De Foe tells us that, in composing this work,
he felt the aid of the Divine presence . . . curious mysticism,
recalling many previous statements by De Foe of aid from his
"demon of Socrates," and explanatory of his preoccupation
with supernatural subjects which led to his writing books on
magic and spiritism. On the other hand, he says that the
stories he relates in the form of dialogues are absolutely true,
that he has concealed the real names of his characters only as a
matter of protection. The explanation for this statement lies
in the psychology of his readers, who wanted to believe what
they read was fact; except for the romances of chivalry and
fairy tales, fiction in those days was taboo.

In *The Family Instructor,* De Foe draws us a picture of the
ideal family life, although it is doubtful whether it came any
where near being the life led at Stoke Newington . . . it is
the way he would have liked to have had it led there: morning
and evening prayers, complete religious instruction given by
the father to his children, strict observance of the Sabbath
with no walking in the parks or profane reading. He also

portrays the ideal head of the house as he himself wished to be: severe, strict, and firm, but just in all of his judgments . . . the pitiless executor of the order of the tyrannical master that the Puritan God is. A beautiful dream, in truth, with his own family united against him and his children lacking all respect for their father. But into this dream he inserts a most realistic touch . . . the oldest son in the family whose story he tells is a disobedient lad who ends his life miserably without getting his father's pardon . . . a subtle bit of warning to Daniel De Foe, Junior, who, we know, was always rebellious to the home discipline . . . so much so that his father felt it his duty to make this public application for his benefit.

The extraordinary success of *The Family Instructor* was a great surprise as well as a great joy to Daniel. Edition after edition succeeded one another both in England and in America during the Eighteenth and the Nineteenth centuries. De Foe could be glad that he had given up his first idea of presenting his subject as a long dramatic poem, and had held himself to clear, straightforward exposition at which he was much more effective and by which the appeal of his work was broadened. Both rich and poor could draw from *The Family Instructor;* as a matter of fact, the young princes of the realm, the children of George I, were reared under the instructions laid down in this book. This was the kind of glory that pleased De Foe, the kind that had no taint of double-dealing upon it. Finding the book a success, he followed it with others of the same type, gaining peace to his soul and money to his purse. He prepared a second volume of *The Family Instructor* and wrote another book, *Religious Courtship,* in which he showed that the happiest marriages were those in which husband and wife followed the same religious practice.

These books are really imaginative dialogues for religious teaching; they are proof of De Foe's strongly implanted Puritanism. There is nothing surprising in their production at this time; it was quite natural for him, as age crept on, to return to the severity of the Roundheads. He thundered furiously and indiscriminately against actors and puppet-shows, along with atheists and blasphemers. He vigorously lashed with his pen the book-sellers who handled obscene books. He severely criticised those who celebrated too uproariously the feast of Christmas. He used the text, "Tempt not the Lord, thy God!" to preach against scientists and the new methods they employed, particularly the practice of vaccination for smallpox.

De Foe's romances are a natural outcome of his mentality. The characters of his imagination, Robinson Crusoe, Moll Flanders, and their younger brothers and sisters relate the ups and downs of their adventurous lives in order to serve as examples to the reader and to warn him against yielding to temptation. Each of these creations, comfortably installed in old age in some peaceful Stoke Newington, looks back over his life and makes his public confession as a gesture of repentance to the God of his ancestors.

XI. DE FOE'S NOVELS

I N 1718, there appeared a second edition of a popular book
by Capt. Woodes Rogers, entitled, *A Cruising Voyage round
the World . . . begun in 1708 and finished in 1711;* it contained, among other things, *An Account of Alexander Selkirk's living alone four years and four months in an Island.*
Its reappearance must have brought back to De Foe's memory
the rough Scotch sailor, Selkirk, who, following a quarrel with
his superior officers, had been marooned on the Island of Juan-
Fernandez, just off the coast of Chili. When he was rescued
in 1709 by Capt. Woodes Rogers, he had become more than
half savage, and it was some time before he was able to talk
intelligibly again.

He was brought back to London in October, 1711; there the
story of his adventures became a nine days' wonder. Richard
Steele made his acquaintance, and Capt. Edward Cooke related his story in a successful book of the moment. De Foe must
have seen Selkirk, but as he was just getting ready for one of
his trips into Scotland, he had had to content himself with
reading all that got into print about this unusual experience
of a man marooned for four years on an island peopled only
by goats. It may have been that De Foe, when he was in Bristol
in 1713, talked with Selkirk, for the rude sailor, his head
turned by public attention and then by public indifference, had
at last sought a friendly harbor in this western city; but the
interviewer could have drawn but little from his subject,
whose experiences had left him somewhat more brutal, more
dissipated, and more morose than he had been. It is possible,

ALEXANDER SELKIRK
the original of Robinson Crusoe, on his island.
The rescue of Selkirk was the greatest sensation of its time.
(From a contemporary print)

though, that De Foe might have planned to write a short treatise on the benefits of solitude, drawing upon Selkirk's experience as a starting point; but Steele anticipated such a move by publishing, on December 3, 1713, in his journal, *The Englishman,* a masterly essay upon Selkirk's adventures. Then more serious matter claimed the attention of all England. Still, busy as De Foe was, trying to win his way into favor with the new Ministry so that he might save his own skin, he never forgot the Hermit of Juan-Fernandez. In 1717, when he had some business dealings with Capt. Thomas Bowry, of the East Indian company, he certainly took the opportunity to study the detailed maps of Selkirk's island which Bowry possessed.

Then, when 1719 found him so peacefully settled at Stoke Newington with but one problem, the necessity for furnishing the book-sellers with enough copy to supply himself with a sufficient income, he bethought him of a subject that must have fitted in with his own secluded life . . . what would a man alone on a desert island do! The first consideration was to avoid taking Selkirk's story and simply adding to it. Selkirk was still alive; therefore, he had better put his own hero's adventures fifty years earlier than the Scotchman's in order to gain the advantage of priority. He chose to make his man an Englishman from York. . . . But what should he name him? One of his old classmates at Newington-Green was Timothy Crusoe; the name had stuck in his memory, but he changed the first part to Robinson, a common surname, especially in his hero's native town. So was created one of the greatest characters in fiction.

There was another and even more important detail to be considered; Juan-Fernandez would inevitably recall the adventures of Selkirk; De Foe must find another location for his story. He had always been interested in Sir Walter Raleigh's account of Guiana, and he made up his mind that his desert

island should be off the coast of South America at the mouth
of the Orinoco river. He chose better than he knew, for there
was so little information regarding these latitudes that he was
pretty safe in inventing his details with a free hand and with
only the needs of his story in mind. The maps of the time show
that geographers generally agreed upon placing an archipelago
at the mouth of the Orinoco, which they pictured as a large
gulf. The most eastern of these islands was in the Atlantic, far
from the mainland. None of these islands was named, and
their outlines were only vaguely suggested. It was one of these
mere dots on the map, then, that De Foe chose for the home
of his shipwrecked hero, transplanting to it the turtles, the
goats, and the cats of Juan-Fernandez; he would have been as
surprised as the next one to know that these animals were
really native to the place. He was not so fortunate in adding
Selkirk's penguins and seals, a blunder which may well be
held against him, since any knowledge of the fauna of the
torrid zone would indicate his error. He did inform himself
as to the proper vegetation for his locality. He accommodated
the physical aspects of the land to Robinson's needs, creating
a clear stream, a wooded hill for an outlook, and a rocky
formation that was easily excavated. Every once in a while
there would crop up in his imagination details that he had
read in connection with Selkirk's story and that have left on
Crusoe's Island the imprint of Juan-Fernandez; such, for example, are the steep clifts where the agile goats lived.

Little by little the subject matter took form in De Foe's
mind; he began to know his character and to see him in
his environment. His masterpiece was all ready then to be
written. He first wrote the sensational title:

*The Life and Strange Surprizing Adventures of Robinson
Crusoe of York, Mariner: Who Lived Eight and Twenty
Years, all alone in an un-inhabited Island on the Coast of*

THE ISLAND OF JUAN FERNANDEZ
where Alexander Selkirk, the original of Robinson Crusoe, was abandoned and later rescued.
(From a contemporary print)

America, near the Mouth of the great River of Oroonoque;
Having been cast on Shore by Shipwreck, wherein all the Men
perished but himself. With an Account how he was at last
strangely deliver'd by Pyrates. Written by Himself.

De Foe took this title to his editor, Taylor, at the Ship in
Paternoster Row, London. Taylor, who had already had some
dealings with De Foe, was immediately struck by the possi-
bilities for success in the sale of a book so captioned and asked
for about 350 pages on the subject.

So it was that, in his study in Stoke Newington, De Foe set
hastily to work on that immortal story. Who has not felt the
charm of those strange adventures created by this needy
author: the capture of Robinson by the pirates of the Barbary
Coast; his flight with the young slave, Xury; his success as a
planter in Brazil; the great tempest and the shipwreck; and,
particularly, his solitary and industrious life on the island; the
coming of the savages; the training of Friday; his sudden and
unexpected deliverance; his delight in returning to England;
and his dramatic crossing of the Pyrenees in mid-winter! Is it
so astonishing that the book has been an immense success
since its first appearance on Saturday, April 25, 1719? It must
be remembered, too, that this success was first based upon the
naïve belief of De Foe's contemporaries that they were reading
the actual autobiographical memoirs of Robinson Crusoe. They
forgot that there had been many fictitious stories about shipwrecked sailors long before this book appeared; they were
simply carried off their feet by the sense of authenticity that
De Foe managed to convey.

De Foe at once followed up his success with further adventures of Robinson; he brought his hero back to the island,
now colonized, told of the quarrels of the inhabitants and of
their fights with the invading cannibals. He described Crusoe's travels to Madagascar, India, and China . . . in the latter

place he engaged in some business transactions . . . and, finally, of his dangerous trip across the continent from Pekin to Archangel. This second volume went on sale, August 20, 1719, and was eagerly received by the public that had so enjoyed the first one. De Foe, as well as his publisher, rejoiced in the jingle of coins that Robinson brought to his empty pockets.

But such success was sure to bring upon him the envy and the cupidity of those who resented his good fortune. The "pirate" book-sellers brought out unauthenticated editions, badly printed on poor paper and full of errors but selling for less money than the official edition. They also made some abridgments of the text, which were acceptable to the public, bored by the long moral and theological commentaries that De Foe had freely inserted into the narrative. De Foe and Taylor first attempted to take legal action against these fraudulent practices, but, finding that they were getting nowhere with it, they gave it up.

One poor writer whose books had not sold well took a vindictive thrust at the unprecedented success of his rival's work. He wrote a sharp criticism of *Robinson Crusoe,* in an attempt to show that this book, praised so extravagantly, was only a hit and miss array of contradictions, untruths, and theories at variance with patriotism and religion. Robinson, he said, was an impossible character, conceived in De Foe's own image, with his author's own mean and common ideas. Gildon developed his envious conclusions at length and achieved a delightful parody of De Foe's title in his own:

The Life and Strange Surprizing Adventures of Mr. D . . . De F . . . of London, Hosier, Who Has liv'd above fifty Years by himself in the Kingdoms of North and South Britain. The various Shapes he has appear'd in, and the Discoveries he has made for the Benefit of his Country. In a Dialogue between Him, Robinson Crusoe, and his Man Friday. With Remarks serious and Comical upon the Life of Crusoe.[1]

This attack annoyed De Foe very much, but it furnished him with a solution to a problem that had been bothering him. He had said that Robinson was a real person and his adventures were true; it seemed that, at any moment, he might be convicted of falsehood. He made up his mind to say, from now on, that his book was the allegorical representation of his own life and that Robinson's misfortunes were his own, transposed to another time and place. He made his plans to present this theory at once in a third volume for which Taylor had been insistently clamoring. He wrote a really brilliant preface in which he set forth this new explanation of his masterpiece. But Robinson had begun to bore him, and he saw no possibility of sending his hero forth, at the age of seventy, upon new adventures around the world. He contented himself with scraps from the bottom drawers of his desk . . . old half-forgotten papers he had written on honesty, Christianity, atheism, warnings and signs from the Lord, the part played by Satan, and so on. He set off this odd collection with a pompous title:

Serious Reflections during the Life and Surprizing Adventures of Robinson Crusoe. With his Vision of the Angelick World. Written by Himself.

This volume appeared in August of 1720. But the public was not to be fooled; they had been told that Robinson was to greet them again with his own thoughts on his solitary life. But the book is a conglomeration of tiresome essays on the most diverse subjects from the lot of bankrupts to the dwelling place of the infernal spirits; Robinson's name appears on only

---

[1] Cf. this very curious pamphlet, edited by Paul G. Dottin in 1924 under the title: *Robinson Crusoe Examin'd and Criticis'd, or a new edition of Charles Gildon's famous Pamphlet, now published with an Introduction and Explanatory Notes, together with an Essay on Gildon's Life.* London, Dent.

a few of the pages. The readers made it clear that they considered themselves cheated. This time Robinson was really dead; philosophy had killed him.

But if the *Serious Reflections* fell flat, the first two volumes of the romance continued to enjoy favor with the English public. De Foe had so truly delineated life on a desert island that writers felt sure of being understood when they wished to refer to such an experience by calling it a "Robinsonad." Every one, the great as well as the humble, endeavored to capture De Foe's style and mannerisms. His unparalleled triumph with the subject led many others to try their hands at it, thus presenting Robinson with a host of imitators and rivals.

Most of the "Robinsonads" had but fleeting success. At least two of them deserve some consideration. The first, published in April, 1727, was:

The Hermit: or the unparalleled Sufferings and surprising Adventures of Mr. Philip Quarll, an Englishman; who was lately discovered by Mr. Dorrington, a British Merchant, upon an uninhabited Island in the South Sea; where he has lived above Fifty Years without any human assistance, still continues to reside, and will not come away.

The book is fairly diverting, but lacks all sense of reality. Quarll made himself some instruments that he needed with the ease of a sleight-of-hand performance. He became quite friendly with the animals that lived on his island; two apes of different species came to him to arbitrate a quarrel they had had upon some subject. . . . Like Robinson he frequently repulsed the cannibals that invaded his land; he took a ship's boy for his "man Friday;" and, in place of a parrot, he had an ape with the fanciful name, Beaufidele, that made pretty little articles out of variegated shells.

The distinguishing characteristic of this "Robinson Crusoe" is its use of a new element . . . the supernatural. Where De

Foe's hero is a practical and commonplace Puritan, Quarll is a mystic. His being on an island completely surrounded by a rampart of rocks, the invisible choir of echoes that repeated and amplified his prayers, the sea monster with the bloody mouth who watched over him to prevent his killing himself in a paroxysm of despair . . . none of these are fully explained. Quarll is visited in his dreams by a spirit who tells him of all that is happening in Europe . . . a detail that De Foe would never have thought of using. But Quarll does not interest the reader as does Robinson, for he is not, like his prototype, a living creature of flesh and blood, and his home is more a Utopian island than a real spot on the earth's surface. This lack of realism has, it seems, caused it to be discarded.

This same element of the marvellous is even more pronounced in *The Life and Adventures of Peter Wilkins* (1750), a combination of *Robinson Crusoe* and *Gulliver's Travels,* by Robert Paltock. His hero is shipwrecked in the latitude of the South Pole, lives for some time on an island in much the same fashion Robinson did, and then makes his way through some caverns that lead to the country of the Glumms and the Gawrys, where the men and women are able to fly. From there on the story becomes simply a fairy tale with a few satiric touches that sustain the interest a little. Nevertheless, it was accounted a "best seller" for half a century, though neither it nor any other work has seriously shaken the secure foundation upon which rests the high fame of *Robinson Crusoe.* Interest has been diverted, but it has always flowed back into the channel of De Foe's masterpiece. Every English child has followed this course which is a part of the great stream of English literature.

France had the same experience. There had been stories of adventure there, too, with situations somewhat analogous to Robinson's; such was *L'Histoire des Sévérambes* (1677), *Les*

Voyages et Aventures de Jacques Massé (1710), and a work by Marivaux, *Les effets surprenants de la sympathie* (1713). But when the first translation of *Robinson Crusoe* appeared in March, 1720, it at once took popular hold of the people. Robinson became the most talked-of individual in the country; Lesage devoted one of his farcical comedies to him; the Marquis de Balleroy, who was exiled in Normandy, inquired about this English character who was the topic of every conversation. The only variation from the general praise came from the priests who considered Robinson a heretic and from the "young bloods" who affected to despise the romance of adventure.

A curious thing is that contemporary acclaim concentrated on Robinson's voyages around the world, and it was not until the appearance of *Émile* (1762), called attention to the great human lesson in one man's experience on a desert island, that this phase of the saga came to be properly appreciated. It was Rousseau who really pointed out the philosophy in *Robinson Crusoe,* and who, by stating that it was the only text book he used in the beginning for Émile, relegated it, at the same time, to juvenile literature. And, as a matter of fact, almost all of the adaptations and abridgments of it that have been made since then have been with the idea in mind of its being read chiefly by children.

There were "Robinsonads" in France as in England, but, in each instance, there was some effort made to put in variations both as to theme and as to locale; the island now became the scene, not of one man's isolated sojourn, but of one family's. Of these French family Robinsons three may be mentioned: *Les mémoires de chevalier de Kilpar* by Gain de Montagnac, appearing in 1768, Grivel's *L'île inconnue, ou Memoirs du chevalier de Gastines,* in 1783, and the *Lolotte et Fanfan* of Ducray-Duminil, in 1788. But, strange to relate, it is the translation of a foreigner, the son of the Reverend Wyss, who in 1813 published at Zurich his *Swiss Family Robinson,* that has won the most lasting place for this type in France as well as in other countries. For more than a century it has continued to hold a definite place in the affections of children. As for stories of youthful Robinsons, it would be impossible to count them. Every year, almost every month, sees the advent of a new one.

In Germany, as in France, Robinson Crusoe fell upon prepared ground; in 1669 *Simplicissimus,* a romance by Grimmelshausen, contains an episode that amounts to a premature "Robinsonad." De Foe's novel, translated into German in 1720, set a new fashion that was adopted even more thoroughly by the Germans than it had been by the French. There was a Robinson for every district and subdivision, for every layer of the social strata . . . there was a Saxon Robinson, a Silisian Robinson, a Brandenburgian Robinson, an Austrian Robinson, a Jewish Robinson, even a Doctor Robinson. One could search the map of the world over without being able to find a spot on the globe that had not been occupied by a Robinson. Most of these books are without any value except to show the general infatuation with the theme. *The Island of Felsenburg,* by Schnabel, a Saxon officer, has some merit; it was published in 1730.

A pedagogue by the name of Campe, inspired by Rousseau's *Émile,* got the idea of building up a dialogue around the central part of De Foe's romance. His book, *Robinson der Jüngere,* appeared in 1779 and was a remarkable success. It was translated into more than a score of different languages and quite eclipsed the original until, with the lessening of Rousseau's influence, there was also a loss of interest in this application of the French master's technique. Campe's book presented a German father who, each evening, related to his attentive children the story of poor Robinson, answering their naïve questions as he went along. The book is even to-day an influence in German pedagogy.

No imitation or variation has been able permanently to take the place of the original. Its appeal has been so general that it has been translated into every written language and has been accepted as a part of the literary background of all civilized nations of Europe as well as of Puritan America and of the Anglo-Saxon world in other lands. It has been re-edited more frequently than any other book except the Bible. Many attempts have been made to dramatize it, but most of them have been unsuccessful; Guilbert de Pixérécourt, the "Shakespeare of the Boulevards," made a spectacular melodrama of the theme and presented it at Saint Martin's in 1805. But, except for vaudeville sketches, pantomime stunts, and ballets, it has proved almost impossible to take the character that De Foe conceived and portrayed in the humdrum reality of living and expect it to show up properly in the glare of the footlights. No, Robinson was meant for armchair enjoyment, and that he shall surely have as long as there are simple, adventurous-minded folk, like the Eighteenth century middle class and active-minded children of all ages and climes.

What are the reasons for this extraordinary success? In the first place, there is no character in literature that grows on the reader more or seems so much like a living being. He is first and foremost a business man; he never speaks of any object without at once giving its money value. He liked "red tape," itemized receipts and detailed contracts. He was given to making careful lists or inventories of everything, whether it was the things he had found on the wreck, the cannibals he had encountered, or the provisions he must take on a voyage. If he was debating some important question; such as, "Should I consider myself a victim or a favorite of destiny?" he would draw up two columns; on the one side list his assets, or the

ONE OF THE FAMOUS STOTHARD ILLUSTRATIONS
for Robinson Crusoe, covering a scene from the latter part of the book.

advantages that the Lord had given him in his solitary life; on the other side his liabilities . . . the inconveniences in his situation. When he had balanced this sheet, he found that the good outweighed the bad. He also kept a journal; just as a merchant would write down each business deal of the day, so did Robinson note everything that he did and just as he did it.

He was a good organizer; he liked to draw up plans ahead of time and carry them out exactly. He had a boresome regard for routine, always holding too closely to the letter of the law. He was intolerant of any play of the imagination, any bit of caprice and had no patience with the dreamer or the sentimentalist. His display of affection for his fellow creatures followed some egoistic or utilitarian design. Beauties of nature did not .stir him, and his love for animals was from the culinary or the gastronomic point of view; he divided them into two classes, those that were good to eat and those that were tasteless or tough. He could see no reasons for going into ecstasies over some winged denizen of the woods without first ascertaining whether it would be better broiled or roasted.

But these faults and eccentricities do not keep Robinson from appealing to the sympathies of the reader, for there is about him a winning simplicity and frankness. He possesses the same self-satisfaction that a child possesses, and with equal candor takes us into his confidence about his hopes, his troubles, and his mishaps. When he sees that his efforts have met with success, he does not hesitate to brag about it with no question in his mind as to modesty, real or assumed. When he makes a mistake, he either acknowledges it penitently, or expresses complete surprise at his having been deceived. For he believes implicitly in his own abilities and, after the coming of Friday, in his own superiority. Fortunately, his religion keeps him from developing an overbearing pride. As a good

Puritan, Robinson must constantly humble himself before the Lord of the Old Testament, whom he regards with a wholesome fear. God and the Devil are his two great dreads. . . . He tries not to displease the One in order to gain His aid against the other. He turned to the Bible for an answer to every difficulty and set to work at once to convert Friday to Protestantism. By this missionary work and by his continued submission to the Will of the Lord, he confidently expected to atone for his past faults. . . . It is as though he had struck a bargain with the Almighty.

It is impossible not to get interested in his activities; he is so persistently energetic and tenacious. He does not begrudge any amount of labor or trouble he is put to in order to finish his task and gain his objective. And he is always just a little bit ahead of events, anticipating every happening so that he can meet it with a calmness and a decisiveness that shows he is a born leader. We rejoice with him in his success because we feel that he deserves it.

He is no angel, nor is he a devil; just an ordinary human being like ourselves . . . a middle class type in his simplicity and his piety, a hard-working, honest business man . . . that is Robinson Crusoe. He does not seem to be a character in a book, but a real individual. De Foe's training explains, to an extent, his ability to create this sense of reality; a journalist by profession and a reporter by temperament, his genius was pruned to the limits of circumstantial invention. He brought out bluntly the little, unexpected details that make us exclaim:

"How could any one have invented that!"

There is, for example, the scene when Robinson, cast upon the shore of his island, sought for traces of his companions and found only "three of their hats, one cap, and two shoes that were not fellows." Or take the whole plan of the book; indeed, there is no plan. The reader is not carried forward, bit by bit,

BOOK PLATE OF GEORGE IV
then Prince of Wales, in a copy of an early edition of Robinson Crusoe.
(Volume in New York Public Library.)

to a foreseen and foreshadowed dénouement. No! People come and go, disappear and reappear, much as they do in real life. Serious events arise without any warning. We are as unprepared as Robinson was for seeing the footprint in the sand that proved he was not alone upon the island. Life itself does not move forward to well-arranged climaxes; the same people are not always playing upon each other's personalities; a lucky day may often be followed by a day of mishaps without our having any ability to foresee it, prepare for it, or prevent it. Of significance, too, is De Foe's simple style, stripped of any touch of artistry; it is exactly the language which a talkative sailor would use in relating his adventures. This is why *Robinson Crusoe* is a masterpiece of realism; it can no more be forgotten than could a page from history be blotted out.

Admiration for the book need not blind us to its faults. De Foe was too ready to assume the rôle of preacher; not satisfied with writing a magnificent epic of human energy and intelligence, he felt himself obliged to stuff his book with pious admonitions and moral precepts. He was writing for the lower class of people, and, as a good Puritan, he must not let slip any chance for teaching them. With that public in mind he keeps his humor, on the whole, quite broad. Friday is a buffoon of the market place, and Robinson's wit is usually lacking in refinement. When De Foe does forget himself and poke a little fun at his readers, he becomes quite witty; he must have smiled to himself when he pictured the perplexity of his readers . . . strict Protestants and patriotic Englishmen . . . when they read of a French Catholic priest, endowed with all virtue, of mild and peaceful Spaniards, and of cruel, wicked British sailors.

The great haste in which the book was written is almost unforgivable; there are so many faults that must be blamed on that. The book is full of repetitions, anticipations, retrospective asides, and, what are even more serious, contradictions and inaccuracies. Robinson had stripped off his clothes to swim to the shipwreck; but when he is ready to start back to shore, he fills his pockets with biscuits. He complained of having no salt for his bread; then he tried diligently to teach Friday to use salt with his meat. He had to give up keeping his detailed journal because he was almost out of ink; but twenty years later he gave the ambassadors to the Spanish wreck written instructions. He had a pipe and some tobacco, yet he frequently lamented that he could not smoke. Oppressed by the night, the wolves, and the snow, why did he stop so many times in crossing the Pyrenees to watch Friday's encounters with the bears! All of his dates and figures are wrong. Friday is both conventional savage and well-trained servant. There is no end to the many times that De Foe contradicts himself, often with but few lines intervening. In fact the underlying theme of the novel may be seriously questioned; a man, after twenty years of solitude would have either gone crazy or reverted to his savage state. But Robinson's intelligence is always clear and appears to increase in clarity as he grows older.

But who thinks of all these things when he is caught up by the vibrant spirit of the book and feels himself a living part of the experience of this unfortunate recluse? Few books have exercised the influence this one has. Everyone has played at Robinson. And, even in maturity, there is a lure in the thought of an island of quiet and solitude where, far from the worries and cares of daily life, one can enjoy a perfect rest, gazing on the vast empty horizons until the footprint of Friday reminds him that in this world man cannot live alone. Then he can plunge again into the turbulent life about him, repeating, perhaps, the kindly, regretful sentiments of a modern romanticist: [1]

[1] Charles Louis Philippe in *La mere et l'enfant*, IV.

GEORGE FOURTH'S COPY OF ROBINSON CRUSOE
Frontispiece and title-page.
(Volume in New York Public Library.)

"Ah, Robinson Crusoe, that was a splendid adventure you had, sailing the high seas, escaping alone from a tragic shipwreck. And that desert island of yours, Robinson . . . I picture you, in your rude hut, your cave, living alone, with the sky overhead and the deserted beach for a playground! You must have been quite happy, Robinson Crusoe! I cannot understand your philosophy, your resignation. I do not even know what your parrot meant by saying, "Robinson, my poor Robinson!" You must have been quite happy, Robinson Crusoe! But it distresses me that you never lived. . . . You were so good and your island was so beautiful. May you rest in peace, Robinson Crusoe, far from the busy world you never even inhabited. You are a fine dream . . . the sort adolescent children have. You are like a dream of good fortune never experienced."

The unlooked-for success of *Robinson Crusoe* made De Foe decide to exploit this vein which he had brought to light. He had some old notes on the brilliant campaign of Gustave-Adolphe in Germany during the Thirty Years War and the Civil War in England between the king and parliament. With a wave of his magic wand, he created his hero, a young nobleman from near Shrewsbury and had him serve first under the proud King of Sweden and then under the "Royal Martyr," Charles I. So did he achieve, without even trying, a historical romance, following the accepted formula: a central character, more or less fictitious, in the midst of circumstances and events that hold pretty closely to actual fact.

De Foe called his book *Memoirs of a Cavalier,* and it was published in May, 1720. Of course, he pretended that he was only editing an authentic manuscript, and it is probable that the public believed him; it was too little impressed with this long-drawn-out succession of military maneuvers, described by a dull and lifeless individual, to offer it any interest at all. De Foe was a good servant to his public, always seeking to please it. He tried again the following month with a wholly different appeal to their literary appetites:

The Life, Adventures and Piracies of the Famous Captain Singleton

This novel, full of unexpected events, was intended to please a public that, in its love for adventure, had made a kind of hero out of the buccaneers. Singleton is a foundling, adopted by an old Portuguese pilot, who took him along to the East Indies. Contact with the coarse and brutal sailors developed the boy's worst side, and he took part in a mutiny against the captain of the ship. When this was discovered, at the last minute, the conspirators were marooned with their arms and supplies on the coast of Madagascar.

After some hesitation as to continuing their way along the shore, they decided to take Singleton's advice and built themselves a boat in which they crossed the Mozambique Channel to the African shore. Here they made a foolhardy attempt to cross the African continent from Mozambique to Angola. They followed the course of the rivers upstream in their boats as far as they could go. Having reached the headwaters, they formed themselves into a caravan with negroes carrying their supplies. Their progress was extremely difficult; they had to cross deserts inhabited by ferocious beasts, to follow impassable mountains, and to skirt immense lakes. But they were well rewarded for all trials, for, after they had ended their journey at the Gulf of Benin, they met up with a former factor for the English Guiana Company who was living with the natives there. He showed them rivers rolling with gold nuggets; so that, although they had been destitute when they left their own country, they returned to it loaded with wealth.

The life Singleton led in London soon stripped him of his whole fortune. But when he got down to penury again, he was ready to set off once more; this time he realized a dream he had long cherished, that of becoming a pirate. He soon rose to be captain of a ship which skimmed the seas at his own command for his own gain. Among the passengers on a vessel that was captured by his men was a merry Quaker, named William, a curious mixture of cynicism and piety. Singleton made him his lieutenant, and they continued their cruising without any serious accidents, touching at Madagascar, the principal resort of buccaneers, and going from there to the Philippines and the Moluccas archipelago. Upon one of the islands of this group, Singleton's men were attacked by savages who took refuge in a hollow tree where the pirates laid siege to them for days. The voyage was otherwise uneventful. On the return trip, they stopped at Ceylon, where William's prudence and foresight saved Singleton from ambush, laid by the cruel and crafty natives. Coming next to the Persian Gulf the astute Quaker there took Singleton to task:

"Now that you are rich," he said to the pirate captain, "have you not enough of this wicked life which will certainly lead you to eternal damnation?"

Singleton accepted this admonition all the more readily because his conscience had been tormenting him with remorse. He and William proceeded to give their companions the slip, taking with them their ill-gotten gains; passing as Persian merchants, they joined a caravan headed for Europe. Singleton married William's sister and did all he could to make his peace with the Lord.

The book was only partly successful either because it was poorly launched by the publisher or because it was considered too monotonous; indeed, it is rather lifeless except for the one character, William, whose acts and sayings form the highlights of the book. De Foe seems to have had a moment of discouragement, and then he was back again, this time with a new vehicle. He had noted the enthusiastic reception given to the translations of the Spanish picaresque novels and made up his mind to try his hand at portraying an English *picara* who was both thief and prostitute. So was conceived the novel that is almost as great as *Robinson Crusoe, The Fortunes and Misfortunes of the Famous Moll Flanders,* published in January, 1722.

Moll was born in the prison at Newgate where her mother, locked up for theft, was made pregnant by a jailer in order to escape hanging. Six months after she had given birth to a daughter, this far from respectable woman was deported to Virginia, leaving her baby with relatives who took so little care of Moll that she was carried off by gipsies. They took her with them about England, abandoning her in Colechester where, dependent on the charity of the town, she was placed in an orphanage and became a good little servant; she attracted the attention of a wealthy middle class woman, who brought her home with her to be a companion to her two daughters.

But Moll's patroness had also two sons, the older of whom came to admire his mother's pretty protégée and, without too much difficulty, made her his mistress. Then the younger brother, more timid and sentimental than the older one, but also susceptible to Moll's charms, asked her to be his wife. Urged by her lover, she finally accepted him, reluctantly, as she was really in love with her seducer; the latter saw to it that his brother was so intoxicated on his wedding night that no embarrassing explanations were necessary. There followed five peaceful and happy years of married life in a small house near London.

But Moll was unlucky; her husband died, and she married a business man who became bankrupt and left her. To avoid being made liable for her husband's debts, she changed her residence, settling on the other side of the Thames where she made the acquaintance of a rich planter from Virginia to whom she gave her hand. She went with him to America, lived with him for several years in perfect happiness, and then, one day, discovered that she had been living with her own brother. Horrified at the incest she had unknowingly committed, she left her husband and returned to England.

She went to Bath, the renowned watering-place and was not slow in getting acquainted with a generous man who became first her friend then her lover. This affair lasted for six years ... until the gentleman became seriously ill and promised the Lord, if he recovered, he would no longer live in sin. When he was convalescing, he told Moll of his resolution, and so she was left once more to take up the struggle for existence alone.

She considered an intrigue with a banker's clerk, who looked after her small fortune with much solicitude; she had already begun to think of marrying him, when she received a more handsome offer. An Irish landowner who was looking for just the woman Moll pretended to be, a wealthy widow, had her come to Liverpool to meet him. As soon as she met him, she fell in love with his good looks; they were married at once, but were scarcely united before they found out that they had fooled each other; both of them were adventurers who had pretended wealth in order to make advantageous marriages. After a moment of chagrin, they laughed at the matter. But the husband refused to submit Moll to a life of poverty. He left her and became a highwayman, while Moll returned alone to London.

She thought again of the banker's clerk, but, as she was pregnant, she could not turn to him. She made the acquaintance of a clever mid-wife who took care of just such cases as Moll's; she even placed the infant in good hands so that the mother could be free to look after herself. She soon married the banker's clerk, who made a model husband, but did not live long.

Once more alone in a hostile world, too old now to rely on her charms to win her way, she reaches the depths of despair. Then, one day, acting upon the guidance of a mysterious voice, she steals a package at an apothecary's shop. After she gets home with it, she finds that it contains some silver-plate, some lace, three pieces of silk, and some small coins. That is the first step . . . she becomes a thief. She meets again the old mid-wife who, having got into difficulties with the law, has to give up her establishment, and has become a receiver of stolen goods. Under her instruction, Moll develops into a real artist at picking pockets and shoplifting. She slips through the hands of the police in the face of the most daring of thefts; relying upon the carelessness of the clerks, she enters the shops and helps herself to very valuable articles; she even steals the necklaces from wealthy children playing in the parks. Furthermore, she paints herself up to appear quite attractive again and makes a conquest of an intoxicated gentleman who, through fear of blackmail, gives her large sums of money and expensive gifts. It is not long until she has become a veritable kleptomaniac, stealing everything that she can lay her hands on, although the small fortune she has amassed makes it unnecessary.

Just one slip, and this brilliant career is ended. She is caught in a hosier's shop in the very act of stealing, is taken to Newgate and condemned to death. But her despair is doubled when she finds among the inmates of the prison, her dear Irish husband, James. Face to face with eternity, she is filled with sincere repentance for her misdeeds. Her piety touches the heart of the chaplain of the prison who intercedes with the judges to have Moll's sentence changed to deportation. Then, with her former husband, James, who has been granted the same favor, she leaves for Virginia. With their combined resources they purchase their freedom as soon as they reach America and set up as planters in the new world. Moll gets hold of her son by her incestuous marriage and, with this dear child and her husband, she passes some very happy years. At the age of seventy she returns to England where she leads a model life and makes up her mind to write her memoirs as a warning and a lesson for posterity.

The Fortunes and Misfortunes of Moll Flanders was a great success. Three editions of it appeared within the year; cheap summaries of it, carrying to the most distant parts of the country the fame of the pathetic heroine, kept a score of hack writers busy.

The appeal of the novel lies in its humanity; De Foe has achieved the somewhat banal effect of winning the reader's sympathetic regard for a whore and a thief. He makes us feel that she is a victim of heredity, of her too responsive temperament, of her seducer's egoism, of some kind of spite, and finally of Society, that makes her an outcast. True, Moll has a calculating and utilitarian mind, but is not that because misfortune has taught her the value of money and of material well-being? She is loyal in love and honest in her dealings with others whenever she can be. She would have been a good wife, a good mother, and an honest, upright woman from the very beginning if circumstances had not brought her face to face with poverty. Who, aware of this London sinner's antecedents and her misfortunes, will dare to cast at her the first stone?

Of course, fastidious Victorian England, horrified at such a novel, closed its eyes and its ears to it. But the book was a great success in France where, since its translation by Marcel Schwob, its naturalism has never shocked any one. For the last ten years or so, it has returned to popularity in England where it now holds a place almost as secure as that of *Robinson Crusoe*.

De Foe was not slow to recognize his success and congratulate himself upon it. The demands upon his purse kept his nose to the grind constantly, and he was always on the hunt for a new subject. During 1720 and 1721 the plague ravaged Marseilles and Provence. Londoners trembled, and the authorities were kept busy, employing the most severe measures for prevention; they were effective as the epidemic did not spread into Great Britain. While all English attention was concentrated on this disease that had taken such a frightful toll in the country in 1665, De Foe called upon his own childish memories of that time and upon everything available in the way of official and personal records to prepare for publication in March, 1722, *A Journal of the Plague Year, Being Observations or Memorials of the Most Remarkable Occurrences, as well Publick as Private, which happened in London during the Great Visitation in 1665. Written by a Citizen who continued all the while in London. Never made Publick before.*

The "citizen" in question, a Puritan saddler of Whitechapel, was, of course, invented by De Foe for his own purposes. He was a mouthpiece for the most frightful descriptions of the devastated City. De Foe was especially good at creating the effect of fear and of desolation. His simple, natural language made his scenes of terror and of death seem unusually awful. Of course the book was written too rapidly; it is badly put together, is full of repetitions, and many of its details are historically incorrect. Nevertheless, the *Journal of the Plague Year* still stands as the best piece of work on the most terrible year that London ever had, the year 1665. De Foe's contemporaries considered it a rather ordinary array of information;

SOLOMON EAGLE, RELIGIOUS ENTHUSIAST
who passed through London streets with a burning brazier on his
head, warning Londoners to repent. De Foe describes him inimitably
in his Plague of London. (From drawing by Cruikshank.)

but the Nineteenth century called it a masterpiece, and critics since then have agreed with this judgment.

Returning again to the picaresque, De Foe brought out, in December of the same year, 1722, a rather uneven novel, parts of which are remarkable while other parts are commonplace and without any interest. This is *The History and Remarkable Life of the truly Honorable Colonel Jacques.* The hero of the story is an orphan, brought up in the streets of London without any idea of good and evil. Falling into the hands of a group of older vagabonds and spurred on by hunger, he becomes, like the rest of them, a clever pickpocket. Perhaps the finest pages De Foe ever wrote are these describing the life of poor London street urchins. When Jack, aware of the danger in his remaining longer in London, flees into Scotland, De Foe, curiously, loses interest in him, though he goes on to show how his hero tries in vain to lead an honest life by joining the army. Soon the prospect of war on the continent causes him to desert and return to his native city. He falls in with an astute captain who carries him off by force to Virginia where he sells him as a slave. But Jack is intelligent and hard-working; he quickly wins his way into the good graces of his master and is made an overseer; his reform measures of discipline by which he wins the confidence and co-operation of his negro workers lead to his early release from bondage after which he sets up as an independent planter. He accumulates a small fortune, is taken with a longing for Europe, and comes back to the Low Countries, going from there down into Italy where he takes part in some military operations. The rest of the book is taken up with the details of the monotonous campaigns in which he took part and the disappointing marriages he contracted. Jack was not lucky in love; he married five times, but the first four wives were either fickle or given to drinking. His fifth wife was a good manager, but she died soon after their mar-

riage. Jack finally returns to Virginia after being mixed up in
the Jacobite insurrection of 1715. There among the workers on
his own plantation is his first wife, quite sorry now for her
past infidelities. Jack magnanimously forgives her and takes
her back. He becomes rather disturbed about the consequences
of his having supported the Pretender and asks for a royal
pardon; while he is waiting for this precious document, he
makes some profitable trips to the Antilles and to Mexico. The
pardon, after considerable trouble, reaches him so that he can
return to England with his wife, leaving the reader to infer
that they "lived happily ever after."

This novel enjoyed popular favor during the life of its
author; then it fell into disrepute among the Victorians, who
were shocked at the recital of Jack's matrimonial experiences.
Of late years critics have praised particularly the first part;
De Foe's realistic picture of the life of a young London pickpocket leaves Dickens's *Oliver Twist* far behind, though the
later book follows in regular sequence the literary precedent
established by the earlier one, for De Foe seems to have written
this book for its beginning incident; the rest of it is only pad-
ding to satisfy his editor's request for a long novel.

Encouraged by his repeated success in the picaresque, De Foe
set to work at once to match the biography of Moll Flanders,
the unfortunate prostitute, with the life of a great courtesan,
loved by princes and even kings. On March 14, 1724, a large
volume, more than 400 pages in length, appeared . . . *The
Fortunate Mistress.*

The heroine of this romance, the Lady Roxana, is the daughter of a French Huguenot who had taken refuge in England.
She is charming, pretty, and well-mannered; at the age of fifteen, she is married to a London brewer. He is a good but
lazy man and is given to gambling. At the end of a few years
he has become bankrupt; one fine morning he leaves without

a word of explanation to his wife and does not return. With no resources Roxana struggles against poverty as long as she can. She has to give up her children since she is unable to support them; she sends them, reluctantly, to some ungracious relatives. Left alone with her faithful servant, Amy, Roxana becomes utterly discouraged; but, as it happens, her landlord, a rich jeweler, has been smitten with her charms and comes to her aid. Out of gratitude for his help she becomes his mistress and follows him when he is called to Paris on business. But their happiness is cut short when the jeweler is assassinated by bandits. A disconsolate but wealthy widow, Roxana is not long without a companion, for her beauty has become celebrated. Her new lover is a prince who takes her with him to Italy. She is happy in being adored by a man whose nobility is exceeded only by his generosity. Later, the prince, filled with remorse at the death of his wife, gives up his mistress; but Roxana is scarcely annoyed. She has a large fortune now and goes to Rotterdam where she has a short intrigue with an honest Dutch merchant; but she refuses to consider matrimony because an ambitious idea has taken root in her mind; she has been the mistress of a prince, why not of a king? She goes to London, sets herself up in magnificent state, gives banquets and masked balls, and finally accomplishes her desire; Charles II, the "merry monarch," is taken with her beauty and, for three years, carries on with her a secret affair. Following that Roxana returns to the social world as the accepted mistress of a great lord and continues to live in this way for a few years longer, until, disgusted with it, she gives up vice and luxury for the sake of a simple life with a good Quakeress. She happens to meet again her old friend, the Dutch merchant; this time he makes himself more agreeable by buying a title of nobility. With this devoted husband, Roxana passes some peaceful, happy days.

But a serious complication arises. The oldest of the children that Roxana has abandoned after her first husband's desertion, has traced her mother and faces her with a demand for the truth. Roxana is wild with fear that her husband will learn through this circumstance of her past life. She has some dramatic escapes from her persistent daughter whom she finally eludes by getting her husband to take her to another city. But the daughter, personifying Divine Vengeance, always turns up in her path, and Roxana seems to be lost. Then suddenly the young girl disappears and with her the faithful servant, Amy, who was willing to commit a crime for her mistress's peace of mind. Roxana, her conscience lacerated with remorse, leaves for Holland where a luxurious home awaits her. But De Foe gives us to understand that the curses of heaven will fall upon this unnatural mother, plunging her into misfortune and leading her to ruin.

The novel is cut short at this point. The author planned, no doubt, to add to it, but he never found the time, and later writers have tried in vain to complete the task. *The Fortunate Mistress* must be considered an unfinished work, but, as it stands, it may be accounted a very impressive one. No brief survey can do justice to the dramatic intensity of certain scenes. It shows great progress in De Foe's art as a novelist; he is now more at ease in handling his characters, leads up to his events more smoothly, and has, in the character of his heroine, with her daring theories of free love, her coquetry, and her inordinate ambition, drawn a strangely vivid, almost modern woman; she is a character well worth studying. Unfortunately, the book, written little by little, lacks arrangement and is particularly marred by its many gross anachronisms; for instance, if Roxana was born in 1683, it is difficult to imagine her becoming the mistress of Charles II, who died in 1685. *The Fortunate Mistress* is really only a sketch beside *The For-*

The Famous ROXANA.

HEROINE OF "THE FORTUNATE MISTRESS"

tunes and Misfortunes of Moll Flanders; but it is a sketch which has many marks of genius, and it is easy to understand why it has been a favorite with the public before and since the Victorian period.

This was the last really creative piece of work that De Foe did. His last novel, *A New Voyage round the World,* published in November of the same year, 1724, is a weak exposition, in the guise of fiction, of the author's theories concerning business and colonization, ideas which he had many times voiced for the benefit of his masters, William of Orange and Harley. It is supposed to be the story of a London merchant who sets out on a long voyage around the world by way of Cape of Good Hope, the Indian Ocean and the Pacific Ocean, returning by South America. The voyage is crowded with events; there is a revolt of the crew, the discovery of gold and of pearls in the Islands of Oceania, a trek across the American continent from the Valdivia to the Argentine coast, crossing the Andes and the pampas. The expedition returned to England loaded with riches, but the incidents of their accumulation are monotonously related. One is constantly aware of the fatigue of the author, who has set out, at any price, to realize on paper what he has never been able to accomplish in his youth. De Foe has, obviously, come to the end of his career as a novelist. He has had his say and contents himself, in the succeeding years, with retouching, upon some editor's orders, the accounts of voyages sent in by sailors or officers, more used to handling grappling irons or swords than pens and inkstands. So it is that we find traces of De Foe's hand in the memoirs of Captain Roberts, who made an exciting voyage among the islands of Cape Verde, in those of Captain Carleton, who took part in the War of the Spanish Succession, and in those of Robert Drury, who lived fifteen years a captive on the island of Madagascar.

De Foe, between 1719 and 1724, that is between the sixtieth

and the seventieth years of his life, wrote all of his immortal works. True, during this time, he did not achieve any great variety of theme . . . he even gives us the same type of individual. Whether his hero is a man or a woman, he is invariably a Puritan business man of London. Those outside the social pale are concerned with illicit businesses; such are Singleton, Jack, Moll, and Roxana. The others like Robinson and the merchant of the *New Voyage,* are good middle class types, whom Providence, in his inscrutable way, has made into globe-trotters. How do De Foe's novels end? Not when wedding bells ring forth a joyous peal, but when the gold has piled up in a great heap in the strong-box . . . when a fortune rather than a wife, has been gained. That is the objective of De Foe's characters as it was of their creator. They are always what De Foe would have been if he had been placed in the same circumstances, whether tragic or fortunate. As a consequence, they are not vague phantoms or painted dummies because they are created in their author's "own image and likeness."

XII. THE HERMIT OF STOKE NEWINGTON

D^{E FOE} settled down to spend his last days at Stoke Newington. He had enlarged his house there on Church
street, flanking the main building with two flat-roofed wings
that were, if possible, more ugly than the original cube of red
brick. But that did not bother De Foe; he sought only comfort.
West of the house and a little to the rear were the stables,
an important part of the menage to the owner, for they represented once more the realization of his youthful dream of
possessing horses and carriages. Behind this extended the
kitchen gardens, carefully enclosed in a brick wall, a part of
which is still standing. Horticulture was quite a fad with De
Foe; one of his favorite pastimes was making unusual pruning
and grafting experiments. Behind his garden was a stretch of
uncultivated land that De Foe called his "pleasure grounds,"
and it was here that his horses grazed.

One of his chief worries was keeping his neighbors' animals
off his property. One evening he surprised a groom just turning his master's horse loose on the grounds of the De Foe property. De Foe was irate at the act but made sure of the intention
to offend before he went to the neighbor and demanded
reparation; the latter, also a quick-tempered man, met the
charge with a broadside of oaths, defending his groom, who
boldly denied De Foe's accusation. The affair threatened to
wear out the combatants, who were almost equally matched in
pugnacity; but mutual friends stepped in to arbitrate the
matter. It was a great to-do over nothing, but De Foe was so
much stirred over it that he interrupted one of his most serious

works, *The Great Law of Subordination,* to insert a detailed account of this petty quarrel.

De Foe was accepted as a very great personage in the village of Stoke Newington. At the parish meeting in April, 1721, the church being heavily in debt, Daniel De Foe and a Captain Whitby were named administrators; they were, no doubt, the two most prominent Non-Conformists in the community and were expected to give a generous sum of money rather than serve in the official capacity to which they had been appointed. The records show that De Foe did, indeed, pay ten pounds to the church in order to be excused from the responsibility assigned him.

But his purse and his personal support were both freely placed at the disposal of the Dissenters at this time. He was recognized for his charity which was dispensed intelligently. One testimony to his philanthropy is contained in a letter written in 1725 by a poor Quaker, Thomas Webb, who had just lost his wife. He wrote:

"And poor and distressed I, left alone, and no one to go and speak to, save only Mr Deffoe, who hath acted a noble and generous part towards me and my poor children. The Lord reward him and his, with the blessings of upper and nether springs, with the blessings of His basket and store."

But at the same time De Foe was leading a worldly enough life, too; his success as a writer of distinction had made him a man of fashion. Well-dressed and well-powdered, he went out frequently on horseback to call upon his friends. His conversation, always lively and interesting, made him a favorite with the ladies, and he prided himself upon his success with women of position. One can imagine, then, his embarrassment when, one day, upon entering a room full of ladies, he embraced them all, as was the custom, and discovered, to his chagrin, that he had included a waiting-woman, whose dress, as fine as her mistress's, had led him into error. He could hear the gossips. "Fie! Did you know Mr Daniel De Foe embraced a lady's maid!"

He took out his fury by writing a severe reprimand addressed to servants who so far forgot their place as to mimic their betters in matters of dress. De Foe was always conscious of class distinctions. He once wrote: "If I must have an intrigue . . . let it be with a woman that shall not shame me. I would never go into the kitchen when the parlour door was open."

The overbearing insolence of domestics seemed to him a sign of national decadence. He was quick enough to belittle them from a distance, but when he had any contact with them, he took care to win their good will. The following anecdote well illustrates the point:

He had gone to a nearby village to call upon a friend, but, not being acquainted with the latter's place of residence and noticing a group of servants gathered in conversation at the end of one of the streets, he approached them and asked for information about the leading citizens of the town. His inquiry released such a volley of abuse against their masters, whom they called misers, thieves, and libertines, that, De Foe says he gave the worthy servants six pence in which to drink his health and led his horse by a roundabout way back to the street on which his friend lived, for he was ashamed to let his informers see him enter the house of one whom they had labeled the "first scoundrel" in the lot.

Along with the gravity of old age, De Foe had also acquired a peevish, fretful outlook on life, declaring that all goodness and beauty had disappeared, that nothing could compare with the days of his own youth. He even railed at his profession as a journalist, accusing himself of *servus servorum*. He complained particularly of the lack of respect:

"The general Contempt put upon old Age by others is now such that it is hardly sufferable by human Nature."

De Foe, his still active mind lodged in a worn-out body, lamented the tastes of the new period, the lack of interest in poetry and the avid demands for accounts of rapes and assassinations. He even went so far, when the death of Marlborough called for a statement of the valuation of life, to express only his sense of its futility:

"What then is the Work of Life?" he questioned. "What the Business of great Men, that pass the Stage of the World in seeming Triumph? . . . Is it to grow great in the mouth of Fame, and take up many Pages in History? Alas, that is no more than making a Tale for the reading of posterity, till it turns into Fable or Romance. Is it to furnish Subject to the Poets, and live in their immortal Rhimes, as they call them? That is, in short, no more than to be hereafter turn'd into Ballad and Song, and be sung by old Women to quiet Children; or, at the corner of a Street, to gather Crowds in aid of the Pickpocket and the Whore."

Vanitas vanitatum was frequently his motto as he grew older, but his Puritan faith would not allow him to yield completely to attacks of the spleen, and he would return now and then to his favorite saying, *Te Deum laudamus*.

The family circle at Stoke Newington was somewhat contracted. The two sons, Daniel and Benjamin, had left long before. Daniel had made a wealthy marriage in March, 1720. Maria, the youngest daughter, had married a Mr. Langley, a "salter" or salt-maker. That left at home only Hannah, Henrietta, and Sophia, together with a young girl whom De Foe familiarly referred to in one of his letters as "Deb the hussy." Mrs. De Foe kept urging her husband to see to their daughters' dowries, but Daniel was much more interested in following his theory that money should be kept in circulation. Whatever he gained in his business deals, he put into other enterprises whose risk or novelty appealed to him. He worked out a fine scheme for putting the idle weavers to work in a sort of co-operative factory. Fortunately, he was led to give up this project before he lost any great sums of money in it. There are two curious records of his business activities: the one, a sample of his cash book for the month of January, 1725, which he included in his *The Compleat English Tradesman* and which is certainly authentic; the other, a notice which appeared in the papers for March 15, 1726, announcing the loss of a pocket book containing some drafts on a number of London business men and listing these drafts; De Foe's name occurs twice for a combined sum of sixty-eight pounds. This may be taken as an indication, though perhaps a weak one of a substantial capital that De Foe might have had invested here and there.

At last Mrs. De Foe's tenacity succeeded in securing for Hannah, who was then past thirty and not likely to marry, a sure income. De Foe's first step in her behalf was to put 800 pounds into stock of the South Sea company . . . so much for his tirades against stock-jobbing. He bought this when the price was low, and he was not wrong in counting on its coming up again. Next, through one of his friends, a minister in Little End, he bought the fine estate of Kingswood-Heath, which was made up of farm buildings, cultivated fields, open heaths, woods, and a fish-pond. This estate, which belonged to the city of Colchester, was to be paid for in two installments of 500 pounds each. Hannah, who became the legal possessor of Kingswood-Heath on September 1, 1723, acting upon the advice of her father, sold a part of her South Sea stock for a price that enabled her to pay the first half of the purchase price of her property. She rented it to Mary Newton of Ipswich on September 29, 1723, for the annual rent of 120 pounds. Finding herself short money when the second payment to the city of

Colchester came due, she mortgaged Kingswood-Heath to her renter for 200 pounds. But either De Foe came to regard this investment as not advantageous enough, or else he was again overtaken by his demon of speculation. . . . Whatever the reason for it, he entered into some rather questionable dealings with his old follower, Ward, the hosier of Coteshill, without saying anything about it to his daughter, although the deal involved building on Kingswood-Heath a factory for making bricks and pantiles. As soon as the plan developed, De Foe approached Hannah to get her to accept it, but Mrs. De Foe interfered and forbade his touching the property of his daughter. De Foe, after some violent quarrels, gave up his idea, although it cost him a trial with Ward. Finally on November 13, 1727, he lifted the mortgage on Kingswood-Heath so that Hannah found herself endowed with a small fortune whose value increased yearly and saved her from any worry about her future.

As for Henrietta and Sophia, young and pretty girls, there was no concern about their marrying. Their mother expressed no anxiety on their account, but she did reflect that, if her husband should die suddenly, she would be without any substantial resources; it would be almost impossible for her to collect the money that Daniel had scattered here and there in enterprises that were known only to himself. She finally succeeded in getting for herself a life-annuity, based upon the value of the house at Stoke Newington. Moreover, when her brother, Samuel Tuffley, died in 1725, he bequeathed to her more than a thousand pounds. With all this she felt quite assured as to her future and could look upon her husband's scatter-brained business deals without too much apprehension.

Now, although his hand had been forced a little, De Foe felt free from worry concerning the welfare of his wife and children when he was no more. He was thankful for this sense of serenity in the midst of encroaching suspicions and mistrust. The calm spirit of the little town was like a benediction to him. The joy he took in his work made the hours seem short to him. His neighbors saw him pass, a great old man, bent with age, irreproachable in bearing and manners. Deep in reflection, he walked slowly under the elms which were later to cast their venerable shade over the childish dreams of Edgar Allan Poe. He would go as far as the old church of Saint Mary, sit there a while under the trees, look with unseeing eyes at the little cemetery and retrace his measured steps to his home, there to set to work on some inspiration he had drawn from his solitary walk. On Sundays he went to the Dissenters' meeting house where whispers of sympathy and of admiration greeted his approach. He did not hesitate to go from time to time during the week to the village taverns . . . the Three Crowns, back of his house, or the Manor, across the way; for, if he could not drink wine, he did always enjoy his beer, the good national drink. He would rail against the importation of foreign intoxicants, such as gin, and also against tobacco.

At regular intervals he went up to London, either for business or for pleasure; he often called at Bateman's, "the first book-seller to the left in Paternoster-Row when turning up from Ave Maria lane," in order to see if he had some old manuscripts or rare books to sell at a reasonable price. De Foe's library had become his great pride, and he tried to add to it all the novelties of the book-sellers. His name and that of his oldest son, who had inherited his father's taste for collecting, may be found on the subscription list for a selection of letters made from the pages of *Spectator*.

Every time that De Foe went up to London by way of Tottenham, he passed by the Academy at Newington Green; the large building was deserted . . . the only inhabitants being the ghosts of dead memories. De Foe would think of those whom he had known there . . . all had departed from this world. He was the only one living of that generation that had dominated England under the reign of William of Orange. He felt himself as lonely as Robinson Crusoe on his desert island; but Daniel's island was peopled with wily and wicked men much more dangerous than the native cannibals who fled, terrified, at the first shot that Robinson fired.

A large cloud appeared to obscure the serenity of his mind. Mist, seemingly dispossessed for the time of all prudence, published in 1720 a series of articles violently critical of English politics which, he assured his public, had ruined the country in order to satisfy the Protestants of the Palatinate. At the urgent request of the House of Lords, Stanhope took measures on June 4, 1720, to have Mist arrested. The latter acknowledged all the incriminating articles as his except one; this one, he said, had appeared while he was on a trip to another city at which time his paper was under the sole supervision of De Foe. Somewhat embarrassed at this, De La Faye, who was conducting the investigation, let Mist go upon bail. For form's sake, then he had to call De Foe for a hearing. The latter also furnished bail to the amount of 200 pounds and brought with him two others who acted as his sureties for the sum of one hundred pounds; one of the two was Daniel's older son, for the two appear now to have reached a friendly understanding of each other.

Mist's influence began to slacken among Tory circles; a word to De Foe from the Ministry, and he set to work with little, underhand maneuvers to pull down the standing of *Mist's Journal*. He began, too, to contribute regularly to the moderate Tory weekly put out by Applebee,[1] Mist's rival. A number of journalists remarked upon De Foe's change of

---

[1] *The Original Weekly Journal or Applebee's Journal*. De Foe's first article in it was in the issue of June 25, 1720.

camp; but Mist appears to have suspected nothing and continued his old relations with him. The two of them came before Lord Chief-Justice Pratt on December the third. De Foe's case was immediately dropped, but Mist was declared guilty and was sentenced to imprisonment in King's Bench. On February 13, 1721, he was condemned to stand twice in the pillory, to pay a fine of fifty pounds, to remain three months in prison, and to furnish sureties for his good conduct for the succeeding seven years.

Three months later two seditious articles appeared in *Mist's Journal*. He was again arrested and again questioned. Mist this time refused to answer and was thrown into Newgate in June. Commenting on this news in *Applebee's Journal*, De Foe urged all other journalists to be more prudent and not to arouse the wrath of a Ministry that was just but active. He went often to Newgate to call upon Mist and to try to draw from him some secrets. He knew how to work his way into Mist's confidence and to be of real help to him; he aided him, for example, in preparing a book of two volumes in which he collected letters that had been published in his *Journal*. De Foe wrote a part of the preface and the dedication of the book which did not come out at once because Mist fell ill. This regrettable incident postponed Mist's hearing until December the ninth. He was at that time acquitted almost without discussion. More than likely De Foe had used his influence in Mist's behalf, for it gave him the upper hand in guiding the policy of an organ that could still be made influential for government purposes, and De Foe did not hesitate to keep Mist constantly reminded of the Administration's clemency towards him.

But the trouble of clearing Mist from his entanglements was not the only bother De Foe had to face during that year, 1721. His bastard son, Benjamin Norton, who had assumed the name of his natural father, had written for the *London Journal* some scandalous articles that caused his arrest on August the twelfth. The second day after they appeared, Benjamin was hurried off to Newgate. De Foe does not appear to have tried to do anything in the matter for his son, who was a living reminder of a past sin. He lay low, all the more because some of the papers at the time published malevolent rumors based, no doubt, on Norton's story. May it not be that De Foe, like Roxana, had been harassed by this son, who had tried to force recognition from his father? And may he not have been vexed at having this dangerous obstacle to his path, brushed aside in this fashion? His regrets for his conduct take off some of the taint from his memory. He did not put himself to much trouble, but he did try to get Norton some sympathy by writing, in *Applebee's Journal,* that this inexperienced young man was, doubtless, the tool of some one higher up, and he directed criticism against the judges who were too ready to pronounce as seditious a pamphlet that was quite inoffensive.

Mist, now, fell more and more under the influence of a Jacobite, named Gayland, who mistrusted De Foe and tried, as far as he could to prevent the latter's having a hand in editing the *Journal.* The Ministry was warned of this new state of affairs, and Mist was arrested once more . . . in May, 1724; De Foe again put the unlucky publisher under obligation to him by arranging for his freedom. Mist, out of gratitude, had to accept De Foe's guidance, and the *Journal* became, once more, the co-operative output of the two men. But in November, the storm, which had been delayed only because of De Foe's uncanny diplomacy, broke forth. Of course, Mist had learned before of De Foe's collaboration with Applebee on the latter's paper, but he had kept still about it because he did not want to lose a valuable helper; now he was to have actual proof that Daniel was also in the pay of the government. After a highly dramatic argument, Mist flung himself upon De Foe with uplifted sword. The latter easily defended himself, wounded his opponent, and disarmed him. That was the end of their relations. De Foe had succeeded in deceiving Mist for eight years without once giving himself away; only circumstances over which he had no control and which are unknown to-day brought his secret double-dealing to light.

From then on, Mist, every time he had an opportunity, insulted his old assistant. De Foe employed his usual tactics in his replies; he posed as a martyr, the victim of the blackest ingratitude from one whom he had served faithfully, whom he had saved from prison and hanging, whose life, when it was at his mercy, he had spared, even though the ungrateful wretch had drawn against him, his generous benefactor. The crowd, ignorant of the details, applauded such magnanimity. De Foe, meanwhile, was busy giving most of his time to the editing of *Applebee's Journal* and robbing it of practically all of its Tory characteristics. De Foe became less and less active for the Ministry because, for some time now, he had had no need for a life pension, and he gained more satisfaction from the peaceful triumphs of his literary work than from sensational achievements in the world of politics. He made a profitable business of writing his novels, moral treatises, and pretended memoirs for an immense reading public.

Like many other pamphleteers, he played up the famous Jack Sheppard, whose dramatic escapes from Newgate had made him the hero of the hour. But De Foe always improved upon the work of his fellow journalists. He manufactured some letters that Sheppard was supposed to have written, published some brilliant interviews he claimed the redoubtable criminal had granted him, and even wrote a wholly fictitious life of the bandit, a manuscript copy of which he had conveyed to the prisoner, and, on the day of his execution, commissioned him to present it before all the crowd to Daniel De Foe for publication. No modern publicity "stunt" has been more ingenious.

Jonathan Wild, police informer, receiver of stolen goods, himself a thief, next claimed De Foe's attention. Wild, when he was taken and condemned to death, had but little sympathy from the crowd that always takes sides against a traitor, even though he belongs to the great brotherhood of criminals. De Foe wrote most of his pamphlets on Wild by drawing from others that had already appeared; but his were better prepared, written more within the grasp of the general public, and were, therefore, given the preference by the readers, who were eager to purchase each fresh statement for the sake of some new sensational detail.

The question as to how De Foe could reconcile his picaresque works with his strict Puritan morality may perhaps best be answered in two ways: he may have considered it a good deed to visit the condemned in their prison cells, joining his pious exhortations with those of the prison chaplain; as far as writing the stories of these lost wretches and selling them . . . that, he, doubtless, considered a purely business proposition which did not affect either his soul or his conscience. He was in the position of a pious book-seller, who, to gain a living, had to sell obscene books. Therefore, he, De Foe, sold his manuscripts to his editors as a commodity that fitted the demand of the public; he must be content to please the taste of his readers, not to form them. Usually, too, he was working upon an order for some book-seller.

The most pretentious order for a book-seller that he filled during the last years of his life was a complete guide to England and Scotland which necessitated his making some trips through the country. He was rather glad for this excuse to settle some business deals that he had under way in other cities.

The educated public had begun for some time to interest itself in geography, both scenic and historic. Camden's great work, *Antiquities of Great Britain,* had been republished in 1720 with various additions that had been made by later scholars. In 1722 the book-seller Macky, had published *A Journey through England, in Familiar Letters, from a Gentleman here to his Friend abroad.* The editor, Strahan, engaged De Foe to match this collection, which had been received with great favor. As a consequence, there appeared between 1724 and 1726 the famous *Tour thru' Great Britain,* in three volumes; it was widely read throughout the whole of the Eighteenth century. In the form of rather poorly organized letters, De Foe presented a detailed guide to some interesting excursions in the country. He had consulted a great number of books before he had started to write; then, fearing that his work would be dull and lifeless, he put aside his authorities and, in his writing, relied upon them very little. He started out with a definite point of view which he maintained . . . that of an intelligent business man who, obliged for his own interests to travel about the country, made up his mind to gather as much information as possible on his way. He gives us freely a wealth of agricultural, industrial, and commercial details; he lists the products of each of the regions, studies the different breeds of horses, and gives minute information about the various city fairs. On the other hand, he was indifferent to the beauties of nature unless they interfered with his own progress, whereupon he storms against the lack of plan in the creation.

De Foe used the notes he had made during his travels in 1684 and 1688 for his descriptions of the parts of England that he had studied at that time. He filled these out with more recently collected data, and, to avoid monotony, interspersed the whole with amusing personal anecdotes. When he touches upon places with which he is not so familiar, such as Wales and the

Highlands of Scotland, he has to turn to his reference books and his style grows heavy and impersonal, loaded with statistics and digressions that are of interest only to the historian or the archeologist.

De Foe himself had not made the seventeen circuits nor the three general tours that, he says in his preface, he had made in order to be able to give his public a faithful and true account of the entire country; his age prevented his making long trips and his work made his presence in London often necessary. Yet he did make, between 1722 and 1725, a series of short trips into neighboring counties; he was called there for business reasons, and he thought it prudent to inform himself as much as possible of that part of the country with which his readers would be more or less familiar. In April, 1722, he went again into the Eastern counties, noting with particular pleasure how both the rural and the urban populations had increased. He even went as far as Harwich, a town that he had not seen since his childhood; he notes that the harbor is in a run-down condition. Ipswich, on the other hand, appeared to him improved, and he began to think seriously of settling there. He did not miss the fair at Bury, pausing to comment upon the pretty women gathered there, though he declared that morals had degenerated, and he lamented the lapse of virtue since the days of his own youth. "O tempora! O Mores!" The following year he went to Norfolk, attended the races at Newmarket, and made a prolonged stay at Cambridge; the business activities in the latter place interested him much more than did the old university, which had not changed. The objective of this short trip seems to have been Yarmouth where, in October, a fish fair was held. There, too, gathered a great number of swallows, ready for their flight to the South; De Foe came to the conclusion that Yarmouth must be the port of debarkation for all English swallows when it came time for them to seek a warmer clime. In preparation for the third volume, which was to deal with the central and northern parts of the country, he took in, during 1724 and 1725, most of the great city fairs, going as far as Liverpool, a city that had grown so rapidly he could not find a familiar spot in it.

The *Tour,* built up from his memories of his former travels, his readings, and his recent observations, was quite personal and as individual as De Foe's novels are; but, after his death, it was re-edited by a number of different writers, particularly by his celebrated successor in novel-writing, Samuel Richardson. These later retouchings have changed the whole spirit of the original text . . . it is no longer De Foe, speaking of his native land as he saw it, no more delightfully intimate stories and details . . . the revised "tourist" is too serious a man to indulge in frivolous asides; he is a methodical and fluent pedagogue, who has added the modern touch of a nature-lover, stopping before such fine sights as the view of the Mersey from Saint James's Walk at Liverpool, to utter some appreciative phrases that are almost lyrical. It is a sentimentalist who speaks; not De Foe. The *Tour* no longer appeals to the small tradesmen of London; it is meant to attract the Pamelas and the Grandisons of Richardson.

De Foe had still one more object up his sleeve with which to attract and interest his public. During the last ten years of his life he devoted a portion of his time to a study of the occult sciences, testing the generally accepted theories concerning supernatural creatures and supernatural events in the light of biblical references and his own experiences. He had already tried out his readers' interest in the marvellous before 1719 with *The Apparition of Mrs. Veal,* and his predictions in the style of Isaac Bickerstaff; he had found them eagerly responsive to such material. Now, relying upon some accurately acquired but rather inferior data, he presented the life of the deaf-mute,

Dickory Croncke, who recovered his powers of speech just before his death and presented his humble philosophy along with some extraordinary predictions.

Meanwhile, the Scotch soothsayer and wizard, Duncan Campbell, whom the *Spectator* had exploited, recognizing a rival in his field, set to work to win back his public with a series of pamphlets and books. He was socially minded and brought together a group of writers of note, among them, William Bond, the author of a ninth apocryphal volume of *Spectator;* Mrs. Haywood, the novelist; and De Foe. On May 2, 1720, Campbell was admitted to kiss the Queen's hand. He presented her Majesty at this time with a copy of his *Life and Adventures,* a book that had been written mostly by Bond, under Campbell's direction, and had been retouched by De Foe, who had revised certain passages to make them more dramatic and had added some chapters on magic and astronomy which were simply brief resumes of parts of Glanvil's and de Beaumont's works on these subjects.

The many pamphlets in praise of Campbell that appeared in the succeeding years are the work of Mrs. Haywood, but De Foe's hand is evident in the one entitled *Friendly Daemon.* To help Campbell sell an anti-epileptic powder he put out, De Foe made up the following story: Campbell, while he was suffering intensely one night, was visited by his guardian angel "clothed in a white surplice, and with a scroll in his hand, containing the following inscription, written in large capitals . . . 'Read, believe, and Practice.'" Under these words was written the formula for this infallible medicine; and, De Foe concluded, following this vision, Campbell made his humanitarian vow to offer, for a very moderate price, to those who had been declared incurable, this secret cure, which he guaranteed to be quick, certain, and economical.

This indicates that De Foe could, upon occasion, treat lightly the subject of spirits; and yet he was quite superstitious, although, as an educated man with good common sense, he resolutely rejected the vulgar beliefs in phantoms, sorceries, and a horned devil. His spiritism was of a higher order. The devil existed, he said, but in the form of a spirit made chiefly of air. He reigned supreme in the atmosphere far from the earth, where he commanded thousands of faithful servants ready, at his bidding, to scatter the seeds of evil in the minds of mankind. As for forebodings, De Foe had always believed firmly in them; back in the year 1711, he had written for his *Review* an article in which he had presented his views on occultism; the successive events of his life had only confirmed him in these earlier conclusions, which he now elaborated upon by adding more evidence from his own experience and his readings.

"I firmly believe," he had written, "and have had much convincing testimonies of it that I must be a confirmed Atheist if I did not, that there is a converse of spirits, I mean those unembodied, and those that are incased in flesh. From whence, else, come all those private notices, strong impulses, involuntary joy, sadness, and foreboding apprehensions, of and about things immediately attending us, and this in the most important affairs of our lives. That there are such things, I think I need not go about to prove; and I believe they are, next to the Scriptures, some of the best and most undeniable evidences of a future existence. . . . I have had, perhaps, a greater variety of changes, accidents and disasters in my short life, than any man, at least more than most men alive; yet I had never any considerable mischief or disaster attending me, but sleeping or waking I have had notice of it beforehand, and had I listened to these notices, I believe might have shunned the evil."

He assembled his ideas in an important treatise, *An Essay on the History and Reality of Apparitions*. The spirits, he declared are beings that stand between men and angels; they possess limited powers and inhabit vast regions of space; they are supposed to advise men when danger threatens them either by dreams or, as in the case of the demon of Socrates, by mysterious whispers in the ears. Such warnings, De Foe considered messages of God's will to men; he explained it in this fashion:

"There is such a drumming in the soul, that can beat an alarm when he pleases, and so loud as no other noise can drown it, no power silence it, no mirth allay it, no bribe corrupt it."

In this curious work De Foe, after explaining his theories concerning the spirits, goes on to ridicule the beliefs of the vulgar with regard to phantoms and dreams. He gives a good deal of space to recounting tales that he had picked up here and there through his various contacts and that he thought would help to make the book popular. He could tell the most horrifying stories of ghosts with a humorous touch at the close by way of relief to the tensed reader. He was quite skeptical about apparitions, questioning every relation of that kind for the hand of the practical joker or the interest somebody might have in frightening the teller. He wrote:

"But above all, I would beg my reading, merry friends, of the thoughtless kind, not to be so much frightened at the apparitions of their own brain; not to start and be frightened when they first make devils by daylight, and then see them in the dark; as they may be assured they will hardly ever see anything worse than themselves, so let them resolve not to be scared at shadows or amused with vapours, mistaking the Devil for an Ass, and tell us of the saucer eyes of a pink-eyed bear; not fancy they see a hearse with headless horses, and take the nightcart for a fiery chariot, which, one would think, they might distinguish by their noses, unless they will own that their fear gave them a worse smell than that of the Devil."

The same point of view dominates in that extraordinary

book, *The Political History of the Devil,* which had a greater run than De Foe himself could have dreamed of. It was Voltaire who first noted that the Italians sang the praises of the saints while the English were establishing the reputation of the devil. De Foe touched a popular chord with this *Political History,* which ran through four editions between 1726 and 1739; a French translation was made at Amsterdam in 1729, and a German translation at Frankfort in 1733; the book was put on the "Index" by Pope Leo XIII and his successors. George Eliot fell under its spell; she speaks of the fascination it had for Maggie Tulliver, the tragic heroine of the *Mill on the Floss.*

De Foe believed in an Evil Spirit that he, like all good Puritans, regarded fearfully. Indeed, he makes considerable effort, in his *Political History,* to avoid drawing down the vengeance of this malignant being by any untoward statement about it. He speaks of it with reserve and even with restraint unless he is speaking of the popular conception of the devil; then he indulges in frankest mockery, poking the finger of scorn at the pervading idea of this hybrid creature, with the trunk and head of a human being, the horns and the feet of a goat, added to the forked tail and wings of a bat.

"Really it were enough to fright the Devil himself," he said, "to meet himself in the dark, dressed up in the several figures which imagination has formed for him in the minds of men."

What De Foe fought against was the anthropomorphism of the crowd. He would raise the religious level of the masses, putting it on a more spiritual plane. As a good Dissenter, he was concerned in eliminating from Protestant England any touch of the dependence on material form which is the distinguishing mark of Catholicism. De Foe even ridiculed, whenever he could, the primitive conception of hell, as a great kitchen where the souls of the damned were in the continuous process of being roasted on a spit. There was a shade of scorn-

ful pity in his mockery of a painter's hell, "represented by a
great mouth with horrible teeth gaping like a cave on the side
of a mountain, with a stream of fire coming out of it, and
smaller devils going and coming continually in and out to
fetch and carry souls the Lord knows whither, and for the
Lord knows what."

As for those folk who claimed to have seen the Devil, De Foe
regarded them all as imposters. How could any one see a dis-
embodied spirit? And what of the men and women "possessed
of the devil," those doing evil for the sheer fun of it. He
distrusted them, especially the women; it seemed to him that
no woman was free from temptation; she was always ready to
lend a willing ear to the suggestions of the "great serpent."
De Foe's advice for insuring the salvation of one's soul was,
keep away from women, particularly the pretty ones; and he
recalled an old saying that beauty is a gift from the devil.

The Political History of the Devil took with its conservative
English public for two reasons: it was a bold subject, and the
author had treated it with a certain audacity, speaking lightly
of the most unutterable things. Then, too, the very fact that
a taboo was placed upon the name of the devil, created a
desire to read this book that sent little shivers of delicious fear
up and down the spine. De Foe himself reviews the reasons for
the success of the book in his preface to the second edition:

"The wise world has been pleased with it, the merry world
has been diverted with it, and the ignorant world has been
taught by it; and none but the malicious part of the world
has been offended at it."

At the present time the devil has dropped in rank to a mere
bugaboo, so that the originality of this work seems to modern
readers insignificant; its chief interest to-day lies in the author's
half serious, half comic criticism of *Paradise Lost;* De Foe took
much pains to show that Milton went quite awry in his treat-

ment of the devil and of hell in the first books of his great
epic poem, and he called upon the Bible and common sense to
help him in his refutation. The book that brought to a close
De Foe's series of occult studies bears the misleading title, *A
System of Magick;* it is really a serio-comic history of the
development of the black science through the ages and is made
up of information drawn from rare books on the subject and
padded with autobiographical details. De Foe did not believe in
sorcery, and he made it the object of the book to disprove any
foundation for such practices, a common one of which was the
"evil eye." The idea of the book was not new, but De Foe's
presentation of the material to make it appeal to the mass of
the people was a departure from previous treatments of the
matter. He took particular pains to strike at the still popular
belief that a great number of men had made a pact with the
devil, which, of course, they had signed with their own blood,
in order to gain some magic power.

But De Foe did not dare come out boldly against oracles
whose predictions and promises had the weight of classic antiquity behind them. And he had some trouble handling the
question of second sight, proofs of which he himself had had
from certain Scotchmen. He had to admit that there were a
number of things in the world that could not be explained
by his philosophy, the philosophy of sound common sense.
Too, there was biblical authority for the gift of second sight,
and, for De Foe, that was authority enough . . . superior, indeed, to what was otherwise apparent to the senses. He had no
ambition to destroy idols and construct new systems. His mind
worked within a quite limited field, stretching from the first
verse of *Genesis* to the twenty-first verse of the twenty-second
chapter of the *Apocalypse.* His horizon was bounded by the
wide open pages of the Holy Book; beyond that, for him, was
only God.

XIII. THE MYSTERIOUS LAST DAYS

D<small>E FOE</small>'s last days held three great joys: his library, his garden, and his youngest daughter, Sophia. She was the only member of the family that found favor in the eyes of the old man; the others maintained a kind of hostile neutrality towards him that, perhaps, aggravated the fits of bad temper and the chronic attacks of sulkiness which made him less and less sociable as time went on.

His enfeebled health kept him from going often to London; rare now were his business trips to the City or his summer walks in the Park. When he joined the London crowds these days, it was to deplore the lapse in public morals, the indifference towards the arts and sciences, and the lack of the wholesome pleasures of his own youth. He would rather remain comfortably at home in Stoke Newington, finding more satisfying companionship among his books. To relieve the monotony of village life and to distract his "three lovely daughters who were admired for their beauty, their education, and their prudent conduct," he would invite to his home young intellectuals who attracted him or wealthy landowners who took an interest in literature. Among these visitors was a young poet and naturalist, named Baker, who interested De Foe in a new language for deaf and dumb that he had just invented. De Foe asked Baker to come and teach them all his new sign language; and the latter, not loath to identify himself with this illustrious journalist, became towards the end of 1724 a frequent visitor at the Stoke Newington home. An important attraction of the place to him was the "three lovely daughters," who, if their father had to keep to his room with the gout, would receive the young man and entertain him either in the garden or at the tea table. It was not long until Baker discovered "the superior excellencies of Miss Sophia." But before declaring his love, on August 17, 1727, he made pretty sure by careful observation that the generous scale of living the family enjoyed must imply a fine dowry for the youngest daughter. Sophia was encouraging enough to justify him in approaching her father; De Foe believed that parents had a right to prohibit an undesirable marriage for their children, but that they had no right to force an unpleasant one upon them. He had found Baker agreeable enough and superior to the general run of young men in what De Foe called this degenerate age, but he said that, since Sophia was the one primarily concerned, she must be consulted first. It was quite apparent that Sophia had no feelings of repugnance towards Baker; quite the contrary, indeed; therefore, the engagement became an accepted fact. Baker was allowed to pursue his courtship on Wednesday, Thursday, and Friday evenings; the other days of the week he could express his devotion in letters addressed to his beloved; these were sometimes lyrical exclamations, sometimes rhetorical questions:

Ah! how can I bear this absence! Absence did I say! How lovers rave! No, you are always with me; your lovely image haunts me day and night, where'er I go, whatsoe'er I do. . . . My Sophy, ah, how I languish for thee! What soft sensations seize me! What fondness inexpressible possesses me whene'er I think of thee! This very moment my soul is stretching after thee with ardent longings. Methinks I fold thee in my eager arms, and bask and pant and wanton in thy smiles; and now I hold thee off and gaze upon thy charms with infinite delight, and now all ecstasy I snatch thee to me, and devour thy lips, strain thee with breathless rapture to my bosom, till feeble mortal faints, unable to endure bliss so excessive, and sinks with joys celestial.

Sophia, who inherited her father's cold and practical temperament, replied with far less lyrical enthusiasm, although she did try her hand at some well-turned phrases. At times she would make some pleasant rejoinder to her fiancé's poetic raptures. Once Baker, in eulogizing her beauty, wrote: "Thou hast dove's eyes." Sophia, good Puritan that she was, recognized the source of the expression from the *Canticle of Canticles* and replied:

"It cost you little pain to copy words. Is the subject grown so dull that you are fain to be beholding to so antiquated a lover?"

But if Baker was at "little pains to copy words," he took considerable pains to see to it that his father-in-law made no mistake about the dowry he had promised to give his youngest daughter upon her marriage. The prolonged and troublesome transactions between Baker and De Foe upon this question grew out of the set purposes of the two men; Baker was bent on getting as much as he could, and De Foe on giving as little as he could. Poor Sophia, worn out by the haggling finally declared that she would be neither bought nor sold. It seems that, when Baker asked for Sophia's hand, De Foe promised a certain sum of money to be given them on their wedding day. Later he retracted this promise on the excuse that his present circumstances would not allow him to part with so much ready money, and he offered, instead, to leave Sophia a much larger sum to be paid after his death, which, he declared, was not far off. He said that he would put this into writing, but Baker preferred a "bird in the hand to two in the bush," and held out for the sum promised at the time of the marriage contract.

Early in December De Foe had a particularly severe attack of
the gout which led Sophia to write her fiancé:

"I fear it is a messenger from that grand tyrant which will,
at last destroy the (to me) so-much-valued structure."

Her fears were unfounded; De Foe recovered quickly, and
the bickering between the two men was resumed. What was
most disturbing to Baker was that De Foe absolutely refused to
tell in what business he intended to invest the money that was
meant for Sophia. He was, doubtless, taken up again with some
unsound speculation, and he seemed to enjoy dragging out the
matter in the hope, no doubt, that Baker, kept waiting, would
marry Sophia without insisting on any sure guarantees from
his father-in-law. But Baker held out for what was promised
and became quite provoking in his language, giving up, even
in his letters to Sophia, the lyrical expressions of his passion
for the prosaic discussion of their business interests. This displeased the girl; she took her father's part and when Baker
called as usual declared that she was ill and could see nobody.
On January 9, 1728, De Foe wrote Baker, reproaching him with
being too demanding, reminding him that there were other
daughters in the De Foe household to be provided for besides
Sophia. Baker relented a little and agreed to accept the deferred
payment if the house at Stoke Newington were put up as
security. De Foe accepted these terms. Then Baker grew suspicious and insisted upon seeing the deed for the house, forcing
the grumbling master to take further measures to protect his
property rights. As a consequence of all these demands and
high-handed measures, a decided coldness sprang up between
De Foe and his future son-in-law, though the latter never allowed the father's trickery to affect his devotion for the daughter. A new obstacle arose. . . . Baker's mother refused to give
her consent to the marriage. The young man's love only in-

creased in the face of opposition, and he wrote his beloved, "I hope, my dearest, neither you nor I are like our parents."

During the last of August De Foe made up his mind to make his final offer. He said he would pay a portion of the dowry he had promised his daughter and give his son-in-law four per cent interest on the rest of it until it was all paid. In case of his death, the oldest daughter, Hannah, would assume the payment from her income on the property in Essex. This offer carried with it the ultimatum to take it or leave it; De Foe was through. Baker accepted it on condition that the interest was raised from four to five per cent. De Foe would not yield the point. Then Baker asked that the property in Essex be put up as security for the payment of the rest of the dowry. And again De Foe refused, saying that he had no right to touch Hannah's belongings. Baker could only accept, and the relations between the two men were re-established on a friendly basis, De Foe even writing the initial article for a new journal, *The Universal Spectator,* that his future son-in-law launched in October.

But it amounted only to a short lull in hostilities, for, as soon as De Foe perceived that Baker was more devoted than ever to Sophia, he made another attempt to get out of his obligations to the lovers. Baker protested in the strongest terms he could think of, and the quarrel grew bitter, reaching a climax in January, 1729. Baker had come to hate his father-in-law, and he wrote bluntly to his fiancée:

"You are my good genius, and your father is my evil one. He, like a curst infernal, continually torments, betrays, and overturns my quiet; you, like a divinity, allay the storm he raises and hush my soul to peace. . . . What your father now designs to do with us I won't pretend to guess, for his purposes are always dark and hideous. . . . I am persuaded he is all deceit and baseness."

On February the first Baker asked Sophia to take poison

with him so that they might die in each other's arms. Sophia
was not enthusiastic over this suggestion, but she was alarmed
at the quarrels that were menacing her happiness, and she
tried in vain to bring the two men to terms. Finally her health
broke down, and she took to her bed. Her father and her lover,
both of whom adored her, were so alarmed at her condition
that they were at once reconciled and readily agreed to whatever she asked. An early wedding was planned; on April the
fifth, De Foe gave his daughter a note for 500 pounds, payable
at his death; he made other arrangements with Baker that
appear to have been quite satisfactory. On April the thirtieth
Sophia De Foe became Mrs. Baker.

But disputes about the money began again in June, and this
time De Foe had an antagonist where before he had had an
ally; Sophia was now on her husband's side against him. The
little quarrels between father and daughter always ended in
touching reconciliations, after which all would agree upon
some new and provisional arrangement. In spite of everything,
these disputes on the question of Sophia's dowry lasted up to
the time of De Foe's death. It was not so much that he was
avaricious as that he sincerely wished the best for his favorite
daughter. His taste for speculation had become again a passion
with him just as the game is to gamblers. His constant need
of more money with which to enter into some eccentric enterprise explains his perverse conduct towards Baker. To get hold
of this money he deemed so necessary, he worked without ceasing up to the last day of his life.

The literary productions of his old age were many and
varied; they consisted mostly of treatises on business, science,
or morals. He came gradually to lose his hold as a journalist;
Mist told around that he was in government pay, and Applebee
got angry with him for placing some of his biographies of
criminals with rival publishers. It reached the place where

De Foe, not as versatile as he used to be in adapting himself to
the tastes of the hour, suffered the mortification of having his
manuscript of *The Protestant Monastery* refused, in November,
1726, by all the book-sellers in the City; he had to bring out
this book at his own expense, as though he were a tyro. Except
for a few comments on the Spanish war, he gave but little space
in his writings to the events of the day; immured in his hermi-
tage at Stoke Newington, he had little opportunity to be informed of the inner workings of state politics and must content himself with the trade aspects as he could judge them
from the seclusion of his study. He did, however, allow himself to put in a word on the controversy aroused by the discovery of the savage child, Peter, who had lived like an animal in the forests of Hanover; he made the incident an example in proof of the excellence of Baker's method for teaching the deaf and dumb, at the same time jeering at Swift whom
he had never forgiven for past insults. Some connection that he
must have established the last months of his life with the
masonic lodge of the Three Crowns at Stoke Newington led
to his writing a pamphlet, which came out November 13, 1730,
and was directed against that traitorous and perjured free-
mason, Prichard.

De Foe grew more and more convinced that the world was
going to the dogs; he resolved to pose as a reformer, crusading
against the prevailing immorality. Fearing that the use of his
own name, tainted as it was with the gossip of dishonesty and
double-dealing would be a handicap, he chose to present his
pious and worthy ideas under the pseudonym of Andrew
Moreton. Steadfast in his Puritanism, he continued to urge the
strict observance of the Sabbath and the suppression of all
theatrical performances. The unprecedented success of *The
Beggar's Opera* infuriated him; he predicted that it would cost
London a frightful disaster of some kind and called down the

wrath of heaven upon Gay with whom also he had an old score to settle.

All of these moral issues have, with De Foe, a practical side. And they were, for the most part, restatements of ideas that he had advanced many times in the course of his long writing career. In the place of gin, he praised the national product, beer; he would substitute for the Universities of Oxford and Cambridge, where the students, far from parental watchfulness, could indulge in all sorts of loose living, a University of London; music was to him but a very good occupation for leisure, a distraction from unwholesome thinking. He presented a bold design to make London the commercial, intellectual, and artistic center of the civilized world. But the particular project that he developed at length was a plan for replacing the night watchmen of London, who were mostly timid and ineffective old men, with some stalwart young fellows who could be paid out of a special fund, created by a tax on property owners and a special tax on bachelors. De Foe's particular grievance with the policing of London leads one to suspect that he himself must have been the victim of a robbery or a night attack. But then, he was always ready to start a campaign directed against some oppression of the people, and the condition of the streets of the City, infested with apaches, prostitutes, thieving and lazy bootblacks, seemed to him a cause worthy of some effort to correct. He had to bring in his favorite hobby, the servant problem. Then, from the depths of a pessimistic depression, he brought forth his idea of a "Protestant monastery," a kind of refuge in which old men could end their days in peace, far from the evils and the drawbacks of life around them. Here again is a recurrence of the desert island motif. . . . At the very end of his life he searches for a calm and solitary place where the turmoil and confusion of his own hectic days could not penetrate.

De Foe was to have one more triumph. With the publication of a small pamphlet in which he outlined his ingenious plan for preventing the escape of street robbers, he won a royal distinction; as one of the leading journals of the day put it:

"On Sunday last (October the sixth) Andrew Moreton Esq. presented to their Majesties at Windsor his Scheme for preventing Street Robberies."

But this distinction won him also the enmity of his jealous rivals and, at the same time, revealed the identity of Andrew Moreton, Esq.

It is particularly for the great educational tracts De Foe wrote during the last years of his life that he is recognized as a moralist: *A New Family Instructor* was published in 1727, repeating many of his formerly expressed ideas, but showing a more experienced hand at work. In the same year appeared a pretentious book that, according to De Foe, would mark the close of his literary work. It came out first under the title, *Conjugal Lewdness: or, Matrimonial Whoredom,* a title that certainly gave impetus to the sale of the book; but it aroused considerable criticism, and the second edition bore the modified head, *Use and Abuse of the Marriage Bed.* But the book does not come up to its alluring title; De Foe said that he wrote it following a terrible confession made to him by one of his friends. It does relate some graphic incidents whose off-color slant is concealed in all the many veils that decency demands; but it seems that many of these scandalous stories refer to contemporaries, rather thinly veiled under initials which do, however, make it impossible to identify them to-day. It may be that the vengeance of some of these individuals so scurrilously treated explains the mysterious circumstances connected with the last days of De Foe.

Daniel left unfinished two long educational tracts: *Of Royall Education,* started in 1728; and a more important one, *The*

Compleat English Gentleman, started in the same year and cut short two years later by the author's flight from his home. He published it, as far as it went, using Baker as agent. The manuscript of this work is interesting in that it reveals some of De Foe's methods of writing. His process of revision instead of simplifying his material, appears to amplify it, as he added at intervals marginal notes and interlinings made up of incidental matter suggested by the original text. It is more or less a display of unnecessary erudition which makes the reading of *The Compleat English Gentleman* a somewhat indigestible experience. Yet the sprightly dialogues and the short anecdotes do relieve the monotony of the lengthy dissertations.

Upon giving up journalism, De Foe began to fancy himself somewhat of a scholar. Like his successors, the philosophers of the Eighteenth century, he wanted to feel that he was informed on every known subject. *His Essay on Literature* (1726), is really a short history of the development of writing. In the same year he brought out *A General History of the Principal Discoveries and Improvements in Useful Arts,* which cost him a good deal of research and filled him with pride; but the work has fallen into oblivion, for it did not come up to its pretentious title.

Erudition with De Foe meant always a study of the practical side of trade. Tradesman by rights, by taste, and by temperament . . . whether he was acting as a pamphleteer, journalist, novelist, or scholar, De Foe was always a tradesman. He was recognized as an authority on economics and could afford to ignore the rebuffs of a young author named Gee, who, in opposition to the old man's works, wrote accurate but dry books. De Foe's talkativeness, expanding into personal anecdotes, amusing digressions, and paradoxical maxims, was the very essence of his genius. His *Compleat English Tradesman* in which he good-humoredly told of his mistakes in order to save others from the same pitfalls, reads like a novel. His scrupulosity was based upon the old saying, "The end justifies the means." Success, interpreted as material gain, was the keynote of his philosophy and, indeed, of his morality. The "compleat tradesman" that De Foe draws for us is just a better De Foe, a lucky De Foe, a clever and prudent De Foe . . . in short, a De Foe who succeeded. Here, as in his novels, he puts himself into the scene and realizes upon paper what he had been able only to visualize in his dreams.

His *Plan of the English Commerce* (1728), judged worthy of a reprinting in 1859, summarizes in 400 pages all that he knew on economics. His last works on this subject are mostly statistics that are of interest only to the historian of the Eighteenth century. But none of these books brings in anything new; Daniel had been for some years only repeating himself. That great voice that had resounded throughout all England for nearly a half-century now, had grown weak and was soon to be silent.

His attacks of illness came upon him more and more frequently. His sufferings had not apparently shackled his mental activities, but the repeated blows had taken toll in energy and moral resistence. Daniel had grown restless and preoccupied; his imagination ran amuck with unreasonable fears. In June, 1729, the trial of Mist's collaborators threw him into such a panic of fear that he fell ill and was not fully recovered until September.

Abruptly, in the summer of 1730, some unforeseen catastrophe made him a fugitive from a mysterious enemy. A letter to Baker, written August the twelfth, gives a few details, but they are stated in such a garbled fashion that they have called forth much flow of ink and many strange theories. But if we suppress from the text the many elements introduced by De Foe to dramatize simple facts, we shall be able to come at the truth and understand the tragedy which ended the days of the great writer.

Early in the year, while he was still comfortably installed at Stoke Newington, content with his quiet pleasures, he had received a blow of some kind from a "wicked, perjur'd and contemptible enemy." Who was this enemy? All that is known of De Foe's last years, of his mania for speculation, and of his usual mysterious dealings leads one to conclude that it must have been one of his creditors, one of those who had imprudently given his capital into De Foe's hands for some investment; when he had come for a reckoning of his money, De Foe had, no doubt, put him off; by the time the matter reached the point that the irate creditor sent his ultimatum, demanding an immediate repayment of his money or he would start judicial proceedings, De Foe, incapable of meeting the obligation and unable to face a prison sentence at his age, had decided to flee, as he had done in 1692.

He legally appointed his oldest son to act as his deputy . . . to look after his property and to see to the needs of the family. He fled from Stoke Newington and sought to hide himself in the maze of streets near Newgate; but this was not the secure asylum for insolvent debtors it had once been. De Foe's persistent creditors must have found him out, or he must have imagined that they did; anyway, in August he burrowed deep into a hiding place about two miles from Greenwich. He wrote regularly to his family but forbade their coming to see him as he feared the house at Stoke Newington was watched and that any one leaving it would be followed. He was alone, ill, alarmed at every noise, making too much of every little happening. As a consequence, when his wife and daughters complained that the oldest son was not looking after them as he had been told to do, De Foe allowed his imagination to build up a frightful picture . . . he saw his poor wife and daughters dying of starvation, begging as alms what was theirs by right, turned away from the door of an ungrateful son.

This is the dramatic interpretation that De Foe gave Baker in his letter of August the twelfth. The whole thing is so exaggerated that critics have been suspicious of it and have evolved two hypotheses: either De Foe was the victim of senile hallucinations, or he had invented the story so that he might be let off paying the rest of Sophia's dowry. But our hypothesis is that De Foe thought he was dealing with real facts which he exaggerated by auto-suggestion. He could not escape his literary genius, even in his intimate correspondence, and his habit, for so many years, of sending "leaders," in the form of letters to journals had habituated him to an elaborate, not to say pompous, style of letter-writing. This letter to Baker carried a postscript on business matters that gives evidence of the writer's lucidity. Furthermore, the whole is as studied and as designedly pathetic as some of his letters to Harley and Godolphin were. Such a metaphor as, "May you sail your dangerous voyage of life with a forcing wind and make the port of heaven without a storm," shows that he did not write without careful reflection.

De Foe's fears lessened in time, and, by early in 1731, he felt safe in taking a permanent abode in London, though he deemed it wise to remain away from Stoke Newington. He took lodgings in the poor and populous district in which he was born . . . Saint-Giles-in-Cripplegate, where a jumble of narrow, crooked streets, blind alleys, and inner courts offered a better place of concealment than a great African desert or a lonely island at the mouth of the Orinoco. A convenient place presented itself in Ropemaker's Alley with a Mrs. Brooks; since he owned three houses quite near, in White Cross Alley, members of his family could come, ostensibly to look after this property, really to see him without arousing the suspicions of those who might be spying on their goings and comings. It seems very unlikely, though, that such watchfulness, if it ever did exist, would have been maintained over such a period of time.

It was here, far from the home that he dared not enter, a few steps from the house in which he was born, that Daniel De Foe slipped quietly away, the evening of April 26, 1731. The parish register states that he died of "lethargy." This would seem to indicate that his was not a soul, tormented with the agony of going, for he did not know that he had reached the end. He simply went to sleep and did not waken. In the language of the great Puritan writer, John Bunyan, he did not cross the Lake of Discouragement nor the Valley of the Shadow of Death. He did not see the Castle of Doubt nor the Giant Despair. He crossed without any trouble the deep river which has neither ford nor bridge. He found himself before the Golden Gate of the Celestial City, near the country flowing with milk and honey, and he listened to the Choir of the Shining Ones, chanting the praises of the All Powerful One.

His remains are interred in the Dissenters' cemetery at Bunhill. The ignorant grave-digger, misunderstanding the name of the great writer, of whom he had, perhaps, never heard a word, wrote him down in his book as "Mr. Dubow." So much for the glory of immortal genius. But De Foe would have been proud of seeing on the register at St. Giles his name, followed by the title that would have pleased him most . . . "Daniel de Foe, gentleman."

De Foe did not leave a will, as he had legally disposed of all his property while he was yet alive. His library contained quite a number of books, for his day, all "in good condition, mostly well bound, gilt, and lettered." They were sold at auction, beginning November the fifteenth, by "Olive Payne, at the Bible in Round Court, in the Strand." Mrs. De Foe continued to live with her daughters at Stoke Newington until her death on December 19, 1732; she was buried at Bunhill-Fields in the same grave with her husband.

These successive deaths in the family threw the De Foes into such confusion that they, apparently, neglected to pay the landlady of the place where Daniel died. She, lacking what was due her, asked, in September, 1733, for legal authority to sell the belongings of the deceased De Foe in order to reimburse herself for what was coming to her; none of the surviving members of the family offered any opposition to this action, leaving one to conclude that they did not consider these belongings of any particular value.

As far as distinction goes, the author of *Robinson Crusoe* was the first and last of his family. His two sons led peaceful lives as honest and contented tradesmen; the elder, Daniel, was established at Hackney where, in 1736, he solicited the post of secretary to the Million Bank. He was one of nine candidates and received one out of the twenty votes cast. A year after this he lost his wife, but the affection he had for a young cousin with whom he corresponded seems to indicate that he did not grieve too much. Benjamin remained for a long time at Norwich; tradition has it that he emigrated to America, and a descendant of his has recently turned up in Australia. As for De Foe's natural son, Benjamin Norton, he continued his harrowing occupation of writing for wages, endorsing for pay the misdeeds of his patrons, living in constant fear of prison. In 1739 he sent to the Duke of Newcastle a series of heart-rending letters, begging for financial aid by which he might bring up the children that remained to him; he said that he had just come from burying his wife and fourteen of his offspring. One of his descendants, called John Joseph, became a bandit and was executed at Tyburn, January 2, 1771.

Hannah De Foe remained unmarried and died, in 1759, at

quite an advanced age. She was buried at Wimborne, her mother's native county, Dorset. Henrietta married a John Burton, excise inspector at Wimborne, by whom she had one son. She died in 1760 and was buried in the same grave with her sister. There is no information to be found concerning Maria Langley, but there are many clues to help us follow the long and happy life of Sophia and her husband; the latter became famous as a naturalist and was made a member of the Royal Society; their two sons achieved some small literary fame and founded a long line of Anglican ministers whose simple piety does honor to the memory of their great ancestor.

The grandson of Daniel De Foe, Junior, great-grandson of the author of *Robinson Crusoe,* was named James De Foe; he followed carpentry as a trade and lived in poverty until the middle of the Nineteenth century, when the biographer, John Forster, moved at his distress, interested himself in the case and made an appeal for his relief. Charles Dickens, the great novelist, De Foe's spiritual son, was the first to respond; he took the initiative in getting up a subscription, the result of which placed the old carpenter in comfortable circumstances to the end of his days. He left a son and four daughters; the *Times,* in 1861, called public attention to the poverty of this little family, and Queen Victoria sent from her own purse a generous donation to them which was renewed yearly and became, in May, 1877, an annual pension of seventy-five pounds. The boy became a sailor and ploughed the seas that his great ancestor had only dreamed of sailing over. He died quite young in 1896 at San Francisco, and his sisters never married; the last survivor among them was Mary-Ann, who died at Hull in May, 1902, the last of the male line in England. There remained only the great-grandson of Sophia, who bore the name De Foe-Baker.

*   *   *   *   *   *   *

In the fields of Bunhill, the burial grounds for London Dissenters, Daniel De Foe sleeps the sleep of the just, awaiting the hour of the resurrection. Near him rest the parents of Cromwell and John Bunyan, the great Puritan, at last arrived at his celestial harbor. They have been joined since by the mystic, William Blake, and Thomas Stathard, the first artist really to understand and successfully to illustrate *Robinson Crusoe*. All of these worthy people have in common their worship of the Lord according to their own interpretation of Holy Scriptures.

De Foe's grave was first marked by one of those white stones that, in the clear moonlight of an evening, give to English cemeteries the appearance of being peopled with an army of phantoms, waiting, in good order, the review which must pass the Sovereign Judge. In 1858, De Foe's headstone was cracked by a bolt of lightning, and the grass that grew up over it soon seemed to obliterate the spot where this great creator of the modern novel lay buried.

The editor of the *Christian World* started the idea of erecting a national monument to De Foe by soliciting from the children of the realm their small subscriptions. Six pences that meant, perhaps, a sweet foregone, began to come in and pile up; some grown-ups who were still young at heart added bigger sums, and at last all was ready to place a fine monument at the head of De Foe's grave. But, in excavating the earth for the base of the stone, the coffin was jarred and fell open. The crowd that gathered rushed forward to carry away some souvenir of the remains of this great man; even the bones of the skeleton [1] were fought over. How the stern Puritan would have shuddered at this act, savoring of the practice of pious Catholics with regard to the relics of the saints.

On September 16, 1870, in the presence of descendants of

[1] The skeleton and the lower jaw were measured; the length of the latter confirms the bull-dog effect that is apparent in most of the photographs of De Foe.

De Foe, the granite obelisk that had been erected on his grave was dedicated. The tall shaft against the lowering gray London sky gave way to a vision of a lonely desert island encircled by a blazing tropical sea. . . .

APPENDIX I

LIST OF DANIEL DE FOE'S WORKS.

No other classical author has tried the patience and sagacity of the bibliographer so much as has De Foe. Most of the time he wrote under the cover of anonymity, and discretion prompted him to conceal, wherever possible, his participation in the political literature of his time.

The first important list of De Foe's works was made by Chalmers in 1786; it contained 174 titles. Wilson, in his *Life of De Foe* which appeared in 1830, increased this number to 210. In 1840 the younger Hazlitt offered a revised list which contained 183 "certain" titles and 52 "doubtful." In the various editions of the *Manual of Bibliography*, Lowndes and his successors contented themselves with compilations of these lists, with the errors they contained.

In his biography of De Foe (1869), Lee made a great effort to revise the lists of his predecessors; by dint of patient research, he attributed to De Foe 254 separate works. Finally, quite recently, (1912) Mr. W. P. Trent, after years of methodical and persistent labor, has given a list which contains 370 titles, in the new volume of the *Cambridge History of English Literature*.

We have used this list as a foundation, but we have firmly set aside a considerable number of occasional writings, which, although their publication was announced in the *Review,* give no evidence of De Foe's hand. On the other hand, we have added several new works, the result of our own research.

The criteria which have guided us in attributing to De Foe works not signed by him are three in number:

1. Evidence given by De Foe himself in his correspondence.
2. The accusations of his contemporaries, especially of his opponents, who were rendered perspicacious by hate or jealousy.
3. Internal evidence in the text, which is generally revealing because De Foe has a very individual style and method of writing.

Nevertheless, since it must be admitted that another author of the same period might have borrowed De Foe's style to the point where he wrote exactly like him, we have prefixed an asterisk to the titles of those works for which we have nothing but the third criterion; we are convinced that these works are indeed De Foe's, but we cannot give indubitable proof.

We have arranged the list chronologically. One glance over the following pages gives evidence of De Foe's prodigious activity. We consider this list an indispensable complement to our biography, for we did not wish to burden the study of the man with an analysis of fugitive pieces. We have tried to make De Foe himself relive, in order that we might better understand his novels. It was only by placing this long catalogue of occasional writings at the end that we have been able to rescue our author from the flood of unimportant and uninteresting pamphlets in which for more than a century criticism has immersed him.

1683

Pamphlet against the Turks. Cf. De Foe, *Appeal to Honour and Justice* (Hazlitt ed.) p. 14-15.

1687

Pamphlet against Addresses to King James Cf. *Review*, VIII, 442.

1691

A New Discovery of an Old Intreague. A Satyr levell'd at Treachery and Ambition: calculated to the Nativity of the Rapparee Plott, and the Modesty of the Jacobite Clergy. Designed by Way of Conviction to the 117 Petitioners, and for the Benefit of those that study the City Mathematics. Printed in the year 1691. (Poem of about 700 lines, reprinted by De Foe in the second volume of his works in 1705.)

Ode to the Athenian Society, by D. F. (poem of 71 lines published for the first time by Gildon in his *History of the Athenian Society,* 1691. Afterwards reprinted in the successive editions of *The Athenian Oracle,* by Dunton).

1697

The Character of the late Dr. Samuel Annesley, by way of Elegy (poem of 261 lines reprinted by De Foe in the first volume of his works in 1703).

Some Reflections on a Pamphlet [by Trenchard, or Moyle] lately published, entitled: *"An Argument shewing that a Standing Army is Inconsistent with a Free Government, and absolutely Destructive to the Constitution of the English Monarchy".* London, Printed for E. Whitlock [in-4º, pp. 28] (a second edition appeared the same year).

1698

An Enquiry into the Occasional Conformity of Dissenters in Cases of Preferment. With a Preface to the Lord Mayor. Occasioned by his Carrying the Sword to a Conventicle [in-4°, pp. 28]. (This pamphlet appeared Jan. 25. De Foe reprinted it in November 1700, with a new preface dedicated to Mr. How. It is this changed edition which is in the first volume of his works.)

An Essay upon Projects. London. Printed by R. R. for Tho. Cockerill at the Corner of Warwick Lane [in-8°, pp. 14 and 336]. (The first edition appeared March 29. To sell remaining copies of the book, the publisher offered it in May 1702 under a different title.)

The Poor Man's Plea, in Relation to all the Proclamations, Declarations, Acts of Parliament, etc., which have been or shall be made or published for a Reformation of Manners, and suppressing Immorality in the Nation [in-4°, pp. 31, 1st ed., March 31, 2nd ed., May 24, 1698; 3rd ed., March 26, 1700] (reprinted by De Foe in the first volume of his works).

An Argument shewing that a Standing Army, with Consent of Parliament is not Inconsistent with a Free Government. London. E. Whitlock [in-4°, pp. 26] (reprinted by De Foe in the first volume of his works).

A Brief Reply to the History of Standing Armies in England [by Trenchard] with some account of the Authors. London [in-4°, pp. 4 and 25].

*Lex Talionis: or an Enquiry into the most proper ways to prevent the persecution of the Protestants in France. London [in-4°, pp. 27] (probably edited only in part by De Foe).

1700

The Pacificator, a Poem. London. Sold by J. Nutt near Stationers' Hall [folio, title and pp. 14] (satirical poem of about 450 lines, which appeared Feb. 20 and was reprinted by De Foe in the second volume of his works).

The Two Great Questions Consider'd. I. What the French King will do, with respect to the Spanish Monarchy. II. What Measures the English ought to take. London [in-4°, pp. 28] (appeared Nov. 15 and was reprinted by De Foe in the first volume of his works).

The Two Great Questions further Consider'd. With some Reply to the Remarks. London [in-4°, pp. 28] (appeared Dec. 2 and was reprinted in the first volume of his works).

1701

The Six Distinguishing Characters of a Parliament Man; address'd to the good People of England. London [in-4°, pp. 22] (this political pamphlet appeared Jan. 4 and was reprinted in the first volume of his works).

The Danger of the Protestant Religion Consider'd, from the Present Prospect of a Religious War in Europe [in-4°, pp. 32] (date of publication: Jan. 9. Reprinted in the first volume of his works).

The True-born Englishman. A Satyr [in-4°, pp. 71]. First edition in Jan. The ninth edition which appeared the same year has an explanatory preface. Constantly reprinted since; editions de luxe, in Elzevirian type, in March

1716, October 1719 ("with a new Preface adapted to the Present Reign"), and November 1721 (this poem is in the first volume of De Foe's works).

*Considerations upon Corrupt Elections of Members to serve in Parliament. London [in-4°, pp. 24] (Jan. 1701).

The Freeholders Plea against Stock-Jobbing Elections of Parliament-Men. London [in-4°, pp. 27] (1st ed., Jan. 23; 2nd ed., Feb. 4. In the first volume).

A Letter to Mr. How by Way of Reply to his Observations on the Preface to the Enquiry into the Occasional Conformity of Dissenters in Case of Preferment. By the Author of the Preface and the Enquiry. Printed 1701. By A. Baldwin in Warwick Lane (published Jan. 24; reprinted in the 1st volume of the works).

The Villainy of Stock-Jobbers detected, and the Causes of the late Run upon the Bank and Bankers Discovered and Considered. London [in-4°, pp. 26; 1st ed., Feb. 11; 2nd ed., Feb. 17] (reprinted in the first volume).

The Succession to the Crown of England Considered. London [in-4°, pp. 38] (political pamphlet in favor of the Duke of Monmouth's family).

Legion's Memorial to the House of Commons [in-4°, pp. 2; given May 14].

The History of the Kentish Petition. London [in-4°, pp. 25; published in August].

The Present State of Jacobitism Considered in two Queries. I. What Measures the French King will take with respect to the Person and Title of the P. P. of Wales? II. What the Jacobites in England ought to do on the same Account. London, A. Baldwin [in-4°, pp. 22].

Reasons against a War with France; or an Argument shewing that the French King's Owning the Prince of Wales as King of England, Scotland and Ireland, is no Sufficient Ground of a War. London [in-4°, pp. 30; published in October] (this pamphlet with the ironic title was reprinted in the first volume of the works).

*A List of one Unanimous Club of Members of the late Parliament, Nov. 11, 1701, that met at the Vine-Tavern in Long Acre. London [in-4°, pp. 4].

The Original Power of the Collective Body of the People of England, Examined and Asserted. With a double Dedication to the King and to the Parliament. London [folio, pp. 24; published Dec. 27] (reprinted by De Foe in the first volume of his works).

1702

Legion's New Paper: Being a second Memorial to the gentlemen of a late House of Commons. With Legion's Humble Address to His Majesty. London [in-4°, pp. 18] (Jan. 1st, 1702; signed T. G. gent).

The Mock-Mourners, a Satyr, by way of Elegy on King William. By the Author of the True-born Englishman. London, W. Gunne [in-4°, pp. 20]. (This poem of 583 lines was reprinted by De Foe in the first volume of his works. By Feb. 23, 1703, the seventh edition was being sold.)

Reformation of Manners. A Satyr. London [in-4°, pp. 32] (poem of about 1500 lines).

A New Test of the Church of England's Loyalty: or, Whiggish Loyalty and Church Loyalty Compared [in-4°, pp. 34] (this political pamphlet was reprinted in the first volume of the works). (June 1702.)

*Good Advice to the Ladies: shewing, that, as the World goes, and is like to go, the best way for them is to keep Unmarried. By the Author of the True-born Englishman (?). 1st ed., Sept. 3; 2nd ed., with additions in 1705 [in-4º, pp. 16] (poem undoubtedly written in part by De Foe and published against his will, for he disavows it in the *Little Review*).

The Spanish Descent. A Poem. By the Author of the True-born Englishman. London [in-4º, pp. 27; November] (poem of 388 lines reprinted in the first volume of the works).

An Enquiry into Occasional Conformity. Shewing that the Dissenters are no Way concerned in it. By the Author of the Preface to Mr. How. London [in-4º, pp. 31]. The 3rd edition (1704) bears a slightly different title. (An Enquiry into the Occasional Conformity Bill.) (Reprinted in the first volume of the works.)

The Shortest Way with the Dissenters: or Proposals for the Establishment of the Church. London [in-4º, pp. 29; December 1st] (reprinted in the first volume of the works).

1703

A Brief Exploration of a late Pamphlet, entitled The Shortest Way with the Dissenters (reprinted in the first volume).

King William's Affection to the Church of England Examin'd. London [in-4º, pp. 26] (this pamphlet reached the 4th edition April 13, the first dating March 25).

More Reformation. A Satyr upon himself. By the Author of the True-born Englishman. London [in-4º, p. 52: 16 July]. This poem of nearly 1,000 lines is reprinted in the 2nd volume of the works.

The Shortest Way to Peace and Union. By the Author of the Shortest Way with the Dissenters. London [in-4º, pp. 26; July 29]. Reprinted in the first volume.

A Hymn to the Pillory. London [in-4º, pp. 24; sold the 29th of July and the following days]. New edition in Feb. 1721. Reprinted in the second volume.

A True Collection of the Writings of the Author of the True-born Englishman, corrected by himself. London [end of July; in-8º, portrait, pp. xii and 465]. (2nd ed. in 1705).

The Sincerity of the Dissenters Vindicated from the Scandal of Occasional Conformity. With some Considerations on a late book, entitled, Moderation a Virtue. London, Price 6ᵈ [in-4º, pp. 27; Sept. 18].

An Enquiry into the Case of Mr. Asgil's General Translation, shewing that 'tis not a nearer way to Heaven than the Grave. By the Author of the True-born Englishman. London. J. Nutt [in-8º, pp. 48] (1st ed., Nov. 4, 1703; (2nd ed. in 1705.)

A Challenge of Peace, addressed to the whole Nation, with an Enquiry into Ways and Means for bringing it to pass. London [Nov. 23; in-4º, pp. 24]. Reprinted in the second volume.

Some Remarks on the First Chapter in Dr. Davenant's Essays concerning Appeals to the People from their Representatives. Printed and sold by A. Baldwin. London [Dec. 10, in-4º, pp. 29]. The 2nd ed. appeared in 1704 with the title: "Original Right; or the Reasonableness of Appeals to the Public", etc.

*The Liberty of Episcopal Dissenters in Scotland as it stands by the laws there truly stated. By a Gentleman. London, in-4°.

Peace without Union. By way of Reply to Sir H— M—'s (Humphrey Mackworth's) *Peace at Home*. London [in-4°, pp. 14]; 1st ed., Dec., 1703; 4th ed. in May, 1704. Reprinted in the second volume.

*The Case of Dissenters, as affected by the late Bill proposed in Parliament for preventing Occasional Conformity. By a Gentleman. London, Printed in the year 1703.

1704

The Dissenters' Answer to the High-Church Challenge. London [Jan. 5; in-4°, pp. 55] (reprinted in the second volume).

An Essay on the Regulation of the Press. Sold by the booksellers of London and Westminster. Price: 6ᵈ [in-4°], Jan. 7.

A Serious Inquiry into this Grand Question: Whether a Law to prevent Occasional Conformity of Dissenters would not be Inconsistent with the Act of Toleration, and a Breach of the Queen's Promise. London [in-4°, pp. 28] (reprinted in the second volume).

The Parallel: or Persecution of Protestants the shortest Way to prevent the Growth of Popery in Ireland. London [in-4°] (political pamphlet reprinted in the second volume).

The Layman's Sermon upon the late Storm. Held forth at an honest Coffee-House Conventicle. Not so much of a Jest at 'tis thought to be [in-4°, pp. 24] Feb. 24.

Royal Religion. Being some Enquiry after the Piety of Princes. With Remarks on a Book, Entitled *a Form of Prayers used by King William*. London, Price 6ᵈ [in-4°, pp. 27], 1st ed., March 18, 1704; 2nd ed., the same year. Reprinted in the second volume.

Legion's Humble Address to the Lords [April, folio, one sheet].

More Short Ways with the Dissenters. London, April 28 [in-4°, pp. 24]. Reprinted in the second volume.

The Dissenters Misrepresented and Represented [in-4°, May]. Reprinted in the second volume.

A New Test of the Church of England's Honesty. London, July 16 [in-4°, pp. 24]. Reprinted in the second volume.

The Storm; or, a Collection of the Most Remarkable Casualties and Disasters, which happened in the late Dreadful Tempest, both by Sea, and Land. London, G. Sawbridge. Price 3 s. 6ᵈ., July 17 [in-8°, pp. viii and 272].

An Elegy on the Author of the True-born Englishman. With an Essay on the late Storm. By the Author of the Hymn to the Pillory. London, Aug. 15 [in-4°, pp. 56]. The two pieces of verse in this brochure were reprinted in the second volume.

A Hymn to Victory. By the Author of the True-born Englishman. London, Printed for John Nutt [in-4°, pp. 52]; 1st ed. in Aug.; 2nd ed., Sept. 9. Numerous doubtful editions. Poem reprinted in the second volume.

The Protestant Jesuite Unmasked. In Answer to the two Parts of *Cassandra*. Wherein the Author [Leslie] and his Libels are laid open, with the True

Reasons why he would have the Dissenters Humbled. With my service to Mr. Lesley. London, Sept. 12 [in-4°, pp. 52].

Giving Alms No Charity, and Employing the Poor a Grievance to the Nation. Being an Essay upon this Great Question: Whether Workhouses, Corporations, and Houses of Correction for Employing the Poor. as now practised in England, or Parish-Stocks in a late Pamphlet entitled: *"A Bill for the better Relief, Imployment, and Settlement of the Poor, etc."* are not mischievous to the Nation, tending to the Destruction of our Trade, and to Encrease the Number and Misery of the Poor, Addressed to the Parliament of England. London, Nov. 18 [in-4°, pp. 28]. Reprinted in the second volume.

The Christianity of the High-Church Consider'd. Dedicated to a Noble Peer [Lord Haversham] [in-4°, pp. 28].

*Queries upon the Bill against Occasional Conformity [folio, pp. 4].

Contributions to the journal: The London Post.

A Review of the Affairs of France, and of all Europe as influenced by that Nation. Being historical Observations upon the Publick Transactions of the World; Purged from the Errors and Partialities of News-writers and petty Statesmen of all sides. With an Entertaining Part in every Sheet, being Advice from the Scandal Club to the curious Enquirers; in Answer to Letters sent them for that purpose. The first volume containing 102 numbers (pp. 424), an appendix translation of the French edict against duels, (pp. 32) and 5 supplements (Scandal-Club, pp. 140) was terminated Feb. 24, 1705 (date of 1st number: Feb. 26, 1704).

1705

The Double Welcome. A Poem to the Duke of Marlborough. London [in-4°, pp. 30] (Jan. 9). Reprinted in the second volume.

A Second Volume of the Writings of the Author of the True-born Englishman. Some whereof never before Printed, Corrected, and Enlarged by the Author. London, Printed and Sold by the Booksellers. Price 6 s. [in-8°, portrait, pp. viii and 479]. The two volumes of works were republished Dec. 28, 1710, with a key; 4th ed., July 1st, 1713.

Moderation maintain'd in Defense of a compassionate enquiry into the Causes of the Civil War etc. In a Sermon preached the 31st of January at Aldgate Church by White Kennet, etc. [by D. F.] [in-4°, pp. 22].

Persecution Anatomized: or an Answer to the following Questions, viz. I. What Persecution for Conscience Sake is? II. Whether any High Church that Promote the Occasional Bill may not properly be called Persecutors? III. Whether any Church whatever, whilst it savours of a Persecuting Spirit, is a true Church? IV. Who are the greatest Promoters of a Nation's Welfare, the High Church, or Dissenters? London [Feb. 22; in-4°, pp. 23].

The Consolidator; or Memoirs of Sundry Transactions from the World in the Moon. Translated from the Lunar Language. By the Author of the True-born Englishman. London, B. Bragg [in-8°, pp. 360]; 1st ed., March 26; 2nd ed. (with additions), Nov. 17. Many extracts from this long satire in prose were published in different pamphlets in London and Edinburgh, probably in pirated editions.

The Experiment; or the Shortest Way with the Dissenters Exemplified. Being the Case of Mr. Abraham Gill, a Dissenting Minister in the Isle of Ely, and a full Account of his being sent for a Soldier by Mr. Fern (an Ecclesiastical Justice of the Peace) and other Conspirators. To the Eternal Honour of the Temper and Moderation of High-Church Principles. Humbly Dedicated to the Queen. London, B. Bragg, March 27 [in-4°, pp. 58]. The 2nd ed. appeared Oct. 19, 1706, with the title: "The Modesty and Sincerity of those worthy English Gentlemen commonly called High Churchmen, exemplified in a Modern Instance".

Advice to all Parties. By the Author of the True-born Englishman. London, B. Bragg, April 30 [in-4°, pp. 24].

The Dyet of Poland. A Satyr. Printed at Dantsick in the year 1705 [London] (May, in-4°, pp. 60) (poem of 1,350 lines).

The High Church Legion: or, the Memorial Examined. Being a New Test of Moderation, as 'tis recommended to all that love the Church of England and the Constitution. London, July 17 [in-4°, pp. 21].

A Declaration without Doors: By the Author of the True-born Englishman. Sold by the booksellers of London and Westminster [in-4°, Oct. 24]. This pamphlet is the resumé of a series of articles in the *Review* (vol. II, pp. 381-428).

The Ballance: or a New Test of the High-flyers of all sides; being a short View of the Rise of our present Factions, with a New History of Passive Obedience, and a Proposal of a Bill against Occasional Conformity that may pass both Houses. London [in-4°, pp. vi and 48] (published under the pseudonym of Philusebiae).

Party Tyranny: Or, An Occasional Bill in Miniature: as now Practised in Carolina. Humbly offered to the Consideration of both Houses of Parliament. London, Nov. [in-4°, pp. 30].

An Answer to Lord Haversham's Speech. By Daniel De Foe [in-4°, pp. 4]. Reprinted from the *Review* of Nov. 24.

A Review of the Affairs of France, with Observations on Transactions at Home; vol. II, containing the numbers from Feb. 27 to Dec. 31, and also 23 numbers of the Little Review or an Inquisition of Scandal; consisting in answers of Questions and doubts, remarks; observations and reflections (from June 6 to Aug. 21). pp. 558.

Contributions to the *London Post.*

1706

A Hymn to Peace. Occasioned by the two Houses joining in one Address to the Queen. By the Author of the True-born Englishman. London, Jan. 8 [in-4°, pp. 60]. Poem of about a thousand lines.

A Reply to a Pamphlet, entitled The Lord Haversham's Vindication of his speech. By the Author of the Review. London, Jan. 15 [in-4°, pp. 32].

The Case of Protestant Dissenters in Carolina; shewing how a Law to prevent Occasional Conformity there has ended in the Total Subversion of the Constitution in Church and State. Recommended to the serious Consideration of all that are true Friends of our Present Government. London [in-4°, pp. 29].

Remarks on the Bill to prevent Frauds committed by Bankrupts. With Observations on the Effect it may have upon Trade. London, April 18 [in-4°, pp. 29].

Remarks on the Letter [by Rawlins] to the Author of the State-Memorial [Toland]. London [in-4°, pp. iv and 32].

An Essay at Removing National Prejudices against a Union with Scotland. To be continued during the Treaty here. Part I. London, B. Bragg, May 4 [in-4°, pp. 30].

(Same Title). Part II, May 28. The two first parts were published together in Edinburgh.

A Plea for the Non Conformists: Shewing the true State of their Case. By Thomas de Laune, who died in Newgate during his imprisonment for this book. Printed 20 years ago, but being seized by the Messenger of the Press, was afterwards Burnt by the Hangman, and Now reprinted from the Author's Original Copy. With a Preface by the Author of the Review. London. Printed and sold by W. and J. Marshall at the Bible in Newgate St., June 6 [in-4°, pp. 66; the preface by De Foe occupies 11 pages].

A Sermon preached by Mr. Daniel De Foe on the Fitting up of Dr. Burgess's Meeting House. Taken from his *Review* of the 20th June, 1706.

A True Relation of the Apparition of one Mrs. Veal, the next Day after her Death, to one Mrs. Bargrave at Canterbury, the 8th of September, 1705. [Which Apparition recommends the Perusal of Drélincourt's *Book of Consolations against the Fears of Death*.] London, Printed for B. Bragg, at the Black Raven. 1st ed., July 5. Joined to the 4th ed. of the book of Drélincourt (Sept. 30). The 2nd phrase of the title was not introduced until the 3rd separate ed. of the De Foe pamphlet on April 9.

Jure Divino: a Satyr. In twelve Books. By the Author of the True-born Englishman. London, July 20 [folio, portrait, pp. xxviii, vii and 346]. An incomplete and defective pirated edition of this great political poem appeared the same day.

The Vision. A Poem. Edinburgh, November. This poem of 124 lines was composed by De Foe to ridicule the solemn discourse of Lord Belhaven in the Scottish Parliament; but always prudent, he made it seem that the Count of Haddington was the author. (Letter to Harley, Nov. 28.)

A Reply to the "Scot's Answer to the British Vision (by Lord Belhaven)". Edinburgh (loose sheet).

A Letter to the Glasgow Men. Edinburgh (loose sheet, 2,500 copies printed). Letter to Harley, December 9.

*An Enquiry into the Disposal of the Equivalent. Edinburgh, 1706.

An Essay at Removing National Prejudices against a Union with England. Part III. By the Author of the two First [Edinburgh; November, in-4°, pp. 35].

A Fourth Essay at Removing National Prejudices; with some Reply to Mr. Hodges, and some other Authors, who have printed their Objections against a Union with England. Part IV [Edinburgh, December, in-4°, pp. 44].

A Review of the State of the English Nation. The third volume (pp. 688) was closed Feb. 6, 1707; it contained 172 numbers.

1707

A Fifth Essay at Removing National Prejudices; with a Reply to some Authors who have printed their Objections against a Union with England. Part V [Edinburgh, January, in-4°, pp. 35].

Two great Questions Considered: I. What is the Obligation of Parliaments to the Addresses or Petitions of the People, and what the Duty of Addressers? II. Whether the Obligation of the Covenant, or other National Engagements, is concerned in the Treaty of Union? Being a Sixth Essay at Removing National Prejudices against the Union. Part VI [Edinburgh, January, in-4°, pp. 31].

The Dissenters in England vindicated from some Reflections in a late Pamphlet called "Lawful Prejudices". Edinburgh [in-4°, pp. 8]. Reprinted in London the same year.

Caledonia. A Poem in Honour of Scotland and the Scots Nation. In 3 parts. Edinburgh. Printed by the Heirs and Successors of Andrew Anderson, Printer to the Queen's Most Excellent Majesty [folio pp. v and 60]. This poem of about 1,000 lines was published by subscription in London, Jan. 28, by Matthews and Morphew.

A Short View of the Present State of the Protestant Religion in Britain, as it is now profest in the Episcopal Church in England, the Presbyterian Church in Scotland, and the Dissenters in both. Edinburgh, March [in-4°, pp. 48], 2nd ed. published in London April 1st.

A Voice from the South; or an Address from some Protestant Dissenters in England to the Kirk in Scotland [May, in-4°, pp. 8]. Reprints of articles published in the May 10 and 15 numbers of the Review.

*A Modest Vindication of the Present Ministry: From the Reflections published against them in a late Printed Paper, Entitled, The Lord Haversham's Speech, etc. With a Review and Balance of the Present War. Evincing, That we are not in such a Desperate Condition as that Paper Insinuates. Humbly submitted to the Considerations of all, but especially to the Right Honourable and the Honourable, the North British Lords and Commoners. By a Well-wisher to the Peace of Britain. London [in-4°, pp. 14].

An Historical Account of the Bitter Sufferings, and Melancholy Circumstances of the Episcopal Church in Scotland, Under the Barbarous Usage and Bloody Persecution of the Presbyterian Church Government. With an Essay on the Nature and Necessity of a Toleration in the North of Britain. Edinburgh [in-8°, pp. 40].

De Foe's Answer to Dyer's Scandalous Newsletter [Edinburgh; in-4°, pp. 3, August].

Dyer's News Examined as to his Swedish Memorial against the Review [September, in-4°, pp. 4].

The Trade of Britain stated; being the substance of 2 papers published in London on occasion of the importation of wine and brandy from North Britain [Edinburgh, in-4°, pp. 8] (Articles from the Review).

A Review of the State of the British Nation. The fourth vol. (pp. 700) contains 175 numbers and ends March 25, 1708.

1708

*Reflections on the Prohibition Act: Wherein the necessity, usefulness and value of that law are invinced and demonstrated. In Answer to a Letter on that subject, From a gentleman concerned in Trade. London [in-8º, pp. 22].

Advice to the Electors of Great Britain; occasioned by the intended Invasion from France [in-4º, pp. 4]. Printed at London and reprinted at Edinburgh.

A Review of the State of the British Nation. The fourth vol. (158 numbers, pp. 632) ended March 31, 1709.

1709

The Scots Narrative Examined; or, the Case of the Episcopal Ministers in Scotland stated; and the late Treatment of them in the City of Edinburgh enquired into. With a brief Examination into the Reasonableness of the Grievous Complaint of Persecution in Scotland and a Defence of the Magistrates of Edinburgh, in their Proceedings there. Being some Remarks on a late Pamphlet, entitled *A Narrative of the late Treatment of the Episcopal Ministers, within the City of Edinburgh,* etc. London. Sold by A. Baldwin in Warwick lane, Feb. 19 [in-4º, pp. 41 and Post-scriptum of pp. x].

The History of the Union of Great Britain. Edinburgh, Printed by the Heirs and Successors of Andrew Anderson, Printer to the Queen's Most Excellent Majesty [folio, portrait, pp. viii, xxxii and 694]. Reprinted at London in 1711.

An Answer to a Paper concerning Mr. De Foe, against the History of the Union [Edinburgh, in-4º, pp. 8].

A Commendatory Sermon. Preached Nov. 4, 1709. Being the Birth Day of King William of Glorious Memory. By Daniel De Foe, London, Printed by J. Dutton, near Fleet Street [in-8º, pp. 8]. Extract from the *Review.*

A Review of the State of the British Nation. The fourth vol. (150 numbers, pp. 600) ended March 23, 1710.

Parson Plaxton of Barwick, in the County of York, turn'd inside out. Satire in verse (about 4 pp. folio) copied in a letter from a certain G. Haviland, dated May, 1709 (cf. *Times,* literary Supp., Feb. 19, 1920).

1710

The Advertisement of Daniel De Foe to Mr. Clark. Edinburgh [in-4º, pp. 8].

A Letter from Captain Tom to the Mob now Raised for Dr. Sacheverell. London. Printed for J. Baker at the Black Boy in Paternoster Row [in-8º, pp.8, March 11].

*A Speech without Doors. London. Printed for A. Baldwin etc. Price 2ᵈ, April 19 [in-8º, pp. 28]. Reprinted at Dublin.

Instructions from Rome in Favour of the Pretender: Inscribed to the most Elevated Don Sacheverillio and his Brother Don Higginsco. And which all Perkinites, Non-jurors, High-Flyers, Popish Desirers, Wooden-shoe Admirers, and Absolute-Non-Resistance Drivers, are obliged to pursue and maintain (Under pain of his Unholinesses Damnation) in order to carry on their intended subversion of a Government, fixed upon Revolution Principles. London J. Baker. Price: 2^d [in-8°, pp. 16, May 11].

An Essay upon Publick Credit: Being an Enquiry, How the Publick Credit comes to depend upon the Change of Ministry or the Dissolution of Parliaments; and whether it does so or no. With an Argument, Proving that the Publick Credit may be upheld and maintained in this Nation; and perhaps brought to a greater Height than it ever yet arriv'd at; Tho' all the Changes and Dissolutions already made, pretended to, and now Discoursed of, should come to pass in the World. London. Printed and Sold by the Booksellers. Price: 3^d, Aug. 23 [in-8°, pp. 28].

A Word against a New Election; that the People of England may see the Happy difference between English Liberty and French Slavery: and may consider well before they make the Exchange. October [in-8°, pp. 23].

A New Test of the Sense of the Nation: Being a Modest Comparison between the Addresses to the late King James, and those to her present Majesty. In order to observe how far the Sense of the Nation may be judged of by either of them. London, October 12 [in-8°, pp. 91].

An Essay upon Loans: or, An Argument proving That Substantial Funds, settled by Parliament, with the Encouragement of Interests, and the Advances of Prompt Payment usually allowed, will bring in Loans of Money to the Exchequer, in spite of all the Conspiracies of Parties to the Contrary: while a just, Honourable, and Punctual Performance on the Part of the Government, supports the Credit of the Nation. By the Author of the Essay upon Credit. London. Printed and Sold by the booksellers, October 21 [in-8°, pp. 27].

A Supplement to the "Faults on both Sides" [Pamphlet by Harley or Clements], Containing the compleat History of the proceedings of a Party ever since the Revolution: in a familiar Dialogue between Steddy and Turn-round, 2 displaced officers of State. Which may serve to explain Sir Thomas Double [title of an extreme Tory pamphlet]; and to show How far the Late Parliament were right in proceeding against Dr. Sacheverell by way of Impeachment. London. J. Baker, price 1 s. [in-8°, pp. 76].

A Review of the State of the British Nation. The seventh vol. (155 numbers) ended March 22, 1711.

1711

Contributions to the journal: The Edinburgh Courant, after Feb. 1st.

Atalantis Major. Printed in Olreeky, the Chief City of the Northern Part of Atalantis Major [Edinburgh, Jan., in-8°, pp. 46].

A Spectator's Address to the Whigs, on the Occasion of the Stabbing Mr. Harley [in-12, pp. 15, March].

Eleven Opinions about Mr. Harley; with Observations. London. J. Baker [May 14, in-8°, pp. 89].

The Secret History of the October Club: From its Original to this Time. By a Member. London [J. Baker] Price 1 s. [in-8°, pp. 86], 1st ed., April 21; 2nd ed., May 10.

Idem. Part II [in-8°, pp. 93], August.

The British Visions: or Isaac Bickerstaff's 12 Prophecies for the year 1711 [in-12°, pp. 29]. Price: 2ᵈ.

An Essay on the South Sea Trade: with an Enquiry into the Grounds and Reasons of the present Dislike and Complaint against the Settlement of a South-Sea Company. By the Author of the Review. London. J. Baker [in-8°, pp. 47], 1st ed., Sept. 6; 2nd ed., Nov. 29.

Reasons why this Nation ought to put a Speedy End to this Expensive War. With a Brief Essay at the probable Conditions on which the Peace now Negociating may be Founded. Also an Enquiry into the Obligations Britain lies under to the Allies, and how far she is obliged not to make Peace without them. London, J. Baker [in-8°, pp. 47]. 1st ed., Oct. 6; 2nd ed., Oct. 11; 3rd ed., Oct. 13.

*Armageddon; or the Necessity of Carrying on the War if such a Peace cannot be obtained, as may render Europe safe and Trade secure. London, J. Baker. Price 6ᵈ [in-8°, pp. 47, Oct. 30].

The Balance of Europe: or, an Enquiry into the respective Dangers of giving the Spanish Monarchy to the Emperor, as well as to King Philip. With the Consequences that may be expected from either. London, J. Baker, Nov. 1st [in-8°, pp. 48].

An Essay at a Plain Exposition of that difficult Phrase: A Good Peace. By the Author of the Review. London, J. Baker. Price 6ᵈ, November [in-8°, pp. 52].

Reasons why a Party among us, and also among the Confederates, are obstinately bent against a Treaty of Peace with the French at this Time. By the Author of Reasons for putting an End to this Expensive War. London, J. Baker. [in-8°, pp. 48]. 1st ed., Nov. 29; 2nd ed., Dec. 8.

The Felonious Treaty; or, an Enquiry into the Reasons which Moved his late Majesty King William of Glorious Memory to enter into a Treaty at two several Times, with the King of France, for the Partition of the Spanish Monarchy. With an Essay proving that it was always the sense of King William, and of all the Confederates, and even of the Grand Alliance itself, that the Spanish Monarchy should never be united in the Person of the Emperor. By the Author of the Review. London, J. Baker, Price 6ᵈ [December, in-8°, pp. 48].

An Essay on the History of Parties and Persecution in Britain, beginning with a brief Account of the Test Act and an Historical Enquiry into the Reasons, the Original, and the Consequences of the Occasional Conformity of the Dissenters; with some Remarks on the several Attempts, already made and now making, for an Occasional Bill. Enquiring how far the same may be esteemed a Preservation to the Church, or an Injury to the Dissenters. London, J. Baker. Price 6ᵈ, Dec. 22 [in-8°, pp. 48].

*The Succession of Spain considered. London. Printed in the year 1711.

An Essay upon the trade to Africa, in order to set the Merits of that Cause in a True Light, and bring the Disputes between the African Company and the Separate Traders into a narrower Compass. London [in-8°, pp. 48].

A True Account of the Design and Advantages of the South-Sea Trade: with answers to all the objections raised against it. A list of the Commodities proper for that Trade; and the Progress of the subscription towards the South-Sea Company. London, Morphew. Price 6ᵈ [in-8º, pp. 38].

A Defence of the Allies and the late Ministry; or Remarks on the Tories new Idol. Being a detection of the manifest frauds and falsities in a late Pamphlet [by Swift] entituled, The Conduct of the Allies and of the late Ministry in the beginning and carrying on the War. London, J. Baker. Price 6ᵈ [in-8º, pp. 46].

*Contribution to the *Protestant Post-boy.*

A Review of the State of the British Nation. The eighth vol. (211 numbers, pp. 848) ended July 29, 1712.

Contribution to the following miscellany: *"A Collection of Original Papers and Material Transactions concerning the late great affair of the Union between England and Scotland. Also an exact Journal of the proceedings of the Treaty as well at London as in Edinburgh. Wherein the Privileges of the Presbyterian Kirk and the Case of toleration of Episcopal Dissenters there are very clearly stated. In 5 parts,* etc. London, Knapton, Cliff, Baker.

1712

The Conduct of Parties in England, more especially of those Whigs who now appear against the new Ministry and a Treaty of Peace. London, Jan. 24 [in-8º, pp. 42].

The Present State of Parties in Great Britain: Particularly an Enquiry into the State Dissenters in England and the Presbyterians in Scotland, their Religions and Public Interests considered as it respects their Circumstances before and since the late Acts against Occasional Conformity in England, and for Toleration of Common Prayer in Scotland. London, J. Baker. Price 5 s. May 17 [in-8º, pp. iv and 352].

*Peace or Poverty. Being a Serious Vindication of Her Majesty and Her Ministers consenting to a Treaty for a general Peace. London, Printed in the year 1712.

The Highland Visions or the Scots New Prophecy: Declaring in 12 Visions what Strange Things shall come to Pass in the Year 1712. Price: 2ᵈ [March 26, in-12, pp. 16].

*The Validity of the Renunciations of Former Powers Enquir'd into, and the Present Renunciation of the Duke of Anjou, impartially consider'd. London. Printed in the year 1712.

*An Enquiry into the Danger and Consequences of a War with the Dutch. London, J. Baker [in-8º, pp. 40].

The Justice and Necessity of a War with Holland, in Case the Dutch do not come into Her Majesty's measures, stated and examined. London.

Reasons against Fighting: Being an Enquiry into this Debate, whether it is Safe for Her Majesty, or her Ministry, to Adventure an Engagement with the French, considering the present Behaviour of the Allies. London, June 7. Price: 6ᵈ [in-8º, pp. 38].

*An Enquiry into the Real Interest of Princes in the Persons of their Ambassadors; and how far the Petty Quarrels of Ambassadors, or the Servants and

Dependants of Ambassadors, one among another, ought to be Resented by
their Principals. With an Essay on what Satisfaction it is Necessary to Give
or Take in such Cases. Impartially applied to the affair of Monsieur Mesnager, and the Count de Rechteren, Plenipotentiaries at Utrecht. London,
J. Baker, September 18 [in-8º, pp. 23].

A Seasonable Warning and Caution against the Insinuations of Papists and
Jacobites in favour of the Pretender. Being a Letter from an Englishman at
the Court of Hanover. London, J. Baker [in-8º, pp. 24].

Hannibal at the Gates; or the Progress of Jacobitism and the Danger of the
Pretender. London, J. Baker [in-12, pp. 40]; 1st ed., Dec. 30; 2nd ed.
(With Remarks on a Pamphlet now Published Intituled *Hannibal not at our
Gates*), in-8º, pp. 48, 1714.

The Review. This journal appeared in a new form from Aug. 9, 1712 to June 11,
1713 (vol. IX, 106 numbers, pp. 212).

1713

A Strict Enquiry into the Circumstances of a late Duel, with some Account of
the Persons concern'd on both Sides [Hamilton and Mohun]. Being a Modest
Attempt to do Justice to a Noble Person Dead, and to the Injured Honour
of an Absent Person Living. To which is added the substance of a Letter
from General McCortney to his Friend. London [in-8º, pp. 45].

Reasons against the Succession of the House of Hanover, with an Enquiry how
far the Abdication of King James, supposing it to be legal, ought to affect
the Person of the Pretender. London, J. Baker. Price 6ᵈ [in-8º, pp. 45];
1st ed., Feb. 21. This pamphlet with the ironic title reached a fourth ed.
in April.

And what if the Pretender should come? or some Considerations of the Advantages
and real Consequences of the Pretender's possessing the Crown of Great
Britain. London, J. Baker, Price 6ᵈ [in-8º, pp. 44], 1st ed., March 26; 2nd
ed. in April.

An Answer to a Question that nobody thinks of, viz. What if the Queen should die?
London, J. Baker. April [in-8º. pp. 44].

An Essay on the Treaty of Commerce with France, with Necessary Expositions.
London, J. Baker [in-8º, pp. 44], 2nd ed. in May.

Nottingham's Politicks Examin'd. Being an Answer to a pamphlet lately published
intituled: Observations upon the State of the Nation. London, J. Baker, 6ᵈ
[in-8º, pp. 34].

The Second-Sighted Highlander. Being 10 New Visions for the year 1713. Printed
in 1713.

A Brief Account of the Present State of the African Trade. London, 1713.

Considerations upon the 8th and 9th Articles of the Treaty of Commerce and Navigation. Now published by Authority. With some Enquiries into the Damages
that may accrue to the English Trade from them. London, J. Baker, June 2
[in-8º, pp. 40].

Some Thoughts upon the Subject of Commerce with France. By the Author of the
Review. London, J. Baker. June (résumé of articles published in the *Review*).

A General History of Trade, and especially considered as it respects British Commerce etc. It appeared in 4 sections (2 a month) in August and September, written for the most part by De Foe. London, J. Baker (each number in-8°, pp. 40).

A Letter from a member of the House of Commons to his Friend in the Country, relating to the Bill of Commerce. With a true copy of the Bill, and an exact list of all those who voted for and against engrossing it. London, J. Baker [in-8°, pp. 46].

Memoirs of Count Tariff. London, J. Morphew; 1 s. [in-8°, pp. 95] (undoubtedly in part by De Foe).

Whigs turned Tories and Hanoverian Tories from their avowed Principles proved Whigs; or Each side in the other Mistaken. Being a plain proof that each Party deny that Charge which the others bring against them; and that neither side will disown those which the others profess. With an Earnest Exhortation to all Whigs, as well as Hanoverian Tories, to lay aside those uncharitable Heats among such Protestants, and seriously to consider, and effectually to provide, against those Jacobites, Popish, and Conforming Tories, whose principal Ground of Hope to ruin all sincere Protestants is from those Unchristian and violent Feuds among ourselves. London, J. Baker.

Union and no Union. Being an Enquiry into the Grievances of the Scots and how far they are right or wrong, who alledge that the Union is dissolved. London, J. Baker [in-8°, pp. 24].

A Letter to the Dissenters. London, J. Morphew. Price 6ᵈ, Dec. 3 [in-8°, pp. 48].

Contribution to the journal: *Mercator,* or Commerce Retrieved. Being considerations on the Subject of British Trade, particularly as it respects Holland, Flanders and the Dutch Barrier, the Trade to and from France, the Trade to Portugal, Spain and the West Indies, and the Fisheries of Newfoundland and Nova Scotia. With other Matters and Advantages accruing to Great Britain, by the Treaties of Peace and Commerce lately Concluded at Utrecht. The whole being founded upon just Authorities, faithfully Collected from Authentick Papers, and now made Publick for general Information. Bi-weekly review which lasted for 181 numbers, from May 26, 1713 to July 20, 1714 (each number a large sheet in-4° printed in two columns).

1714

The Scots Nation and Union Vindicated from the Reflections cast on them in an Infamous Libel entitled, *The Public Spirit of the Whigs,* etc. [by Swift]. In which the most Scandalous Paragraphs contained therein are fairly quoted and fully answered. London, Printed for A. Bell. Price 6ᵈ March [in-4°, pp. 28].

A Letter to the Whigs, expostulating with them upon their present Conduct. London, 1714.

A View of the Real Danger of the Protestant Succession. London, J. Baker, 6ᵈ, April [in-8°, pp. 44] (ironic title).

A Brief Survey of the Legal Liberties of the Dissenters, and how far the Bill, now Depending, Consists with preserving the Toleration inviolably. Wherein the

Present Bill is published, and also the Toleration Act at large, that they may be compar'd with one another. London, J. Baker, 6^d [in-8º, pp. 39].

Reasons for Impeaching the Lord High Treasurer, and some others of the Present Ministry [ironic title]. London, J. Moore, 6^d, April [in-8º, pp. 39].

The Remedy worse than the Disease; or, Reasons against passing the Bill for preventing the Growth of Schism. To which is added a brief Discourse of Toleration and Persecution, shewing their Unavoidable Effects good or Bad; and Proving that neither Diversity of Religions, nor Diversity in the Same Religion, are Dangerous, much less Inconsistent with good Government. In a Letter to a Noble Earl. London, J. Baker, June 9 [in-8º, pp. 48].

Contributions to the journal: *The Monitor,* April 22 to Aug. 7 [each number, 1 sheet in-4º].

Contributions to the journal: *The Flying Post and Medley* (of which Hurst was the owner), from July 27 to Aug. 21 (1 sheet folio, appearing three times a week).

Advice to the People of Great Britain, with respect to 2 Important Points in their future Conduct; I. To what they ought to expect from the King; II. How they ought to behave to him. London, J. Baker, Oct. 7 [in-8º, pp. 40]. Reprinted in Dublin (G. Risk, bookseller).

*Impeachment, or No Impeachment: Or an Enquiry how far the Impeachment of certain Persons at the present Juncture, would be consistent with Honour and Justice. London, J. Moore, 3^d [in-8º, pp. 23].

A Secret History of One Year (1688, compared to 1714). London, J. Baker [in-8º, pp. 40].

The Secret History of the White Staff. Being an Account of Affairs under the Conduct of Some late Ministers; and of what might probably have happended if Her Majesty had not died. London, J. Baker [in-8º, pp. 71]. 4 editions appeared in October. [The greatest part of this treatise and of the following ones was the work of De Foe.]

Idem. Part. II [in-8º, p. 71]. 1st ed., Oct. 27 (3rd ed. appeared before the end of the year).

1715

The Secret History of the White Staff, etc. Part III [in-8°, pp. 80]. 1st ed., Jan. 29 (the three sections were made into one pamphlet).

Strike while the Iron's Hot, or Now is the Time to be Happy. Humbly propos'd, upon His Majesty's late most gracious Injunction. London, Keimer 6^d, [in-8°, pp. 43].

Treason Detected, in an Answer to that Traiterous and Malicious Libel entitled English Advice to the Freeholders of England. Humbly offer'd to the Consideration of all those Freeholders who have been poyson'd with that malicious Pamphlet [by Bishop Atterbury]. London, Keimer, 6^d [in-8º, pp. 35]. 1st ed., Jan.; 2nd ed., Feb.

A Friendly Epistle by Way of Reproof, from one of the People called Quakers to Thos. Bradbury, a Dealer in many Words. London, Keimer, 6^d [in-8º, pp. 39], Feb. 19. 5th ed., 1715.

An Appeal to Honour and Justice, tho' it be of his Worst Enemies, by Daniel De Foe; Being a True Account of his Conduct in Public Affairs. London, Baker [in-8°, pp. 58], Feb. 24.

The Family Instructor: in 3 Parts. I. Relating to Fathers and Children. II. To Masters and Servants. III. To Husbands and Wives. By way of Dialogue, with a Recommendatory Letter by the Rev. Mr. S. Wright. London, E. Matthews [in-12, pp. 444]. 1st ed., March 31; 2nd ed., corrected by the author, without the Wright letter, September 17. The 8th ed. appeared in 1720, the 16th in 1766, etc.

The Secret History of the Scepter, or the Court Intrigues in the late Reign. London, Keimer, 1 s. [in-8°, pp. 48] (largely composed by De Foe). A second edition appeared under a slightly different title.

The Secret History of the Secret History of the White Staff [Harley], Purse [Harcourt] and Mitre [Atterbury]. Written by a Person of Honour.

Memoirs of the Conduct of Her late Majesty and her last Ministry, relating to the separate Peace with France. By the Right Hon. the Countess of —. London, Keimer, 1 s. [in-8°, pp. 80] (partly by De Foe).

A Sharp Rebuke from one of the People called Quakers to Henry Sacheverell, the High Priest of Andrews, Holborn. By the same Friend that wrote to Thos. Bradbury. London, Keimer, 6ᵈ [in-8°, pp. 35], March.

A Seasonable Expostulation with, and Friendly Reproof unto James Butler, who by the Men of this World is styled the Duke of Ormond, relating to the Tumults of the People. By the same Friend that wrote to Thos. Bradbury, the Dealer in many Words, and Henry Sacheverell, the High Priest of Andrews, Holborn. London, Keimer, May 31 [in-8°, pp. 31]. Reprinted at Dublin [by Thos. Humes, in-8°, pp. 24].

A Letter to a Merry Young Gentleman intituled Tho. Burnett Esq. (one of the Justices of the Court of Common Pleas). In Answer to one writ by him to the Right Hon. the Earl of Halifax; by which it plainly appears the said squire was not awake when he writ the said letter. London, J. Morphew, 4ᵈ [in-8°, pp. 24].

Burnet and Bradbury, or the Confederacy of the Press and Pulpit for the Blood of the Last Ministry. London, 1715.

*Some Reasons offered by the late Ministry in Defence of their Administration. London, Morphew, 1 s. [in-8°, pp. 78].

*The Folly and Vanity of Impeaching the late Ministry Considered. London, 1715.

History of the Wars of his present Majesty Charles XII King of Sweden; from his first Landing in Denmark to his Return from Turkey to Pomerania. By a Scots Gentleman in the Swedish Service. London, A. Bell [in-8°, pp. 400]. A compilation largely written by De Foe. 1st ed., July 6.

Idem. With a Continuation to his Death [History, pp. 1-248; Continuation, pp. 249-402], May 21, 1720.

A Hymn to the Mob. London, July 14, 6ᵈ [in-8°, pp. 40]. Poem of about 800 lines.

*A Remonstrance from some Country Whigs to a member of a Secret Committee. London, J. Morphew, 6ᵈ [in-8°, pp. 40].

The Fears of the Pretender turn'd into the Fears of Debauchery. Proposed, without Ceremony, to the Consideration of the Lords spiritual and temporal; with a hint to Richard Steele esq. London, Keimer, 6ᵈ [in-8º, pp. 38].

The Second-Sighted Highlander. Being 4 visions of the Eclypse and something of what may follow. London, Baker 6ᵈ [in-8º, pp. 46].

Some Methods to supply the Defects of the late Peace, without entring into a New War. London, 1715.

*A Second Letter from a Country Whig to his Friend in London, relating to the matter of Impeachments. London, Morphew, 6ᵈ [in-8º, pp. 38].

Bold Advice: or, Proposals for the Entire rooting out of Jacobitism in Great Britain. Address'd to the present Ministry. London, J. Moore, 6ᵈ [in-8º, pp. 43].

Some Considerations on the Danger of the Church from her own clergy. Humbly offer'd to the Lower House of Convocation. London, J. Roberts, 6ᵈ [in-8º, pp. 40].

*An Attempt towards a Coalition of English Protestants. To which is added Reasons for restraining the Licentiousness of the Pulpit and Press.

An Account of the Conduct of Robert Earl of Oxford. London, T. Warner 1 s. [in-8º, pp. 99]. Reprinted in 1717 with the title: "Memoirs of some transactions during the late Ministry of Robert, Earl of Oxford".

Humble Address to our Soveraign Lord the People. London, J. Baker, 6ᵈ [in-8º, pp. 36].

A View of the Scots Rebellion. With some Enquiry into what we have to fear from the Rebels? And what is the properest method to take with them? London, R. Burleigh in Amen corner. Oct. 15. Price 6ᵈ [in-8º, pp. 40].

*The Traitorous and Foolish Manifesto of the Scots Rebels Examined and Exposed Paragraph by Paragraph. London, R. Burleigh, 6ᵈ [in-8º, pp. 32].

A Trumpet, Blown in the North, and Sounded in the Ears of John Ereskine, called by the Men of the World, Duke of Mar. By a Ministering Friend of the People called Quakers. With a word of Advice and Direction to the said John Ereskine and his Followers. London, Keimer, 6ᵈ [in-8º, pp. 38].

An Account of the Great and Generous Actions of James Butler (late Duke of Ormond). Dedicated to the Famous University of Oxford [ironic title]. London, J. Moore, 6ᵈ, Dec. [in-8º, pp. 48]. Reprinted in 1718.

1716

Some Account of the Two Nights Court at Greenwich; wherein may be seen the Reason, Rise and Progress of the late Unnatural Rebellion against his Sacred Majesty King George, and his Government. London, J. Baker [in-8º, pp. 72]. Reprinted at Edinburgh. In large part the work of De Foe.

*An Essay towards Real Moderation. London, Morphew, 3ᵈ [in-8º, pp. 15], 2nd ed. in 1716.

*Some Thoughts of an Honest Tory in the Country upon the late Disposition of some People to revolt. London, 1716.

The Conduct of some people, about pleading guilty, With some reasons Why it was not thought proper to shew mercy to some who desired it. London [in-8°, pp. 23]. Reprinted at Dublin.

Some Considerations on a Law for triennial Parliaments. With an Enquiry: I. Whether there may not be a Time, when it is necessary to suspend the Execution of such Laws as are most essential to the Liberties of the People. II. Whether this is such a Time or No? London, J. Baker, April [in-8º, pp. 40].

*Arguments about the Alteration of Triennial Elections of Parliament. In a letter to a Friend in the Country. London, Gray, 1½ d [folio, pp. 6].

*The Triennial Act impartially Stated. London, 1716.

*A True Account of the Proceedings at Perth, the Debates in the Secret Council there, and the Reasons and Causes of the suddain finishing and breaking up of the Rebellion. Written by a Rebel. London, J. Baker [in-8º, pp. 72]. (Reprinted in 1845 in vol. II of the Spottiswoode Miscellany.) Probably revised by De Foe.

An Essay upon Buying and Selling of Speeches, in a Letter to a Worshipful Justice of the Peace, being also a Member of a certain Worshipful Society of Speech-makers. London, J. Baker, 6ᵈ [in-4º, pp. 39].

*Remarks on the Speeches of William Paul, Clerk, and John Hall of Otterburn Esq.; executed at Tyburn for rebellion the 13th. of July, 1716. In which the Government and Administration, both in Church and State, are vindicated from the treasonable Reflections and false Aspersions thrown upon them in those Speeches, which are inserted at length, as they were delivered to the Sheriffs. London, Baker and Warner, 6ᵈ [in-8º, pp. 38].

The Layman's Vindication of the Church of England, as well against Mr. Howell's charge of schism, as against Dr. Bennett's pretended Answer to it. London, Bell and Baker [in-8º, pp. 79].

*Secret Memoirs of the New Treaty of Alliance with France [Jan. 4, 1717]; in which some of the First Steps in that remarkable Affair are discovered; with some Characters of Persons. London, J. Roberts [in-8º, pp. 36].

Secret Memoirs of a Treasonable Conference at Somerset House, for deposing the Present Ministry, and making a new turn at Court. London, F. More, 1 s. [in-8º, pp. 78]. In part the work of De Foe.

Collaboration, Contribution, beginning with May, to the monthly review: Mercurius Politicus: Being monthly Observations on the Affairs of Great Britain; with a Collection of the Most Material Occurrences. By a Lover of Old England. London, J. Morphew, 1 s. [each number, brochure in-8º from 60 to 100 pages].

Editing, beginning with June, Dormer's News Letters (each number, one sheet, folio) (lithographed).

1717

Memoirs of the Church of Scotland, in 4 Periods: I. The Church in her Infant State, from the Reformation to Queen Mary's Abdication. II. The Church in its Growing State, from the Abdication to the Restoration. III. The Church in its Persecuted State, from the Restoration to the Revolution. IV. The Church in its Present State, from the Revolution to the Union. With an Appendix of Some Translations since the Union. London, E. Matthews [in-8º, pp. 233, 196 and 9], April 26. Republished by the Rev. W. Wilson in 1845 (with introd. and notes).

Minutes of the Negociations of Mons. Mesnager, at the Court of England, Towards the Close of the last Reign. Wherein some of the Most Secret Transactions of that Time, relating to the Interest of the Pretender, and a Clandestine Separate Peace are detected and laid open. Written by himself. Done out of French. London, S. Baker, June 17 [in-8º, pp. 326], 2nd ed., 1717; 3rd ed., July 8, 1731; 4th ed., 1736.

A Declaration of Truth to Benjamin Hoadley, one of the High Priests of the Land, and of the Degree whom Men call Bishops. By a Ministering Friend who writ to Tho. Bradbury, a Dealer in Many Words. London, E. Moore, 6ᵈ [in-8º, pp. 31].

*An Expostulatory Letter to the Bishop of Bangor, concerning a book lately published by His Lordship, entitled: A Preservative against the Principles and Practices of English Nonjurors. London, E. Smith, 6ᵈ [in-8º, pp. 30].

*The Danger of Court Differences; or the unhappy effects of a Motley Ministry; occasion'd by the Report of Changes at Court. London, Printed in the year 1717.

The Quarrel of the School-boys at Athens, as lately acted at a School near Westminster. London, J. Roberts, Price 6ᵈ [in-8º, pp. 38]. (Ironic relation of stormy sessions of Parliament.)

An Impartial Enquiry into the Conduct of the Right Honourable Charles, Lord Viscount Townshend, London. A. Dodd [in-8º, pp. 76]. Justification of Townshend's acts.)

An Argument proving that the Design of Employing and Ennobling Foreigners is a treasonable Conspiracy against the Constitution, dangerous to the Kingdom, an Affront to the Nobility of Scotland in particular, and dishonourable to the Peerage of Britain in General. With an Appendix, wherein an Insolent Pamphlet entitled *The Anatomy of Great Britain* is anatomiz'd, and its design and authors detected and exposed. London, Price 1 s. [in-8º, pp. 102] (3 editions in 1717).

Fair Payment no Spunge. London, in-8º, printed in the year 1717.

A Farther Argument against Ennobling Foreigners in answer to the two parts of the State Anatomy (by Toland). London, printed in the year 1717, in-octavo.

*What if the Swedes should come? With some Thoughts about keeping the Army on Foot, whether they come or not. London, 1717, in-8º.

*A Short View of the Conduct of the King of Sweden. London, 1717, in-8º.

The Repeal of the Act against Occasional Conformity Consider'd. London, 1717, in-8º.

The Question fairly stated, Whether Now is not the Time to do Justice to the Friends of the Government, as well as to its Enemies? And whether the old excuse of its Not being a proper season will serve any longer? Stand by your friends, do Justice to your Enemies, and fear no Body. London, J. Roberts, J. Harrison, A. Dodd. Price 6ᵈ [in-8º, pp. 33].

The Danger and Consequence of disobliging the Clergy consider'd, as it relates To making a Law for regulating the University, and repealing some Laws which concern the Dissenters. In a letter to a noble lord in Oxfordshire. London, Baker, April 9, 1717, 6^d [in-8°, pp. 38].

The Conduct of Robert Walpole, esq. From the beginning of the reign of her late Majesty Queen Anne to the present time. London, T. Warner, 1 s. [in-8°, pp. 66].

*A General Pardon consider'd in its Circumstances and Consequences. London, 1717, in-8°.

*The Report reported: or, the weakness and injustice of the Proceedings of the Convocation in their censure of the Lord Bishop of Bangor, Examin'd and Expos'd. Judge righteous Judgment. London, S. Baker, 6^d [in-8°, pp. 39].

A Vindication of Dr. Snape, in answer to several libels lately published against him. With some further remarks on the Bishop of Bangor's sermon. By which it will plainly appear who is the truest friend of the Church, the bishop or the Dr.-O Tempora! O Mores! . . . London, Dodd. 6^d [in-8°, pp. 32].

Mr. Benjamin Hoadley. Against the Right Reverend Father in God Benjamin, Lord Bishop of Bangor; or, an humble reply to His Lordship's *Answer to the Rev. Dr. Snape's letter occasion'd by that great Prelate's Sermon,* preach'd before the King at St. James's, March 31, 1717. London, T. Warner [in-8°, pp. 48].

*The Old Whig and Modern Whig revived in the Present Divisions at Court. London, 1717, in-8°.

A Letter to Andrew Snape, occasion'd by the Strife that lately appeared among the People called Clergy-men. By the Author of the Declaration of Truth. London, T. Warner, Aug. 24, 6^d [in-8°, pp. 30]. (Pamphlet against Snape, in quaker style.)

The Conduct of Christians made the Sport of Infidels. In a letter from a Turkish Merchant at Amsterdam to the Grand Mufti at Constantinople: on occasion of some of our National follies, but especially the late Scandalous Quarrel among the Clergy. London, S. Baker, 6^d [in-8°, pp. 38].

Observations on the Bishop's Answer to Dr. Snape. By a Lover of Truth. London, S. Baker, 6^d [in-8°, pp. 34].

Contributions to *Mist's Journal:* The Weekly Journal, or Saturday's Post (each number, 12 pp., small folio), starting with n° 37 (Aug. 24th).

A Curious Little Oration, Delivered by Father Andrew, concerning the Great Quarrels that divide the Clergy of France. Translated from the 4th ed. of the French by Dan. De Foe. 3^d [in-8°, pp. 20] (2nd ed. in 1717).

Contributions to the journal: *Mercurius Politicus.*

Contributions to *Dormer's News Letter.*

1718

Mr. De la Pillonnière's Vindication: being an Answer to the 2 School-masters, and their boys' Tittle Tattle, wherein the Dispute between Dr. Snape and Mr. Pillonnière is set in a true light. By the Author of the Layman's Vindication. London, T. Warner, 6^d [in-8°, pp. 34].

Memoirs of Publick Transactions in the Life and Ministry of his Grace the
D. of Shrewsbury. In which will be found much of the History of Parties,
and especially of Court Divisions, during the last Four Reigns; which no
History has yet given an Account of. London, T. Warner, 2 s. [in-8⁰, pp. 139].
May 6.

The Case of the War in Italy Stated. Being a Serious Enquiry, how far Great
Britain is Engaged to concern itself in the Quarrel between the Emperor
and the King of Spain. London, T. Warner, 6ᵈ [in-8⁰, pp. 34].

Memoirs of the Life and Eminent Conduct of that Learned and Reverend Divine, Daniel Williams, D. D. With some Account of his Scheme for the
Vigorous Propagation of Religion, as well in England as in Scotland, and
several other Parts of the World. Address'd to Mr. Peirce. London, E. Curll.
Price 2 s 6ᵈ Bound [in-8°, pp. 86].

*Some Persons vindicated against the author of the *Defection* [Tindall]; and that
writer convicted of Malice and Falsehood. R . . . W . . . esq. "Much Malice
mingled with but little wit" (Dryden). London, Boreham, 6ᵈ [in-8⁰, pp. 40].
(Justification of Townshend and of Walpole).

The *Defection* farther Consider'd, wherein the resigners, as some would have
them stil'd, are really deserters. London, Boreham, 6ᵈ [in-8⁰, pp. 38].

Considerations on the Present State of Affairs in Great Britain. London, J. Roberts [small in-4⁰, p. 40].

The Family Instructor. Vol. II. In 2 Parts: I. Relating to Family Breaches, and
their obstructing Religious Duties. II. To the Great Mistake of mixing the
Passions, in the Managing and Correcting of Children. With a great variety
of Cases of Setting Ill Examples to Children [in-12, pp. vi and 404] (in 1766
the 8th edition appeared).

*A Vindication of the Press: or, an Essay on the Usefulness of writing, on Criti-
cism and the Qualification of Authors. London, 1718.

Contributions to the following miscellany: *A Continuation of Letters Written by
a Turkish Spy at Paris* [by J. P. Marana]. Giving an Impartial Account to
the Divan at Constantinople of the most remarkable Transactions of Europe,
and Discovering several Intrigues and Secrets of the Christian Courts, especially
of that of France: continued from the year 1687 to the year 1693. Written
originally in Arabick, Translated into Italian, and from thence into English.
London, 1718.

A Brief Comment upon His Majesty's Speech: Being Reasons for strengthening
the Church of England by taking off the Penal Laws against Dissenters.
By one called a Low-Churchman. London, T. Warner, 6ᵈ [in-8°, pp.
38].

A History of the session of the present Parliament, with a correct list of both
houses. London, Boreham, 1 s. 6ᵈ [in-8⁰, pp. 136]. (Collection of official
documents edited by De Foe and preceded by an introduction against Boyer.)

Contribution to the tri-weekly journal: *The Whitehall Evening Post,* founded
by De Foe September 18 (each number, 4 pp. in-4⁰ in 2 columns).

Contributions to *Mercurius Politicus.*

Contributions to *Dormer's News Letter* (up to Aug.)

Contributions to *Mist's Journal*: The Weekly Journal or Saturday's Post.

1719

A Friendly Rebuke to One Parson Benjamin; Particularly Relating to his Quarrelling with his own Church and Vindicating Dissenters. By one of the People called Quakers. London, E. Moor, 6ᵈ [in-8°, pp. 32], Jan. 10.

The Life and Strange Surprizing Adventures of Robinson Crusoe, of York, Mariner: Who lived eight and twenty Years all alone on an uninhabited Island on the Coast of America, near the Mouth of the Great River of Oroonoque; Having been Cast on Shore by Shipwreck, wherein all the Men perished but himself. With an Account how he was at last strangely delivered by Pyrates. Written by Himself. London. Printed for W. Taylor, at the Ship in Paternoster Row [in-8°, Front., pp. 364], April 25 (2nd ed., May 12; 3rd ed., June 6; 4th ed., Aug. 8, etc.).

The Farther Adventures of Robinson Crusoe. Being the Second and Last Part of his Life, and of the Strange Surprizing Accounts of his Travels Round three Parts of the Globe. Written by Himself. To which is added a Map of the World, in which is Delineated the Voyages of Robinson Crusoe. London, Printed for W. Taylor, at the Ship in Paternoster Row [in-8°, pp. 373], Aug. 20.

Some Account of the Life and most Remarkable Actions of George Henry, Baron de Goertz, Privy Counsellor and chief Minister of State to the late King of Sweden. London, Bickerton [in-8°, portrait, pp. 46], May.

A Letter to the Dissenters. London, J. Roberts, 6ᵈ [in-8°, pp. 27], May.

The Anatomy of Exchange Alley; or a System of Stock-Jobbing; proving that Scandalous Trade, as it is now carried on, to be knavish in its private Practice, and Treason in its Publick. Being a clear Detection: I. Of the private Cheats, used to deceive one another. II. Of their Arts to draw Innocent Families into their Snare, understood by their new Term of Art, viz. Being let into the Secret. III. Of their Raising and Spreading false News, to ground the Rise or Fall of Stocks upon. IV. Of the Dangerous Consequences of their Practices, and the Necessity there is to Regulate or Suppress them. To which is added some Characters of the most Eminent Persons concern'd now, and for some years past, in carrying on this pernicious Trade. By a Jobber. London, Smith and Warner, 1 s. [in-8°, pp. 64], July 11 (2nd ed., March 26, 1720).

Contributions to the following work: *History of the Reign of King George,* from the Death of her late Majesty Queen Anne to the 1st of August, 1718. Collected from the most authentick vouchers; supported by evidence of fact, and entirely unconcern'd in the separate interest of persons or parties. To be continued yearly. London, Printed for N. Mist in Carter lane, 1719 [in-8°, pp. 252 and 232, indexes].

The Just Complaint of the Poor Weavers truly represented, with as much answer as it deserves to a Pamphlet lately written against them, entitled *"The Weaver's Pretences Examin'd,* etc." London, Boreham [in-8°, pp. 43], August.

A Brief State of the Question between the Printed and Painted Callicoes and the Woollen and Silk manufacture, as far as it relates to the Wearing and using of Printed and Painted Callicoes in Great Britain. London, Boreham [in-8°, pp. 48].

The Dumb Philosopher: or Great Britains Wonder, containing: I. A Faithful and very Surprizing Account, how Dickory Cronke, a Tinner's Son, in the County of Cornwall, was born Dumb, and continued so for 58 years; and how, some Days before he Died, he came to his Speech. With Memoirs of his Life, and the manner of his Death. II. A Declaration of his Faith and Principles in Religion: With a Collection of Select Meditations composed in his Retirement. III. His Prophetical Observations upon the Affairs of Europe, more particularly of Great Britain from 1720 to 1729. The whole extracted from his original Papers, and confirmed by unquestionable authority. To which is annexed, His Elegy, written by a young Cornish Gentleman of Exeter College in Oxford. With an Epitaph by another Hand. London, Bickerton, 1 s. [in-8°, pp. 64], October 14 (2nd ed., May 27, 1720).

*Charity still a Christian Virtue; or an Impartial Account of the Tryal and Conviction of the Rev. Mr. Hendley for Preaching a Charity Sermon at Chisselhurst. And of Mr. Campman and Mr. Harding, for Collecting at the same Time the Alms of the Congregation. At the Assizes held at Rochester, on Wedn. July 15, 1719. Offered to the Consideration of the Clergy of the Church of England. London, Bickerton. 1 s. [in-8°, Front., pp. 72], October 16 (pamphlet probably revised and edited by De Foe).

The King of Pirates: Being an Account of the Famous Enterprizes of Captain Avery, the Mock King of Madagascar; with his Rambles and Piracies, wherein all the Sham Accounts formerly published of him are detected. In Two Letters from himself, one during his Stay at Madagascar, and one since his Escape from thence. London, Bettesworth. 1 s. 6ᵈ [in-8°, pp. vi and 93], December 10 (2nd ed. in 1720).

Contributions to the journal: *The Daily Post* (each number 2 pp., small f°). Founded by De Foe Oct. 4.

Contributions to the journal: *Mercurius Politicus.*

Contributions to *Mist's Weekly Journal.*

Contributions to the *Whitehall Evening Post.*

*Contributions to the journal: *The Manufacturer*: or the British Trade truly Stated. Wherein the Case of Weavers and the Wearing of Calicoes are considered (beginning with October 30) (bi-weekly).

1720

The Chimera: or, the French Way of Paying National Debts Laid Open. Being an Impartial Account of the Proceedings in France for Raising a Paper Credit, and Settling the Mississippi Stock. London, T. Warner, 1 s. [in-8°, pp. 76], Jan. 5.

An Historical Account of the Voyages and Adventures of Sir Walter Raleigh. With the Discoveries and Conquests he made for the Crown of England. Also a particular Account of his Several Attempts for the Discovery of the

Gold Mines in Guiana, and the Reason of the Miscarriage, shewing, That it was not from any Defect in the Scheme he had laid, or in the Reality of the Thing itself, but in a Treacherous Discovery of the Design and of the Strength he had with him to the Spaniards. To which is added, An Account how that Rich Country might be now with Ease, Possess'd, Planted and Secur'd to the British Nation, and What immense Wealth and Increase of Commerce might be raised from thence. Humbly proposed to the South-Sea Company. London, W. Boreham, 1 s. [in-8º, pp. 55]. The brochure bears the date 1719 but it was not out until Jan., 1720.

The Trade to India, critically and calmly consider'd and prov'd to be destructive to the General Trade of Great Britain, as well as to the Woollen and Silk Manufacturers in Particular. London, W. Boreham, [in-8°, pp. 45], Feb. 13.

The History of the Life and Adventures of Mr. Duncan Campbell, A Gentleman, who though born Deaf and Dumb writes down any Stranger's Name at First Sight; and their Future Contingencies of Fortune. Now living in Exeter Court, over against the Savoy in the Strand. London, E. Curll, 5 s. [in-8º, pp. xxiv and 320], May 3, 1720, 2nd ed., Aug. 4; 3rd ed. under the title The Supernatural Philosopher, 1728; 4th ed., Dec. 21, 1728. (This work is only partially by De Foe.)

Memoirs of a Cavalier: or a Military Journal of the Wars in Germany and the Wars in England. From the year 1632 to the year 1648. Written threescore years ago, by an English Gentleman, who served first in the Army of Gustavus Adolphus, the Glorious King of Sweden, till his Death, and after that in the Royal Army of King Charles the First, from the Beginning of the Rebellion to the End of the War. London, Bell, Osborn, Taylor, and Warner [in-8º, pp. vi and 338], May 24.

The Life, Adventures and Piracies of the Famous Captain Singleton: Containing an Account of his being set on Shore in the Island of Madagascar, his Settlement there, with a Description of the Place and Inhabitants: Of his Passage from thence in a Paraguay, to the Main Land of Africa, with an Account of the Customs and Manners of the People: His great Deliverances from the Barbarous Natives and Wild Beasts: Of his meeting with an Englishman, a citizen of London, amongst the Indians. The great Riches he Acquired, and his Voyage Home to England. As also Captain Singleton's Return to Sea, with an Account of his many Adventures and Pyracies with the famous Captain Avery and others. London, Brotherton, Graves, Dodd and Warner [in-8º, pp. 344], June 4.

The Case fairly stated between the Turky Company and the Italian Merchants. By a Merchant. London. Printed in the year 1720 [in-8º, pp. 48]. (Pamphlet written against the company and its commercial monopoly.)

Serious Reflections during the Life and Surprizing Adventures of Robinson Crusoe. With his Vision of the Angelick World. Written by Himself. London, W. Taylor [in-8°, front., pp. viii, 270 and 84].

*A Letter to the Author of the Independent Whig. Wherein the Merits of the Clergy are consider'd; the Good vindicated and the Bad expos'd. With some Account of the late Controversy in the Church. By One who has no Dependence on Church, State or Exchange-Alley. London, A. Moore, 6ᵈ [in-8°, pp. 32].

*A Letter to the *Independent Whig* occasion'd by his Consideration of the importance of Gibraltar to the British Empire. London, A. Moore, 6ᵈ [in-8°, pp. 36].

The Compleat Art of Painting. A Poem. Translated from the French of M. Du Fresnoy. By D. F. Gent. London, T. Warner, 1 s. [in-8°, pp. 53].

Contributions starting with June 25 to: *Applebee's Original Weekly Journal.*

Contributions up to September to *Mercurius Politicus.*

Contributions in October-November to the journal *The Director.*

Contributions up to June to the *Whitehall Evening Post.*

Contributions to *Mist's Weekly Journal.*

Contributions to the *Daily Post.*

1721

*A Vindication of the Honour and Justice of Parliament against a Scandalous Libel, Entituled *the Speech of John A—* [Aislabie] *Esq.* London, A. More, [in-8°, pp. 36], February.

A True State of Public Credit; or a short view on the Condition of the Nation, with respect to our present Calamities. And some Considerations how they may be redress'd and the Landed and trading interest advanced. As also some necessary observations on the conduct of the Bank, in this critical Juncture. Dedicated to the Right Honourable Sir John Fryer, Bart., lord mayor of the City of London; occasion'd by the City petition to the Honourable House of Commons. London, T. Warner, [in-8°, pp. 32], May.

Contributions to *Mist's Journal.*

Contributions to *Applebee's Journal.*

Contributions to the *Daily Post.*

1722

A Collection of Miscellany Letters, selected out of Mist's Weekly Journal, 4 vol., 12 mo., Jan. 9. Republished June 26 in 2 vol. in-8°.

The Fortunes and Misfortunes of the Famous Moll Flanders, who was born in Newgate, and during a Life of continued Variety, for Threescore years, beside her Childhood, was Twelve years a Whore, Five Times a Wife (whereof once to her own Brother), Twelve years a Thief, Eight years a Transported Felon in Virginia, at last grew Rich, liv'd Honest, and died a Penitent. Written from her own Memorandums. London, W. Chetwood, T. Eddin (dated 1721) [in 8°, pp. xiii and 424], 1st ed., Jan. 27; 2nd ed. (by Brotherton, pp. iv and 366), July 23; 3rd ed. (by Chetwood), December 21 (reprinted Nov. 2, 1723). Abridged edition published by Read July, 1723.

Due Preparations for the Plague, as well for soul as body. Being some seasonable thoughts upon the Visible approach of the present dreadful contagion in France; the properest measures to prevent it, and the great work of submitting to it. London, E. Matthews, J. Batley, 12ᵐᵒ [pp. xi and 272]. 1 s. 6ᵈ., Feb. 8.

Religious Courtship: Being Historical Discourses on the Necessity of Marrying
Religious Husbands and Wives only. As also of Husbands and Wives being
of the same Opinions in Religion with one Another. With an Appendix of
the Necessity of taking none but Religious Servants, and a Proposal for the
better Managing of Servants. London, E. Matthews [in-8°, pp. iv and 358],
Feb. 20.

A Journal of the Plague Year. Being Observations or Memorials of the most
Remarkable Occurrences, as well Publick as Private, which happened in London during the Great Visitation in 1665. Written by a Citizen who continued
all the while in London. Never made Publick before. London, E. Nutt,
Roberts, Dodd [in-8°, pp. 287], March 17 (reprinted in 1754 under the
title: *The History of the Great Plague in London*).

*A Brief Debate upon the Dissolving of the late Parliament. Printed in the year
1722 (April).

*A History of the Archbishops and Bishops who have been Impeach'd and at-
tainted of High Treason, from William the Conqueror to this Time. With
an account of their impeachments and defences, the character of their persons in prosperity and adversity, their public and private charities and bene-
factions: as also the Behaviour of those who suffer'd death. Extracted from
the best Historians, ancient and modern. London, J. Roberts. 1 s. [in-8°,
pp. 75], September (compilation undoubtedly in part by De Foe and occasioned by the arrest of the Bishop of Rochester).

The History and Remarkable Life of the truly Honourable Colonel Jacque, vul-
garly called Col. Jack, who was born a Gentleman; put 'Prentice to a Pickpocket; was 26 years a Thief, and then kidnapped to Virginia; came back
a Merchant; was 5 Times married to 4 Whores; went into the Wars, be-
haved bravely, got Preferment, was made Colonel of a Regiment, came
over, and fled with the Chevalier, is still abroad Completing a Life of
Wonders, and resolves to die a General. London: Brotherton, Payne, Mears,
Dodd, Chetwood, Grave, Chapman, Stagg [in-8°, pp. vii and 399], December 20; 2nd ed., Jan. 19, 1723; 3rd ed., 1724.

Contributions to *Mist's Journal*.
Contributions to *Applebee's Journal*.
Contributions to the *Daily Post*.

1723

*An Impartial History of the Life and Actions of Peter Alexowitz, the present
Czar of Muscovy: from his Birth down to this present Time. Giving an
Account of his Travels and Transactions in the Several Courts of Europe.
With his Attempts and Successes in the Northern and Eastern Parts of the
World. In which is intermixed the History of Muscovy. Written by a British
Officer in the Service of the Czar. London. W. Chetwood, J. Stagg, J. Broth-
erton and T. Edlin. 5 s. [in-8°, pp. 420]. Compilation probably directed by
De Foe. A new edition appeared in 1725 under the title: *A True, Authen-
tick, and impartial History . . . etc. . . .*

Contributions to the *Daily Post*.
Contributions to *Mist's Journal*.

Contributions to *Applebee's Journal*.
N. B.—During the whole year De Foe was preparing his Tour through Great Britain.

1724

The Fortunate Mistress; or, a History of the Life and Vast Varieties of Fortunes of Mademoiselle de Belau; afterwards called the Countess of Wintelsheim in Germany. Being the Person known by the name of the Lady Roxana, in the Time of King Charles the Second. London: T. Warner, W. Meadows, W. Pepper, S. Harding and E. Edlin [in-8°, Front., pp. iii and 407], March 14. New edition, with continuation, in 1745. Abridged by F. Noble (1775).

The Great Law of Subordination Consider'd: or, the Insolence, and Unsufferable Behaviour of Servants in England duly enquired into. Illustrated with a great Variety of Examples, Historical Cases and Remarkable Stories of the Behaviour of some particular Servants, Suited to all the Several Arguments made use of as they go on. In Ten Familiar Letters. Together with a Conclusion, being an Earnest and Moving Remonstrance, to the Housekeepers and Heads of Families in Great Britain, pressing them not to cease using their Utmost Interest (especially at this Juncture) to obtain sufficient Laws for the effectual Regulation of the Manners and Behaviour of their Servants. As also a Proposal, containing such Heads, or Constitutions, as would effectually answer this great End, and bring Servants of every class to a just (and yet not a Grievous) Regulation. London, S. Harding, etc. 3 s. 6ᵈ [in-8°, pp. ii and 302], April 4 (new ed. in 1726 under the title: *The Behaviour of Servants in England*).

Considerations on publick Credit. In a letter to a member of Parliament. London, J. Roberts, 4ᵈ [in-8°, pp. 23].

*Some farther Account of the Original Disputes in Ireland, about farthings and halfpence, in a discourse with a Quaker in Dublin. London [in-8°, pp. 47].

A Tour thro' the whole Island of Great Britain; divided into Circuits or Journies. Giving a Particular and Diverting Account of whatever is Curious and worth Observation, viz: I. A Description of the Principal Cities and Towns, their Situation, Magnitude, Government and Commerce. II. The Customs, Manners, Speech; as also the Exercises, Diversions, and Employment of the People. III. The Produce and Improvement of the Land, the Trade and Manufactures. IV. The Seaports and Fortifications, with the Course of Rivers, and the Inland Navigation. V. The Publick Edifices, Seats and Palaces, of the Gentry and Nobility. With useful Observations on the whole, Particularly fitted for the Reading of Such, as Desire to Travel over the Island. By a Gentleman. London: G. Strahan, Mears, Francklin, Chapman, Stagg, Graves; vol. I, May 23 [in-8°, engraving of the siege of Colchester in 1648, pp. vii, 140, 121, and 127] (a few de luxe copies sold at 10 s).

A Narrative of the Proceedings in France, for Discovering and Detecting the Murderers of the English Gentlemen, Sept. 21, 1723, near Calais. With an

Account of the Condemnation and Sentence of Joseph Bizeau and Peter Le Febvre. Two Notorious Robbers, who were the principal Actors in the said Murder; particularly in the killing Mr. Lock. Together with their Discovery and manner of perpetrating that execrable Murder; and also large Memoirs of their Behaviour during their Torture, and upon the Scaffold; their impeaching Several other Criminals, and a brief History of their Past Crimes, as well in Company with their former Captain, the famous Cartouche, as Since his Execution. In which is a great Variety of Remarkable Incidents, and Surprizing Circumstances, never yet made publick. Translated from the French. London: Printed for J. Roberts in Warwick Lane, 2 s. [in-8º, pp. 108], Aug. 17.

*The History of the Remarkable Life of John Sheppard. Containing a Particular Account of his Many Robberies and Escapes. Including his last Escape from the Castle, at Newgate. Printed and Published by John Applebee, 1 s. [in-8º], October 19 (2nd ed., Oct. 26; 3rd ed., Nov. 12).

A New Voyage round the World, By a Course never Sailed before. Being a Voyage undertaken by some Merchants, who afterwards proposed the setting up of an East India Company in Flanders. Illustrated with Copper Plates. London.: A. Bettesworth and W. Mears [in-8º, p. 208 and 205], Nov. 9.

A Narrative of all the Robberies, Escapes etc. of John Sheppard, Giving an Exact Description of the Manner of his Wonderful Escape from the Castle in Newgate, and of the Methods he took afterwards for his Security. Written by himself during his Confinement in the Middle Stone Room, after his being retaken in Drury Lane. To which is Prefixed a true Representation of his Escape, from the condemned Hold, Curiously Engraven on a Copper Plate. The whole Published at the particular request of the Prisoner. London, Applebee, 6ᵈ [in-8º, front., pp. 31]. November 17 (2nd ed., Nov. 18; 3rd ed., Nov. 19; 4th ed., Nov. 20; 5th ed., Nov. 21; 6th ed., Nov. 28; 7th ed., Dec. 12; 8th ed., Dec. 20).

Contributions to the *Daily Post*.
Contributions to *Mist's Journal* (up to Oct. 21).
Contributions to *Applebee's Journal*.

1725

Everybody's Business is Nobody's Business; or, Private Abuses, Publick Grievances. Exemplified in the Pride, Insolence and Exorbitant Wages of our Women Servants, Footmen, etc. By Andrew Moreton, Esq., June 5; 2nd ed., June 9; 3rd ed. [in-8º, pp. 34], June 14; 4th ed., June 19; 5th ed. (with preface), July 24, etc.

A Tour thro' the whole Island of Great Britain. Vol. II, with a Map of England and Wales by Mr. Moll [in-8º, pp. viii, 192 and 200; index of the two first vol., pp. xxxvi], June 8.

The True, Genuine and Perfect Account of the Life and Actions of Jonathan Wild. Taken from good Authority, and from his own Writings. London, J. Applebee [in-8º], June 8 (2nd ed., June 10; 3rd ed., June 12, etc.).

An Account of the Conduct and Proceedings of the late John Gow, alias Smith, Captain of the late Pirates, executed for Murther and Piracy, committed on board the George Galley, afterwards called the Revenge; with a Revelation of all the horrid Murthers they committed in Cold Blood. As also of their being taken at the Islands of Orkney, and sent up prisoners to London. London, J. Applebee, 1 s. [in-8°, pp. viii and 62], June 11.

The Complete English Tradesman, In Familiar Letters, Directing him in all the several Parts and Progressions of Trade—viz. I. His acquainting himself with Business during his Apprenticeship. II. His Writing to His Correspondents, and obtaining a general Knowledge of Trade, as well what he is not as what he is employ'd in. III. Of Diligence, and Application, as the Life of all Business. IV. Cautions against Over-Trading. V. Of the ordinary Occasions of a Tradesman's Ruin; such as Expensive Living, Too early Marrying, Innocent Diversions, Giving and Taking too much Credit, Leaving Business to Servants, Being above Business, Entering into Dangerous Partnerships, etc. VI. Directions in the several Distresses of a Tradesman, when he comes to fail. VII. Of Tradesmen Compounding with their Debtors, and why they are so particularly severe. VIII. Of Tradesmen ruining one another, by Rumour and Scandal. IX. Of the Customary Frauds of Trade, which even honest Men allow themselves to practise. X. Of Credit, and how it is only supported by Honesty. XI. Directions for Book-keeping, punctual paying Bills, and thereby maintaining Credit. XII. Of the Dignity and Honour of Trade in England, more than in any other Countries; and how the Trading Families in England are mingled with the Nobility and Gentry, so as not to be separated, or distinguished. Calculated for the Instruction of Our Inland Tradesmen, and especially of Young Beginners. London; Ch. Rivington [in-8°, pp. xv and 447], September 11. Second edition. To which is added a Supplement, Containing:

> I. A Warning against Tradesmen's Borrowing Money upon Interest. II. A Caution against that Destructive Practice, of drawing and Remitting, as also discounting Promissory Bills, meerly for a supply of Cash. III. Directions for the Tradesman's accounts, with brief but plain Examples, and Specimens for Book-Keeping. IV. Of keeping a Duplicate or Pocket Ledger, in Case of Fire. London, Rivington [in-8°, pp. xx, 368 and 148 pp. of Supplement], September 10, 1726. (Supplement alone, 1 s.)

Contribution to the *Daily Post* (up to April 27).
Contribution to *Applebee's Journal*.

1726

The Friendly Daemon; or the Generous Apparition. Being a True Narrative of a Miraculous Cure newly performed upon that famous Deaf and Dumb Gentleman Dr. Duncan Campbell. By a familiar Spirit, that appeared to him in a white surplice, like a Cathedral Singing Boy. London, J. Roberts [in-8°, pp. 39] (in part by De Foe).

A Brief Historical Account of the Lives of the Six notorious Street-robbers who were executed on Wednesday April 6, at Kingston, viz: Wm. Blewet, Edw.

Burnworth, Emmanuel Dickenson, Thomas Berry, John Higgs, and John Legee; with a particular relation of their early introduction into the desperate trade of Street-Robbing, and especially of Murther, and of several Robberies which they and others of their gang have been concern'd in. London, A. Moor. 6ᵈ., April 9.

The Political History of the Devil, As well Ancient as Modern. In two Parts. I. Containing a State of the Devil's Circumstances, and the Various Turns in his affairs, from his Expulsion out of Heaven, to the Creation of Man. With remarks on the Several Mistakes concerning the Reason and Manner of his Fall. Also his Proceedings with Mankind, ever since Adam, to the first planting of the Christian Religion in the World. Part II. Containing his more Private Conduct down to the present Times; His Government, his Appearances, his Manner of Working, and the Tools he works with. London, T. Warner [in-8º, Front., pp. iv and 408], May 7 (2nd ed., April 20, 1727; 3rd ed., 1734, etc.).

Mere Nature Delineated; or a Body without a Soul. Being Observations upon the young Forester lately brought to Town from Germany. With suitable Applications. Also a Brief Dissertation upon the Usefulness and necessity of Fools, whether Political or Natural. London, Warner, 1 s. 6ᵈ [in-8º, pp. 123], July 23.

An Essay upon Literature; or, an Enquiry into the Antiquity and Original of Letters. Proving that the two Tables, written by the Finger of God in Mount Sinai, was the first Writing in the World; and that all other Alphabets derive from the Hebrew. With a short view of the methods made use of by the Ancients to supply the want of Letters before, and improve the use of them, after they were known. London, Th. Bowles [in-8º, pp. 127].

*Unparallel'd Cruelty: or, the tryal of Captain Jeane of Bristol. Who was convicted at the Old Bailey for the Murder of his Cabin-boy, who he put to death in the most horrid and barbarous Manner that ever was heard of. To which is added An account of his life and conversion both before and after his Condemnation; with his dying Speech and Behaviour at the place of execution. London, T. Warner, 6ᵈ [in-8º, pp. 35].

A Tour thro' the whole Island of Great Britain. Vol. III, Which completes this Work, and contains a Tour thro' Scotland etc. With a Map of Scotland by Mr. Moll [in-8º, carte, pp. iii, 239 and 230, index], Aug. 13 (2nd ed. of the Tour, 3 vol., June 15, 1727).

A Brief Case of the Distillers and of the Distilling trade in England, Shewing How far it is in the interest of England to encourage the said trade, as it is so considerable an advantage To the Landed interest, To the trade and navigation, To the publick revenue and To the employment of the Poor. Humbly recommended to the Lords and Commons of Great Britain in the present Parliament assembled. London, T. Warner, 1 s. [in-8º, pp. 52].

A General History of the Principal Discoveries and Improvements in Useful Arts. Particularly in the Great Branches of Commerce, Navigation, and Plantation in all Parts of the known World. A work which may entertain the Curious with the view of their present state, prompt the Indolent to retrieve those inventions that are neglected, and animate the Diligent to advance and perfect what may be thought wanting. London, J. Roberts [in-8°, pp. viii and 307 and index]. (This work was published monthly in 4 parts—Oct., 1726, Jan., 1727.)

The Four Years' Voyages of Capt. George Roberts. Being a Series of Uncommon Events which befel him in a Voyage to the Islands of the Canaries, Cape de Verd, and Barbadoes, from whence he was bound to the coast of Guiney. The manner of his being taken by Three Pyrate Ships, commanded by Low, Russel and Spriggs, who after having plundered him, and detained him ten days, put him aboard his own Sloop, without provisions, water, etc.: and with only two boys, one of eighteen, and the other of eight years of age. The Hardships he endured for above twenty days, till he arrived at the Island of St. Nicholas, from whence he was blown off to sea (before he could get any sustenance), without his boat and biggest boy, whom he had sent ashore; and after four days of difficulty and distress, was shipwrecked on the unfrequented Island of St. John, where, when he had remained near two years he built a vessel to bring him off. With a particular and curious Description and Draught of the Cape de Verd Islands, their Roads, Anchoring Places, Nature and Productions of the Soils; the Kindness and Hospitality of the Natives to Strangers; their Religion, Manners, Customs and Superstitions. Together with Observations on the Minerals, Mineral Waters, Metals, etc.; Salts, and of the Nitre with which some of these Islands abound. Written by Himself, and interspersed with many pleasant and profitable Remarks, very instructive for all those who use this Trade, or who may have the misfortune to meet with any of the like distresses either by Pyracy or Shipwreck. Adorned with several Copper-Plates. London, A. Bettesworth [in-8°, pp. 458].

*Some Considerations upon Street-Walkers. With a Proposal for Lessening the Present Number of them. In two letters to a Member of Parliament. To which is added A letter from one of those unhappy Persons, when in Newgate, and who was afterwards executed, for picking a Gentleman's pocket, to Mrs.— in Great P—ney Street. London, A. Moore, 6ᵈ. [in-8°, pp. 18], October 15. New ed. in Jan., 1727.

The Protestant Monastery, or, a Complaint against the Brutality of the Present Age. Particularly the Pertness and Insolence of our Youth to Aged Persons. With a Caution to People in Years how they give the Staff out of their own Hands, and leave themselves to the Mercy of others. Concluding with a Proposal for Erecting a Protestant Monastery, where Persons of small Fortune may End their Days in Plenty, Ease and Credit, without Burthening their Relations, or accepting Publick Charities. By Andrew Moreton, Esq. Author of Everybody's Business is Nobody's Business. London, W. Meadows [dated 1727] 6ᵈ. [in-8°, pp. viii and 31], November 26 (new edition in 1727).

A System of Magick; or, a History of the Black Art. Being an Historical Account of Mankind's most early Dealings with the Devil, and how the Acquaintance on both Sides first began. London, J. Roberts [in-8°, front., pp. v and 403], Dec. 19 (2nd ed., with additions, Jan. 16, 1731).

Contributions to *Applebee's Journal* (up to March).

1727

The Evident Approach of a War: and Something of the Necessity of it, in order to Establish Peace and Preserve Trade. To which is added an Exact Plan and Description of the Bay and City of Gibraltar. London, J. Roberts, 1 s. 6d. [in-8°, Plan, pp. 59], Jan. 11.

Conjugal Lewdness: or, Matrimonial Whoredom. London, T. Warner [in-8°, pp. iv and 406], Jan. 30. Reprinted June 10 under the title: A Treatise concerning the Use and Abuse of the Marriage Bed. Shewing. I. The Nature of Matrimony, its Sacred Original, and the True Meaning of its Institution. II. The gross abuse of Matrimonial Chastity from the Wrong Notions which have possessed the World, degenerating even to Whoredom. III. The Diabolical practice of attempting to prevent Child-bearing by Physical Preparations. IV. The fatal Consequences of clandestine, or forced Marriages, thro' the Persuasion, Interest, or Influence of Parents and Relations, to wed the Person they have no love for, but oftentimes an Aversion to. V. Of unequal Matches as to the Disproportion of Age; and how such many Ways occasion a Matrimonial Whoredom. VI. How married Persons may be guilty of Conjugal Lewdness, and that a Man may in effect make a Whore of his own Wife. Also many other Particulars of Family Concern.

The Evident Advantages to Great Britain and its Allies from the approaching war: especially in matters of Trade. To which is added two curious Plans, one of the Port and Bay of Havana; the other of Porto-Bello. London, J. Roberts, 1 s. [in-8°, pp. 44], Feb. 11.

A Brief deduction of the Original, Progress and Immense Greatness of the British Woollen Manufacture. London, Printed in the year 1727.

An Essay on the History and Reality of Apparitions. Being an Account of What they are, and What they are not; Whence they come and Whence they come not; As also how we may distinguish the Apparitions of Good and Evil Spirits, and how we ought to behave to them. With a great Variety of Surprizing and Diverting Examples, never published before. London, J. Roberts, etc. [in-8°, pp. vi and 395], March 22. Reprinted in November, 1728 by the editor Peele under the title: The Secrets of the Invisible World Disclos'd: or, An Universal History of Apparitions, Sacred and Prophane, under all Denominations; whether Angelical, Diabolical, or Human Souls Departed . . . etc. . . . By Andrew Moreton, Esq. 5s. (2nd ed., Feb. 13, 1729).

The Compleat English Tradesman. Volume II. In Two Parts. Part. I. Directed chiefly to the more Experienc'd Tradesmen; with Cautions and Advices to them after they are thriven, and suppos'd to be grown rich, viz. I. Against Running out of their Business into needless Projects and Dangerous Adventures, no Tradesman being above Disaster. II. Against Oppressing one another by Engrossing, Underselling, Combinations in Trade etc. III. Advices, that when he leaves off his Business, he should part Friends with the World; the great Advantages of it; with a Word of the Scandalous Character of a Purse-proud Tradesman. IV. Against being litigious and vexatious, and apt to go to Law for Trifles; with some Reasons why Tradesmen's Differences should if possible all be ended by Arbitration. Part II. Being useful Generals in Trade, describing the Principles and Foundation of the Home Trade of Great Britain, with large

Tables of our Manufactures, Calculations of the Product, Shipping, Carriage of Goods by Land, Importation from Abroad, Consumption at Home etc. by all which the infinite number of our Tradesmen are employ'd, and the General Wealth of the Nation rais'd and increas'd. The whole calculated for the use of our Inland Tradesmen, as well in the City as in the Country. London, Ch. Rivington [pp. xiv and 298 and 176]. May 13. New edition (2 volumes), Aug. 10, 1728.

A New Family Instructor; in Familiar Discourses between a Father and his Children, on the most Essential Points of the Christian Religion. In Two Parts. Part. I. Containing a Father's INSTRUCTIONS to his Son upon his going to Travel into Popish Countries; and to the rest of his Children, on his Son's turning Papist; confirming them in the Protestant Religion, against the Absurdities of Popery. Part. II. Instructions against the Three Grand Errors of the Times; viz. 1. Asserting the Divine Authority of the Scriptures; against the Deists. 2. Proofs, that the Messias is already come, etc.; against the Atheists and Jews. 3. Asserting the Divinity of Jesus Christ, that he was really the same with the Messias, and that the Messias was to be really GOD; against our Modern Hereticks. With a Poem upon the Divine Nature of JESUS CHRIST, in Blank Verse. By the Author of the Family Instructor. London, T. Warner [in-8°, pp. xv and 384] (new edition in 1732).

Parochial Tyranny: or, the Housekeeper's Complaint against the insupportable Exactions and partial Assessments of select Vestries. With a plain Detection of many Abuses committed in the Distribution of Public Charities. Together with a Practical Proposal for Amending the Same: which will not only take off great Part of the Parish Taxes now subsisting, but ease Parishioners from Serving troublesome Offices, or paying exorbitant Fines. By Andrew Moreton, Esq. London, W. Meadows, 6 d [pp. 36], Dec. 9.

1728

Augusta Triumphans: or, the Way to make London the most Flourishing City in the Universe. I. By Establishing a University where Gentlemen may have Academical Education under the Eyes of their Friends. II. By an Hospital for Foundlings. III. By forming an Academy of Sciences at Christ's Hospital. IV. By Suppressing Pretended Mad-Houses, where many of the fair Sex are unjustly confined, while their Husbands keep Mistresses etc. and many Widows are locked up for the Sake of their Jointure. V. To Save our Youth from Destruction, by clearing the Streets of impudent Strumpets, suppressing Gaming Tables, and Sunday Debauches. VI. To Save our lower class of People from utter Ruin, and render them useful, by preventing the immoderate use of Geneva. With a frank Exposition of many other common Abuses, and incontestable Rules for Amendment. Concluding with an Effectual Method to prevent Street Robberies, and a Letter to Col. Robinson, on Account of the Orphan's Tax. By Andrew Moreton Esq. London, J. Roberts [in-8°, pp. 63], 1 s., March 16; 2nd ed. 1729. Abridged edition in 1730, under the title: The Generous Projector, or a Friendly Proposal to prevent Murder and other enormous Abuses, by Erecting an Hospital for Foundlings, etc.

A Plan of the English Commerce. Being a Compleat Prospect of the Trade of this Nation. As well the Home Trade as the Foreign. In 3 Parts. Part. I. Containing a View of the present Magnitude of the English Trade, as it respects, 1 The Exportation of our own Growth and Manufacture; 2 The Importation of Merchant Goods from Abroad; 3 The Prodigious Consumption of Both at Home. Part. II. Containing an Answer to that Great and Important Question now depending, whether our Trade, and especially our Manufactures, are in a declining Condition or No? Part. III. Containing several Proposals entirely new, for Extending and Improving our Trade, and Promoting the Consumption of our Manufactures in Countries, wherewith we have hitherto had no Commerce. Humbly offered to the Consideration of the King and Parliament. London, C. Rivington, 5s [in-8°, pp. 368], March 23.
    2nd ed. in 1730 [pp. iv, 368 and 40]: To which is added an APPENDIX, containing a View of the Increase of Commerce, not only of England, but of all the Trading Nations of Europe, since the Peace with Spain. The whole Containing several Proposals, entirely new, for Extending and Improving our Trade, etc. (New ed., Jan. 13, 1731.)

An Impartial Account of the late famous siege of Gibraltar: to which are added, most accurate plans of the town, and of the approaches and camp of the Spaniards. With many remarkable transactions never made publick before. By an officer who was at the taking and defence of Gibraltar by the Prince Hesse of glorious memory; and served in the town during the last siege. London, T. Warner [in-8°, pp. 51].

The Military Memoirs of Captain George Carleton; From the Dutch War, 1672, in which he served, to the Conclusion of the Peace at Utrecht, 1713. Illustrating some of the Most Remarkable Transactions, both by Sea and Land, during the Reigns of King Charles and King James II, Hitherto unobserved by all the Writers of those times; Together with an Exact Series of the War in Spain; and a Particular Description of the several Places of the Author's residence in many Cities, Towns, and Countries; Their Customs, Manners, etc. Also Observations on the Genius of the Spaniards (Among whom he continued some Years a Prisoner); their Monasteries and Nunneries, especially that fine one at Montserrat; and in their Public Diversions, more particularly their famous Bull Feasts. London, E. Symon, May 18 (2nd ed., July 27; 3rd ed., 1741). Book edited and revised by De Foe.

Some Considerations on the Reasonableness and Necessity of Encreasing and encouraging the seamen. Founded on the gracious expressions in their favour contained in His Majesty's Speech from the Throne. With some proposed Schemes for the effectual performing it without prejudice either to the Navy or the Commerce. Never made publick before. London, J. Roberts, 1 s. [in-8°, pp. 51].

The Universal Spectator: no 1 (October 12); leading article by De Foe.

Second Thoughts are Best: or a Further Improvement of a late Scheme to Prevent Street Robberies. By which our Streets will be so strongly Guarded, and so gloriously Illuminated, that any part of London will be as safe and pleasant at Midnight, as at Noonday, and Burglary totally impracticable. With some Thoughts for Suppressing Robberies in all the Publick Roads of England, etc. Humbly offered for the good of his Country, Submitted to the Consideration

APPENDIX I

of the Parliament, and Dedicated to his Sacred Majesty George II. By Andrew Moreton Esq. London, W. Meadows. 6d. [in-8°, pp. 24], October 12.

Street Robberies considered. The reason of their being so frequent, with probable means to prevent 'em. To which is added, 3 short Treatises: 1. A Warning for Travellers: with Rules to know a Highwayman, and Instructions how to behave upon the Occasion. 2. Observations on Housebreakers. How to prevent a Tenement from being broke open. With a Word of Advice concerning Servants. 3. A Caveat for Shopkeepers: with a Description of Shoplifts, how to know 'em, and how to prevent 'em; also a Caution of Delivering Goods: With the Relation of several Cheats practised lately upon the Publick. Written by a Converted Thief. To which is prefix'd some Memoirs of his Life. London, J. Roberts, 1 s. [in-8°, pp. 72], Nov. 12 (largely the work of De Foe).

1729

* Fog's Weekly Journal: article in the Jan. 11th number.

Reasons for a War, in Order to Establish the Tranquillity and Commerce of Europe. London, A. Dodd and R. Walker, without Temple Bar; E. Nutt and F. Smith, at the Royal Exchange, and Sold by the Booksellers and Pamphlet Shops, Mercuries and Hawkers of London and Westminster, 6d. [in-8°, pp. 32], March.

An Enquiry into the Pretensions of Spain to Gibraltar, as founded on Her late Majesty's letter to the Catholick King: together with a copy thereof, and a brief answer to the said pretensions. London, R. Walker, 6d. [in-8°, pp. IV and 22], 2nd ed. same year.

An Humble Proposal to the People of England, for the Encrease of their Trade and Encouragement of their Manufactures; whether the present Uncertainty of Affairs issues in Peace or War. By the Author of the Compleat English Tradesman. London, C. Rivington [in-8°, pp. 59], March 15.

Madagascar: or, Robert Drury's Journal, during 15 Years captivity on that Island. containing: 1. His voyage to the East Indies and short stay there. 2. An account of the shipwreck of the Degrave on the island of Madagascar, the murder of Captain Younge and his ship's company except Admiral Bembo's son and some few others, who escap'd the hands of the barbarous natives. 3. His being taken into captivity, hard usage, marriage and variety of fortune. 4. His travels through the island, and description of it; as to its situation, product, manufactures, commodities, etc. 5. The nature of the people, their customs, wars, religion and policy; as also the conferences between the author and some of their chiefs, concerning the Christian and their religion. 6. His redemption from thence by Captain Mackett, commander of the Prince of Wales in the East India Company's service, his arrival to England and second voyage thither. 7. A Vocabulary of the Madagascar language. The whole is a faithful narrative of Matters of facts, interspers'd with variety of surprising incidents, and illustrated with a sheet Map of Madagascar and cuts. Written by himself, digested into order, and now published at the request of his Friends. London, printed and sold by W. Meadows . . . and by the author at Old Tom's Coffee house in Birchin Lane. Price, bound 6 s. [in-8°, pp. xvi and 464].

APPENDIX I

The Advantages of Peace and Commerce, with some remarks on the East India Trade. London, J. Brotherton, 1 s. 6ᵈ. [in-8°, pp. 40].

1730

A Brief State of the Inland or Home Trade of England, and of the oppressions it suffers and the dangers which threaten it from the invasion of Hawkers, Pedlars, and clandestine traders of all sorts. Humbly presented to the Present Parliament. London, T. Warner [in-8°, pp. 70].

*The Perjur'd Free Mason detected; and yet the honour and Antiquity of the Society of Free-masons preserved and defended. By a Free Mason. London, T. Warner, 6ᵈ. [in-8°, pp. 32].

An Effectual Scheme, for the immediate Preventing of Street Robberies, and suppressing the other Disorders of the Night: With a Brief History of the Night-Houses, and an Appendix relating to those Sons of Hell, called Incendiaries. Humbly Inscribed to the Right Honourable, the Lord Mayor of London. London, J. Wilford, 1 s. [in-8°, pp. 72] (dated 1731 but published late in 1730).

Posthumous Works.

The Compleat English Gentleman, edited by Bülbring (London, D. Nutt), in 1890.

Of Royall Education, edited by Bülbring (London, D. Nutt), in 1895.

APPENDIX II

I

BIOGRAPHIES OF DE FOE

A. *General Studies.*

AITKEN (G. A.): *Romances and narratives by Daniel De Foe*: General Introduction (London, 1895) (very good study).

Athenaeum (The): 1894, 2, p. 521: *Wright's life of De Foe* (review of Wright's biography).

BALLANTYNE and SCOTT: Biography of De Foe (*Scott's Prose Works*, vol. IV, and *Tegg's ed. of De Foe's works*, vol. XX).

BASTIDE (Ch.): *Daniel De Foe*: introduction (Paris, La Renaissance du Livre).

British Quarterly Review: 1858, 1869.

Century: September 1893 [*The author of Robinson Crusoe, by* M. O. W. Oliphant].

CHADWICK (Wm.): *The life and times of Daniel De Foe: with remarks digressive and discursive* (London, 1859).

CHALMERS (A.): *Life of De Foe*, 1787.

CHASLES (Ph.): *Daniel De Foe, auteur de Robinson Crusoë* (2nd vol. of the *Dix-huitième siècle en Angleterre*, Paris, 1846).

CIBBER: *Lives of the Poets*, vol. IV (London, 1753).

CLARK (T. A.): *Daniel De Foe* (New York, Parker).

Cornhill Magazine: 1871 *(Daniel De Foe)*.

Correspondant: article by W. H. Robinson in issue of July 10, 1872.

DAWSON (G.): *Biographical lectures* (ed. by G. Saint-Clair, London, 1886), *Daniel De Foe.*

DENNIS (J.): *Studies in English literature* (London, 1876), *Daniel De Foe.*

DOTTIN (P.): *Robinson Crusoe examin'd and criticis'd: or, a new edition of Charles Gildon's famous pamphlet*, etc. (London, 1923).

Eclectic Review: July, 1851.

Edinburgh Review: January, 1830; October, 1845.

FORSTER (J.): *Daniel De Foe* (London, 1855).

HAZLITT (Wm. junior): *Works of De Foe*, introduction (London, 1840).

HEARNSHAW (F. J. C.): *The Social and Political Ideas of Some English Thinkers of the Augustan Era 1650-1750*, London, 1928.

Lectures on Protestant Nonconformists (London, 1853): *Daniel De Foe*, by the Rev. H. S. Brown.

LEE (Wm.): *Daniel De Foe, his life and recently discovered writings* (London, 1869), vol. I.

Literary Guide (The): article by F. J. Gould, April, 1927.

London Quarterly Review: 1881.

MASEFIELD (J.): *Masters of Literature, De Foe;* introduction (London, 1909).

MEYNADIER (G. H.): *The Works of Daniel De Foe* (New York, 1903), introduction.

MINTO (Wm.): *Daniel De Foe* (English Men of Letters, London, 1879).

Musée des Familles, XXXIII, 1865-66, article by Jules Janin.

North American Review: July, 1913 (*The Author of Robinson Crusoe*, by Edith Wyatt).

RANNIE (D. W.): *Daniel De Foe* (The Stanhope essay, Oxford, 1890).

Revue hebdomadaire: 1920 (article by M. G. Grappe).

RUSSELL (W.): *Eccentric Personages*, vol. I (London, 1864).

Saturday Review: Nov. 3, 1894 (analysis of Wright's biography).

SHARP (R. F.): *Architects of English literature,* p. 43-53 (London, 1900).

Spectator: Jan. 5, 1895.

Tait's Magazine: 1859.

TRENT (W. P.): *Daniel De Foe, and how to know him* (Indianapolis, 1916).

Westminster Review: 1830.

WHERRY (A.): *Daniel De Foe* (London, 1905).

WHITTEN (W.): *Life of De Foe* (London, 1900).

WILSON (W.): *Memoirs and the life and times of De Foe,* 3 vol. (London, 1830).

WINDSOR (A. L.): *Ethica,* vol. IV (London, 1860).

WOTTON (M. E.): *Word portraits* (London, 1887).

WRIGHT, (T.): *Life of De Foe* (London, 1894).

B. Special Studies.

Academy (the): March 14, 1891 (*De Foe and Mary Astell*, by K. B. Bülbring). September 9, 1899 (*A masterly lie*). Dec. 30, 1905 (*De Foe and Selkirk at Bristol*, by Charles Wells).

Archaeologia Cantiana, vol. XXXI, p. 61 (*De Foe and Kent*, by Wm. Minet).

Athenaeum (the): 1889, I, p. 472 (*De Foe's brick-kilns*, by G. A. Aitken). 1890, II, p. 257 (*De Foe's birth and marriage*, by G. A. Aitken). 1894, II, p. 862 (*De Foe in trouble*, by G. A. Aitken).

Catholic Presbyterian (the): Feb., 1883 (*De Foe and his church*, by W. Anderson).

Contemporary Review: vol. 57 (1890), p. 232 (*De Foe's wife*, by G. A. Aitken) [corrected in the *Athenaeum*, 1890 and in this book].

DAVIS (A. McFarland): *A Bibliographical puzzle* (Cambridge, Mass., 1910).

DAY (G.): *Daniel De Foe, the tile-maker of Tilbury, Essex* (from the *Essex Review*, January, 1896).

Englische Studien, 1924, "Defoe and Milton," by W. Fischer.

English historical review: April, 1900 (*De Foe and Harley*, by Thomas Bateson). Jan., 1907 (*An unpublished political paper by Defoe*, by G. F. Warner).

English studies: June, 1921 (*De Foe and Swift*, by W. van Maanen).

Gentleman's Magazine: Dec., 1901 (*The apparition of Mrs. Veal*, by R. H. Bretherton).

GÜCKEL (W.) and GÜNTHER (E.): *Daniel Defoe's und J. Swift's Belesenheit und Literarische Kritik*, Leipzig, 1925.

Horner (S.): *Brief account of the ceremony of unveiling the monument . . . of Daniel De Foe* (Southampton, 1870).

Judas discovered and catch'd at last: or Daniel De Foe in Lobs Pound (London, 1713).

Just reprimand to Daniel De Foe [by J. Clark] (London, 1706).

Nation (the) (New York), Sept. 17, 1908 (*New light on De Foe's life,* by W. P. Trent), June 6, July 11, August 29, 1907 (*Bibliographical notes on De Foe,* by W. P. Trent).

Nineteenth Century (the): Jan., 1895 (*De Foe's Apparition of Mrs. Veal,* by G. A. Aitken).

Notes and Queries: Feb. 16, 1850 (*Daniel De Foe and his ghost stories*); Aug. 31, Oct. 12, Nov. 9, 1850 (*Gravesend boats*); Nov. 1, 1851 (*De Foe and Mercator*); Oct. 18, 1851 (*De Foe's house*); April 24, 1852 (*De Foe's descendants*), and May 15, (*id.*); June 19, 1852 (*Boyer's attacks*); May 3, 1856 (*De Foe's death*); July 16, Sept. 3, Oct. 8, 1859, and April 20, 1861 (*De Foe's descendants*); June 18, 1864 (*The storm*); Dec. 31, 1864 and Jan. 21, 1865 (*Letters to De La Faye*); Feb. 17, 1866 (*De Foe's Library*); Oct. 17, 1868 (*De Foe at Halifax*); May 8, 1869 (*De Foe's letter to Keimer*); June 12, 1869, Feb. 12, 1870 (*De Foe, Boyer and Mesnager*); March 19, 1870 (*De Foe's father*); Oct. 29, 1870 (*Corrections to Lee's work*); June 14, 1871 (*Mercey De Foe*); April 3, 1875 (*Correspondence between De Foe and John Fransham, of Norwich*); Sept. 18, 1875 (*Benjamin De Foe*); June 17, 1882 (*De Foe's picture*); May 19, 1883 (*the Edinburgh Courant*); Jan. 26, 1884 (*Unknown letter*); June 4, 1887 (*Benjamin De Foe*); Aug. 11, 1888 (*De Foe and Webb*); Sept. 21 and Nov. 2, 1895 (*The Apparition at Launceston*); April 14, 1900 (*De Foe's difficulties about* 1692); Feb. 2, April 13, 1901 (*De Foe's descendants*); March 15 and April 19, 1902 (*De Foe at Tooting*); June 14, 1902 (*De Foe and the Saint-Vincent eruption of* 1718); July 12, 1902 (*De Foe's descendants*); June 12, 1909 (*De Foe's wife*); Dec. 24, 1910 (*De Foe's chapel*).

Publications of the Modern Language Association of America, December, 1925: "The Indebtedness of Oliver Twist to Defoe's *History of the Devil,*" by M. H. Law.

Republican Bullies (the) (London, 1705).

Review of English Studies, January, 1929: "An Unrecognized Work of Defoe?" by G. C. Moore Smith.

Revue germanique: July, 1923 (*Daniel De Foe mystificateur, ou les faux mémoires de Mesnager,* par Paul Dottin).

Robinson (E. F.): *De Foe in Stoke Newington* (London, 1889).

The True-born Hugonot (London, 1703).

II

General Literary Studies on De Foe's Works

Academy (the): May 26, 1906 (*De Foe as sociological novelist,* by E. A. Baker).

Blackwood's magazine: Oct., 1869 (*A great Whig journalist*).

Bookman (the): Nov., 1915 (*Advance of the English novel,* II, by W. L. Phelps).

BURTON (R.): *Masters of the English novel* (New York, 1909).

CHASLES (Ph.): *Les romans de De Foe et les pseudonymes anglais au dix-huitième siècle* (vol. II of the *Dix-huitième siècle en Angleterre*).

DAWSON (W. J.): *Makers of English fiction* (New York, 1905).

EHRENTHAL (H. N.): *English Novelists* (London, 1894).

ELTON, (O.): *Frederick York Powell*, vol. II, *Essay on Daniel De Foe* (Oxford, 1906).

JACKSON (H.): *The great English novelists* (London, 1908).

JACOB (G. E.): *De Foe's Projects, Ein Beitrag zur Characteristick De Foe's und seiner Zeit* (Leipzig, 1921).

JEAFFRESON (J. C.): *Novels and novelists*, vol. I (London, 1888).

Journal des Débats: July 22, 1908 (*De Foe, précurseur du naturalisme*, by A. Filon).

JUSSERAND (J.): *Le roman anglais et la réforme littéraire de De Foe* (Brussels, 1887).

LAMB (Ch.): *De Foe's secondary novels* (in *Eliana*).

LANIER (S.): *The English novel* (New York, 1900).

LYALL (A.): *Studies in literature and history* (London, 1915).

MITCHELL (D. G.): *Old story-tellers* (New York, 1878).

MORGAN (C. E.): *The rise of the novel of manners* (Columbia U. P., 1911).

National Review (the): 1856 (*De Foe as a novelist*).

PILON (E.): *Portraits de Sentiment, Daneel De Foe* (Paris, 1913).

Revue Anglo-Américaine: Dec., 1923 (*Daniel De Foe et les sciences occultes*, by P. Dottin).

SAINTSBURY (G.): *Selections from De Foe's minor novels, introduction* (London, 1892).

STEPHEN (Leslie): *Hours in a Library*, vol. I (*De Foe's novels*) (London, 1874).

III

COLLECTIONS OF AND SELECTIONS FROM DE FOE'S WORKS

AITKEN (G. A.): *Later Stuart Tracts* (Collection *An English Garner*, Vol. II and VII, London, 1903). Contains an extract from the *Essay upon Projects* (Education of Women), extracts from the *Review* and the prefaces to each of the 7 volumes, and the following works: *True-born Englishman, Legion's Memorial, History of the Kentish Petition, Shortest way, Hymn to the Pillory*, and *Appeal*.

AITKEN (G. A.): *Romances and narratives by Daniel De Foe* (London, 1895). Vol. I. II and III: *Robinson Crusoe and Woodes Rogers's and Steele's Accounts of Selkirk*. Vol. IV: *Duncan Campbell*. Vol. V: *Cavalier*. Vol. VI: *Singleton*. Vol. VII and VIII: *Moll Flanders* and *Appeal*. Vol. IX: *Plague Year*. Vol. X and XI: *Colonel Jack, Everybody's Business*, and *Protestant Monastery*. Vol. XII and XIII: *Roxana*. Vol. XIV: *New Voyage*. Vol. XV: *Due Preparations, Dumb Philosopher, Mrs. Veal, Isle of Saint-Vincent*. Vol. XVI: *King of Pirates, Cartoucheans in France, Life of John Sheppard, Narrative of all the robberies, Life of Jonatham Wild, John Gow, Lives of six notorious Street-robbers*. (Preface and introduction to each work; illustrations by Yeats.) (At the present time, the best edition of De Foe.)

BASTIDE (Ch.): *Daniel De Foe* (Paris, les cent chef-d'œuvres étrangers). Contains *Mrs. Veal* and extracts from *Robinson Crusoe, Plague Year, Moll Flanders* and *History of the Devil* (in French).

BOHN's edition (London, 1854): *The novels and miscellaneous works of Daniel De Foe.* Vol. I: *Singleton, Colonel Jack.* Vol. II: *Cavalier, Captain Carleton, Dumb philosopher, Everybody's business.* Vol. III: *Moll Flanders, Devil.* Vol. IV: *Roxana,* Mother Ross [not by De Foe]. Vol. V: *Plague Year,* Fire of London [not by De Foe]. *Storm, Poetical essay on the Storm, True-born Englishman.* Vol. VI: *Duncan Campbell, New Voyage, Seasonable warning, Answer to a question, Reasons against the succession, What if the Pretender.* Vol. VII: *Robinson Crusoe* (vol. I and II).

DE FOE: *A true collection of the writings of the author of the True-born Englishman* (London, 1703). Contains: *True-born Englishman, Mock-mourners, Character of Annesley, Spanish descent, Original power, Free-holder's plea, Reasons against a War, Argument showing that a standing army . . ., Danger of the Protestant religion, Villainy of Stock-jobbers, Six distinguishing characters, Poor man's plea, Enquiry into the Occasional Conformity of Dissenters, Two great questions considered, Two great questions farther considered, Enquiry into Occasional Conformity shewing . . ., New Test of the Church of England's loyalty, Shortest way, Brief explanation, Shortest way to peace.*
A second volume, etc. Contains: *New discovery, More reformation, Elegy, Storm, Hymn to the pillory, Hymn to Victory, Pacificator, Double welcome, Dissenter's Answer, Challenge of Peace, Peace without Union, More short ways, New Test of the Church's honesty, Serious Inquiry, Dissenters misrepresented, Parallel, Giving Alms, Royal religion.*

HAWKINS: *Selections from De Foe* (London, 1922).

HAZLITT's edition (London, 1840-41). *The Works of Daniel De Foe.* Vol. I: Life of Defoe, *Appeal,* Chronological catalogue of De Foe's works, *Colonel Jack, Roxana, Moll Flanders, Cavalier, New Voyage.* Vol. II: *Plague Year, Carleton,* Christian conversation [not by De Foe], *Inquiry into the Occasional Conformity of Dissenters, Letter to Mr. How. Inquiry into Occasional Conformity shewing . . ., Shortest way, Dumb Philosopher, Brief explanation, Sincerity of the Dissenters, History of the Kentish Petition, Legion's memorial, Original power, Original right, Reasons against the succession, What if the Pretender . . ., Singleton,* Murderers of the English gentlemen [not by De Foe], *Mrs. Veal, Duncan Campbell,* Campbell's Pacquet [not by De Foe], *Use and Abuse.* Vol. III: *Robinson Crusoe* (3 parts), *Humble proposal, Essay upon projects, Remarks on the Bill . . ., Essay upon publick credit, Essay upon loans, Essay on the South-sea trade, Essay on the treaty of commerce, Further observations, True-born Englishman, Jure Divino.*

LEE (Wm.): Daniel De Foe, etc. vol. II and III [periodical articles written by De Foe between 1716 and 1729].

MASEFIELD (J.): *Masters of Literature: De Foe* (London, 1909) (excellent selections).

MEYNADIER's edition (New York, 1905): *The Works of Daniel De Foe* [exactly like the Aitken edition except that the preface and the introductions are different and *Everybody's Business* and *Protestant Monastery* are replaced by *True-born Englishman* and *Shortest way*].

MORLEY (H.): *De Foe's earlier life and chief earlier works* (London, 1889) [contains: *Essay upon projects, True-born Englishman, Shortest way, Hymn to the pillory, Consolidator, Mrs. Veal*].

MORLEY (H.): *Longer works in English Prose*, ch. VII [extracts from *Robinson Crusoe*].

MORLEY (H.): *Shorter works in English Prose*, ch. VII [extract from *Essay upon Projects*: Education of women, *Shortest way* and *Review* of Feb. 9, 1704].

MORRIS's edition: *De Foe's novels* (Phil. 1906); complete unexpurgated edition de luxe, 8 vol. [contains the novels, *Due Preparations* and *King of Pirates*]. Republished in 1914 under the title *Complete works*: unexpurgated edition (Sully and Klinteich, eds.).

NIMMO's *Selections from De Foe* (ed. by Keltie) (Edinburgh, 1869) [contains the novels and long extracts from *Complete Tradesman* and *Duncan Campbell*].

QUILLER-COUCH (A. T.): *Selections from Walton, Bunyan and De Foe* (Oxford, 1913) [For school use].

SAINTSBURY (G.): *Selections from De Foe's minor novels* (London, 1892) [well chosen selections from the minor novels and from *The Storm*].

SCOTT's edition: *The novels of Daniel De Foe* (Ballantyne, Edinburgh, 1810), 12 vol. [contains the novels and the following works: *Dumb Philosopher, Devil, Mother Ross* [not by De Foe], *Storm, True-born Englishman, Duncan Campbell*, and *Reasons against the succession* . . . Notes by Walter Scott and biographical introduction by Ballantyne]. Same edition in 7 volumes (London, 1887).

TEGG's edition: *The novels and miscellaneous works of Daniel De Foe* (ed. by Sir G. S. Lewis) (Oxford and London, 1840). Vol. I: *Robinson Crusoe*. Vol. II: *Further Adventures*. Vol. III: *Singleton*. Vol. IV: *Moll Flanders*. Vol. V: *Colonel Jack, Mrs. Veal*. Vol. VI: *Cavalier*. Vol. VII: *New Voyage*. Vol. VIII: *Carleton*, Mother Ross [not by De Foe]. Vol. IX: *Plague Year, Consolidator*. Vol. X: *Devil*. Vol. XI: *Roxana*. Vol. XII: *System of Magic*. Vol. XIII: *History of Apparitions*. Vol. XIV: *Religious Courtship*. Vol. XV and XVI: *Family Instructor*. Vol. XVII and XVIII: *Complete tradesman, Humble proposal, Augusta triumphans, Second thoughts*. Vol. XIX: *Duncan Campbell, Dumb philosopher, Everybody's business*. Vol. XX: Life of De Foe by Chalmers, List of De Foe's works, *Appeal, Seasonable warning, Reasons against the succession. What if the Pretender, Answer to a question. True-born Englishman*.

TRENT (W. P.): *Daniel De Foe and how to know him* (Indianapolis, 1916) [at the end of each chapter, well chosen extracts from De Foe, especially from rare pamphlets].

WALKER (J.): *Selections of De Foe's writings*, 3 vol. [extracts from the novels, *True-born Englishman and Original Power*].

ADDITIONAL BIBLIOGRAPHY

ATKINSON (G.): *Les relations de voyages au Dix-septième siècle*, Paris, 1925.

Tour Through Great Britain, Everyman Library, 2 vol., 1928.

ANDREAE (G.): *The Dawn of Juvenile Literature in England*, Amsterdam, 1925.

COPPLESTONE (Bennet): *Dead Men's Tales*, Edinburgh, 1926.

English Journal, January, 1927, article by F. R. Howes.

HUTCHINS (H. C.): *Robinson Crusoe and Its Printing, 1719-31*, Columbia University Press, 1925.

JACKSON (H. E.): *Robinson Crusoe, Social Engineer*, New York, 1923.

Library, June, 1927: "Two Hitherto Unrecorded Editions of *Robinson Crusoe*," by H. C. Hutchins.

MICHELET (J.): *Nos Fils*, Flammarion, pp. 429-434.

Nation-Athenaeum, Feb. 6, 1926, article by Virginia Woolf.

Neophilologus, Oct., 1925: "*Krinke Kesmes* und Defoe's *Robinson Crusoe*," by L. Brandl.

Philological Quarterly, April, 1925: "Grimmelshausen's *Simplicissimus* and Defoe's *Robinson Crusoe*," by E. G. Gudde.

STEVENSON (R. L.): *Memories and Portraits and Other Fragments*, "A Gossip on Romance."

THOMPSON (T. A.): *The Theology of Robinson Crusoe*, Holborn Review, Jan., 1925.

UHRSTRÖM (W.): *Studies in the Language of Robinson Crusoe*, Upsala, 1907.

ULLRICH (H.): *Defoe's Robinson Crusoe: Die Geschichte eines Weltbuches*, Leipzig, 1924.

University of California Chronicle, April, 1923: "On the Tediousness of Defoe and *Robinson Crusoe*," by R. P. Utter.

Memoirs of a Cavalier, Constable, 1926 (Uniform edition with *Moll Flanders* and *Roxana*).

Moll Flanders and *Roxana*, Simpkin, The Abbey Classics.

ELISSA-RHAIS (R.): "Une influence anglaise dans *Manon Lescaut*," *Revue de Littérature Comparée*, Oct., 1927.

WILLIAMS (Orlo): *Some Great English Novels*, London, 1926.

INDEX

INDEX

317

cil of Regents, 180; dismissal of, 144; honors of, 156; illness of, 162; pacificism of, 116, 131; resentment of *Atalantis Major*, 155; Secretary of State, 125; Speaker of the House of Commons, 97; stabbed by Marquis de Guiscard, 156; a Tory, 152; trial of, 186
Havana, proposed seizing of, 84
Haywood, Mrs., the novelist, 242
Hepburn, Colonel, 193 and *n.*
Hermit, The, by Philip Quarll, 204
High church
  See Anglican church
High-flyers, the, iii, 92, 93, 94, 111, 124, 127, 128, 130, 131, 147, 150, 165, 166, 181
Highlanders, presence of, in Edinburgh, 139
Highlanders, of Scotland, 141, 147, 240
Historical Manuscript Commission, Reports of, v, 86
Historical romance, created by De Foe, 213
History of the Union, The, attacked, 150, 151; plan for, 141
Hoaxes, of De Foe, *True-Born Englishman,* 81; *The Shortest Way,* 93-95, 106; *An Answer to a Question nobody thinks of,* 171-176; *Reasons against the Succession of the House of Hanover,* 171-176; *What if the Pretender should come?,* 171-176; *Memoirs of M. Mesnager,* 186
Hog, Robin, *A Hue and Cry after Daniel De Foe,* 167
Holland, 38, 67, 126; visited by De Foe in youth, 28
Hollingsworth, the Reverend, married De Foe, 39
Horseback riding, De Foe's enjoyment of, 27, 129, 228
Horticulture, De Foe's interest in, 227
Hosier, De Foe a, 37
Howe, John, attach on De Foe, 71, 78, 88, 100
Hudibras
  See De Foe, early literary bent
Hue and Cry after Daniel De Foe, 144, 145, 167 *n.*
Huguenot refugees, 48, and *See* Deffoe or Defo
Humor, of De Foe, 211

Hurst, Christopher, friend of De Foe, 127, 129, 132
Hurt, in charge of the *Flying-Post,* 181
Hymn to the Pillory, The, 106, 107

Industrial towns, De Foe's interest in, 133
Inquisition, fires of, witnessed by De Foe, 32
Investigation, Harley's political, 127
Irony, of *The Shortest Way,* 93
Isaac Bickerstaff's 12 visions of the year 1711, 155, 241
Italians, De Foe's judgment of, 31
Italy, visited by De Foe in youth, 28

James II, Duke of York; 45, 47, 48, 50, 53, 54, 91
James III, followers of
  See Jacobites
Janeway, printer of De Foe pamphlets, 173, 176
Jacobites, the, iii, 144, 146, 150, 152, 154, 158, 161, 162, 165, 180, 181, 183, 191, 192, 222; hymn, 166; pamphlets, 172
Jacobitism, of Mist, 185; of the Scotch, 137, 141; of the Queen, 161, 187
Journal, Mist's, 189-193; *of the Plague Year,* 220; *des Sçavants,* 74
Journalism, De Foe drawn to, 117; first investigation in, 116; talent in, 139, 149, 190, 192, 210, 248
Journey through England, A, 239
Juan-Fernandez, 198, 200
Judas discover'd and caught at last, pamphlet against De Foe, 176
Jure Divino, 83, 100, 110, 134; publication of in 1706, 117
Juvenal, 66
Juvenile literature, Robinson Crusoe a part of, 206

Keimer, Quaker book-seller, aided by De Foe, 194
Kent, people of, 87, 116
Kentish petition, 87
King's Bench
  See Prisons
Kingswood-Heath, estate of, purchased by De Foe for Hannah, 231, 232

Projects, Essay upon, 75
Protectionist, De Foe a, 159
Protestant cause, 45, 53, 54, 84; nunnery, 62
"Protestant flail," 26, 27
Protestant, Post-Boy, The, 162; *Monastery, The,* 4, 254
Protestants, of the Palatinate, 234
Protestantism, of *Robinson Crusoe,* 210; of William and Mary, 45
Prynne, contemporary poet, 109
Pseudonym, of De Foe, Sir Timothy Caution, 191; Alexander Goldsmith, 129, 137, 157, 254; Claude Guilot, 154, 161; Andrew Moreton, 254; of Mist, *See* Mist, pseudonym of
"Publicity stunt," De Foe's, 237
Puritanism, of De Foe, 12, 13, 43, 71, 77, 194, 196, 210, 230, 238, 254, 264; of James Foe 2; of the *Review,* 123
Puritan, 76, 205; cities, 133; God, 196; litany, 84
Puritans, oppression of, 7; and *Review,* 124; Scotch, 145; and Monmouth, 51.

Quaker style, De Foe's use of, 165, 187
Quakers, 103, 188, 194, 215
Quarll, Philip, 204, 205
Queen's Bench, De Foe imprisoned in, *See* Prisons
Queensbury, Duke of, 137, 145

Races, at Aylesbury, 42, 160; at Hambleton Down, 161; at Newmarket, 42, 70, 240; at Pontefract, 146
Raleigh, Sir Walter, 199; De Foe's claim of, as ancestor, 3
Realism, 205; of *Robinson Crusoe,* 210, 211
Reasons against the Succession of the House of Hanover, 171, 176, 177
Reasons why this nation ought to put an end to this Expensive War, 159
Reformation of manners, 75, 76, 77, 103
Regents, Council of, 180, 181
Rehearsal, The, paper opposed to De Foe's *Review,* 120, 121
Religious Courtship, 196
Religious, fanaticism in 1679, 26

Reporter, De Foe a, 135, 136, 210
Restlessness of De Foe, 40
Review, the, 12, 41, 119, 121, 122, 126, 129, 134, 135, 149, 155, 156, 162, 163, 164, 166, 168, 177, 243; description of, 118; end of, 178, 179; first appearance of, 117; popularity of, 123, 124; quotations from, 48, 68, 83, 128, 142, 147, 148, 165, 169
Revolution, political (1688), 54, 182
Revue Germanique, 159 *n.*
Richardson, Samuel, 241
Ridpath, Whig journalist, 168, 174, 175, 181
Roberts, Memoirs of Captain, 225
Robinson Crusoe, 170, 182, 197, 199-203, 205, 220, 226, 234, 255; allegory of, 5, 103; criticism of, 208-213; philosophy of, 206; style of, 12
Robinsonads, 204; in France, 206; in Germany, 207
Robinson der Jüngere, 207
Robinson Crusoe Examin'd and Criticis'd, by Gildon, 203 *n.*
Rochester, Lord, influence on De Foe, 38, 70, 102
Rogers, Capt. Woodes, 198
Rome, De Foe's judgment of, 33
Roscomon, influence of, on De Foe, 38
Rosseau, 206, 207
Roxana, Lady, 222, 226, 236
Royall Education, Of, posthumous work, 256
Ryswick, peace of, 70

Sacheverell, Doctor, fanatic against Dissenters, 91, 92, 94, 99, 147; attacked by De Foe, 148, 187; popularity of, 106, 148
Saint Bartholomew, Great Fair of, 16
St.-Botolph's-in-Aldgate, De Foe's marriage in, 39
St.-Giles-in-Cripplegate, 2, 6, 260, 261
St. Michael's, parish of, De Foe's shop in, 37
Saint-Vincent, Island of, 189, 190
Sault, Richard, on staff of *Mercury,* 74
Savage, on De Foe's mistress, 71
"Scandalous Club," 118
Schwob, Marcel, transator of *Moll Flanders,* 219
"Scoop," De Foe's, 190